The Rationalization of Miracles

During the Counter-Reformation in southern Europe, Catholic Church officials developed rules to legitimize miracles performed by candidates to sainthood. *The Rationalization of Miracles* uncovers a tacit understanding between central religious officials and local religious activists. Each group had a vested interest in declaring miracles: Catholic Church leaders sought legitimacy in the wake of the crisis of faith created by the Protestant Schism, and religious acolytes needed Church approval to secure a flow of resources to their movements. The Church's new procedure of deeming miracles "true" when there were witnesses of different statuses and the acts occurred in the presence of a candidate's acolyte served the needs of both parties. And by developing rules and procedures for evaluating miracles, the Church rationalized the magic at the root of the miracles, thereby propelling the institution out of a period of institutional, political, and social uncertainty and forming the basis of modern sainthood.

Paolo Parigi is Assistant Professor in the Sociology Department at Stanford University. He received his PhD from Columbia University in 2008.

The Rationalization of Miracles

PAOLO PARIGI

Stanford University

CAMBRIDGE
UNIVERSITY PRESS

CAMBRIDGE UNIVERSITY PRESS
Cambridge, New York, Melbourne, Madrid, Cape Town,
Singapore, São Paulo, Delhi, Mexico City

Cambridge University Press
32 Avenue of the Americas, New York, NY 10013-2473, USA

www.cambridge.org
Information on this title: www.cambridge.org/9781107013681

First published 2012

Printed in the United States of America

A catalog record for this publication is available from the British Library.

Library of Congress Cataloging in Publication Data
Parigi, Paolo, 1973–
The rationalization of miracles / Paolo Parigi.
p.   cm.
Includes bibliographical references and index.
ISBN 978-1-107-01368-1 (hardback)
1. Canonization – History.   2. Miracles – History of doctrines.
3. Catholic Church – Doctrines.   4. Counter-Reformation.
5. Church history – 16th century.   I. Title.
BX2330.P37   2012
235'.2409–dc23   2011043731

ISBN 978-1-107-01368-1 Hardback

A Giada ed Elsie, perchè la magia sia sempre una parte delle vostre vite.

Contents

Figures and Tables

Figures

Tables

Terms: Latin and Other Foreign Languages

Bolla (Latin): Papal bull issued proclaiming the beatification or canonization of a candidate to sainthood.

Caelestis Hierusalem cives (Latin): Decree reforming the procedures for canonization, issued by Urban VIII in 1634.

Caput mundi (Latin; "head of the world"): Latin expression to indicate Rome.

Coda mundi (Latin; the "tail of the world"): The expression that the poet and play writer Piero l'Aretino used to mock the Catholic Church and Rome.

Credo (Latin): Apostles' Creed.

Dies Natalis (Latin; "the day of birth"): In the Church's terminology, this indicates the day the candidate passed away and transitioned to Paradise.

Fama sanctitatis (Latin "fame of sanctity"): One of the official requirements for reaching canonization.

Per Viam Cultum (Latin): The procedures through which established religious cults were judged by the Congregatio.

Per Viam Non Cultum (Latin): In contrast to the procedural path previously described, this path was reserved for recently deceased candidates who did not have an established religious cult.

Processus Super Cultum Non Adhibito (Latin): A type of trialto to verify that the candidate to sainthood had not been worshipped during the fifty years following his death. It became the first trial in the canonization proceedings after the reforms of 1642.

Risorgimento (Italian; "The Resurgence"): Refers to a period of Italian history that began with the Council of Vienna (1815) and culminated with the proclamation of Rome as the capital of the nascent Italian Kingdom in 1871.

Siglo de Oro (Spanish; "Golden Century"): Refers to a period of Spanish history that goes from the Reconquista (1492) to the Treaty of the Pyrenees (1659). It marked the military, political, and cultural ascendance of Spain over Europe.

Preface

This book would not exist without the encouragement, support, and help of many people. I started thinking about a project for my dissertation during the summer of 2003 while visiting my family in Florence. My advisor, Peter Bearman, was spending his sabbatical year in Genoa, and so I took the opportunity to visit him. I spent a day with Peter talking about a paper we were writing together and about potential future projects. On my way back to Florence, Peter gave me a ride to the train station on his Vespa. Few know it, but the unfortunate truth is that Peter is a terrible Vespa driver. He had no idea how to handle the unruly Italian traffic, and after a car passed us on the right side because we were proceeding too slowly in the middle of a lane, I was certain we were going to get hurt. Indifferent to the peril around us, Peter kept talking about projects, and I kept nervously agreeing. We made it to the station safely, but I worried about Peter driving back. I comforted myself with the thought that he would simply perform the same trick as before, of tackling potential problems directly and without much hesitation. For getting me safely to the station that night and for teaching me more than how to be a sociologist, thank you Peter.

In the days following the memorable Vespa ride I kept thinking about the only sentence that I had been able to understand from Peter. He said (or I understood): "Did you know that ancient Rome had more than one million inhabitants?" What was he talking about? In the three hours it took me to get back to Florence I thought about several possible answers. Finally, I settled on the following – Peter was suggesting that if I wanted to go back to Italy to write my dissertation I should focus on Rome, possibly ancient Rome. So I did.

I quickly discovered, however, that doing historical sociological work on ancient Rome would require a deep knowledge of several ancient languages and the ability to travel to archives scattered throughout the Mediterranean basin. Although tempted, I opted to maintain the focus on the Eternal City but to study a more contemporary period and one closer to my interests in formal rules and organizations. In my search for potential topics, I stumbled on a directory that listed in great detail all of the holdings of the archives in the Vatican. This became the basis for building my project about the special commission that, since the end of the sixteenth century, has investigated the miracles and the deeds of candidates to sainthood. The immense archive of the commission resides in large part in the Vatican.

Columbia University awarded me a scholarship to go back to Rome, and so my family and I packed everything and left New York in August 2004. The three years that followed would represent a period of great joy, intellectual growth, and personal challenge for me. My second daughter was born in Rome; the archives of the Vatican, and in particular the Apostolic Library, proved to be truly incredible places for conducting research; and my mother's mental health significantly deteriorated. All of these ups and downs would have been simply too much to handle if it weren't for my wife, Amy, who stood patiently by my side. Simply said, without her the project behind this book would have never been completed. To her, my eternal gratitude and deep love.

In the years since we moved back to New York and then to California, many people have commented on pieces of the manuscript. Dan Lainer-Vos gave me precious suggestions on how to handle theoretical aspects of my argument connected with Max Weber's theory of rationalization; Mark Granovetter helped me with framing the argument in the organizational literature; Harrison White was a constant source of inspiration and encouragement; Roberto Rusconi guided me through a dense historical literature on modern sainthood; and John-Paul Ferguson helped me to bring the historical details in line with the analytical argument of the book. Kathy Gilsinian read multiple drafts of what was then my dissertation. The editorial comments of Esther Cervantes were extremely illuminating and always on point. My colleagues at Stanford, Tomás Jiménez, Monica McDermott, and Rebecca Sandefur, read an earlier draft of the manuscript and provided great comments. I also would like to thank my editor at Cambridge, Robert Dreesen, for believing in this project. Other people, too many to mention, also contributed indirectly to the manuscript by engaging in conversations with me about a most unusual topic for scholars of organizations – the production of miracles. To all of them goes my gratitude. This book was completed while I was in residence at the Institute for Research in the Social Sciences at Stanford University. I would like to thank Karen Cook and Chris Thomsen for creating an environment conducive to research.

This book is dedicated to my two daughters. Their lives, like those of many young girls, are full of magical things. At the moment, therefore, they have no use for a book about the importance of magic. My hope is that once they are older they will find this book useful for understanding the importance of maintaining some magic in their lives.

Palo Alto, August 19, 2011

What Is This Book About?

It may not be obvious, but miracles are an integral part of modern life. Believers usually refer to miracles when describing events that defy scientific explanation. In the most popular sense, a miracle is a statement about the boundaries of science – and of medicine in particular, given that the majority of miracles, at least in the Christian world, are healings. Beyond this broad meaning, a miracle also has a more specific meaning for Catholics – it is one of the proofs required to achieve sainthood. This book focuses on this latter meaning and contends that if the modern Christian world still has people with supernatural powers capable of performing miracles, it is because of the reforms to sainthood that the Catholic Church introduced during the seventeenth century. These reforms fixed the characteristics of miracles and, consequently, of the people capable of performing them – the candidates to sainthood.

Despite the centuries that separate us from the religious world of the seventeenth century, some of the enduring characteristics of a miracle that were established back then can be detected in the story of a miraculous event that occurred in Ferndale, Washington, a town forty miles south of Vancouver, British Columbia, Canada, in the winter months of 2006.[1]

During the last minute of a basketball game, a young boy, Jake Finkbonner, was pushed from the back and hit the basketball hoop with his lips. This seemingly innocuous injury opened up a chain of events that would bring Jake to the brink of death. The next morning Jake woke with his face completely swollen and was rushed to the hospital by his parents, Donny and Elsa. There, the doctors diagnosed that Jake had contracted

---

[1] A report on the event was aired on National Public Radio on April 22, 2011.

the flesh-eating bacteria called strep-A. Like something in a horror movie, the bacteria had begun eating Jake's face – and it was spreading fast. As Dr. Richard Hopper later reported to National Public Radio, "It's almost as if you could watch it moving in front of your eyes. The redness and the swelling – we would mark it, and within the hour it would have spread another half-inch." Because of the speed with which the disease spread, the doctors could not stop it. They told Donny and Elsa that their son would probably die.

A priest, Reverend Tim Sauer, was called to give the boy the last rites. Noticing that the boy was half Lummi Indian, Sauer also invited his parishioners at St. Joseph's Catholic Church to pray for the intercession of Kateri Tekakwitha, a Mohawk who converted to Catholicism three hundred fifty years ago. Kateri also had scars on her face, caused in her case by smallpox. John Paul II beatified her in 1980. Since then she has been on the list of candidates for sainthood; to reach that achievement, she would need to perform another miracle.

Soon, many other people in the community began praying for Jake and, in a true display of the positive effects of living in a connected world, people in Denver, London, and Israel also began to pray for him. In the midst of all of this, a representative of the Society of Blessed Kateri visited Jake at the hospital and gave Elsa a pendant with the Blessed Kateri's image on it. Elsa placed it on Jake's pillow. Elsa would later recall that it was at that time that the disease stopped progressing. The next morning, as his doctors prepared Jake for surgery, they were startled by the discovery. It was a miracle, in the popular sense of the word. The boy was saved. The officials of the Vatican are currently investigating whether the inexplicable sequence of events can be considered a true miracle according to the Catholic Church.

The doctors' impotence in the face of an unstoppable disease makes its retreat a miracle in the broad sense that Catholics share with other Christians. A miracle is something that science cannot explain. What gives the event the potential to be a Catholic miracle is the belief that it occurred through the intercession of the Blessed Kateri because of her position in Heaven close to God. A miracle is the proof of someone's sanctity, as ultimately established by the pope.

To begin unpacking how this latter and narrower meaning of a miracle came to be, we need to focus on a small detail in the preceding narrative – the pendant and the person who brought it to the scene. Not only did the miracle that saved Jake occur only after an object with the image of Kateri was placed on him, but it is also important that the person who provided the image was a representative of Kateri's Blessed Society. As I will show in the book, representatives of the candidate are the crucial actors in modern sainthood. The rules that govern their behavior today developed during the seventeenth century through a tense cooperation between the central officials of the Church, represented by a special commission created to investigate candidates for sainthood and their deeds, and local religious activists – such as the representative of Kateri in the story of Jake's miracle – grouped around a given candidate.

This book is not at all concerned with establishing whether miracles are true or false. Instead, the aim of my analysis is to understand the social and cultural process that created the institutional field of modern sainthood. This process has been studied mainly by historians of the Church, scholars of religion, and people interested in early modernity. My analysis takes an unusual perspective in that it brings an organizational approach to this historical material. The story told in this book is therefore one of organizational adaptation and the transformation of an organizational environment, rather than one of history or religion. I use historical details about religious beliefs during the seventeenth century to build an analytical framework that is firmly part of organizational theory.

Introduction

In the hectic days following Filippo Neri's death, in 1595, a seven-year-old boy named Angelo fell into a coma. His desperate mother called several doctors, all of whom proved unsuccessful at awakening the boy. Angelo's brother decided to visit the church in which Neri's body lay exposed, taking some rose petals from Neri's casket. Back home, he scattered the petals on Angelo, who suddenly woke up and began playing. The second miracle occurred in 1603 when Felicia Sebastiani, a pregnant woman, fell ill as a consequence of a mosquito bite. She remained in bed for four days before her concerned relatives secured some of Neri's relics from one of his followers. Sebastiani ate some of the relics in a broth. The next day, she began bleeding and spat blood from her mouth. Though she lost her child, she survived (*Il primo processo*).

The emotional power of the first story makes it resemble more closely what readers today would consider a miracle. But it was the second story that the church approved as a true miracle, while it rejected the first (*Relationes Super Vitae et Sanctitate*). The difference lies in who provided the relics: in the first case it was one of Neri's acolytes who brought the relics that saved Sebastiani; no acolytes were involved in the second case. The Catholic Church's approval of the acolyte-assisted event as a miracle, despite the greater apparent impact of the event that involved no acolytes, is what we would expect if the Church were interested in strong, structured mobilizations above all. The Church did have this interest during the seventeenth century.

The key to understanding this outcome lies in the procedures that the Catholic Church had crafted at that time in an effort to distinguish true miracles from false and in how local religious activists acted and reacted in light of those procedures. In the aftermath of the Protestant Schism (1517), the central officials of the Church, organized into a special commission charged with investigating candidates for sainthood, and local religious activists, organized around the charismatic religious leaders who became candidates, discovered a common interest in producing true miracles.

This convergence of interests was one of many changes born of the religious turmoil of the sixteenth century. For centuries prior to that, Roman authorities had been, at worst, suspicious and, at best, dismissive of local manifestations of religious fervor. At the same time, local religious activists ignored Rome's religious laws, except when they were promulgated by the sword of an army or the Inquisition. Each set of actors had its own operational definition of *miracle*; each recognized its own saints as capable of performing such miracles. In a geographically, socially, and culturally segmented world, the two groups could ignore each other for the most part. The shape of sainthood before the Protestant Schism exemplified two of the problems of the Medieval Church: its lack of control over local organizations, and thus a constant threat of schismatic movements, and a general disinterest in people's lives that allowed a diffuse ignorance among ostensible believers about even the most basic tenets of Christianity.

The Protestant Schism, which threatened the unity of the Church, and the invention of the printing press, which made heterodox ideas much more widely and readily available, changed the relationship between central officials and local religious activists. Gutenberg's invention vastly increased the circulation of ideas (Ginzburg 1970; Moran 1973; Thomas 1983; Israel 1999), creating a social world at once more integrated and more heterogeneous than the one it had replaced (Durkheim 1997). The diffusion of heterodox religious ideas occurred throughout Europe, though it was stronger in the economic and cultural capitals of the continent: in Northern and Central Italy, Mediterranean Spain and France, and the Netherlands (Braudel 1992).

In this increasingly heterogeneous and increasingly integrated context, answering the Protestant challenge required the Church to regain legitimacy among ordinary people and assume control over local religious activism. Taking control too firmly could alienate ordinary people, who could then follow the example of the schismatics if they so chose, but allowing too much local autonomy would undermine the Church's authority, which was already under threat from the Protestant challenge. Some of the Church's more confrontational tools in its bid for control, such as the Inquisition, are familiar, but this book examines the less familiar, cooperative side of the process – how the Church adjusted its rules to incorporate and shape local religious activism, and what local activists had to gain in establishing a positive relationship with Roman authorities.

I call this process the rationalization of miracles in order to stress its connection to Max Weber's thesis about the rationalization of religion in northern Europe and to highlight what was unique about the process as it happened in southern Europe. For Weber, Puritanism represented the conclusion of the process of rationalization, but this research suggests that Puritanism was only one of the paths taken by the spirit of rationalization in Europe. The other path is the one that the Catholic Church followed in southern Europe and that developed from the legal tradition of Roman law (Gauthier 1996). The aim of this book, therefore, is to show that the rules for adjudicating miracles established by the Church during this period, along with the actions of local religious activists, reorganized magic rather than expelled it, and that this reorganization was part of the rationalization impulse that swept Europe during the sixteenth century. Furthermore, the reorganization of magic was the rational process by which the Church regained its lost legitimacy among ordinary people and established control over local activists.

With respect to canonization procedures, rationalization meant that the content of a supernatural event ceased to be the criterion by which it was declared (or denied) to be a miracle, and by which its performer could be labeled a saint. Acolytes – a candidate's early followers – went from house to house performing miracles on behalf of their leader after his death, thereby keeping his memory alive throughout his canonization trial, which by Church law could not begin until after the candidate was deceased.[1] What mattered instead of the miracles' content was their social form: true miracles knit together believers of different kinship groups and social statuses. Paradoxically, miracles deemed true were no longer those that imitated the acts of Jesus, as in the Middle Ages, but those that addressed the needs of local audiences within an inclusive form. A true miracle united people of different walks of life, turning the saint into someone capable of creating a mobilization that overcame the social cleavages dividing local communities. This form was beneficial to the Church, which needed to reestablish its legitimacy and authority with

---

[1] This book refers to candidates for sainthood using the masculine. This is because the large majority of candidates in the period of analysis that this book covers were men.

a socially broad audience, as well as for the potential saint's followers, who needed the approval of Rome to establish his legitimacy and authority locally. By the second half of the seventeenth century, once local religious activists learned the form that true miracles were supposed to have, candidates for sainthood began performing fewer wonders, albeit all of the correct type. The social form of these few miracles was uniformly inclusive.

Keeping all of this in mind, it may now be less surprising that the miscarriage described earlier was deemed a true miracle and the resuscitation deemed a false one. The key difference is that the miscarriage involved one of Neri's acolytes, who brought in the relic that healed the woman, while the resurrection did not involve Neri's acolytes. Acolytes, in creating and nurturing a local social movement in support of the canonization effort, created the social conditions for the occurrence of miracles after the candidate's death. Rome used acolytes to gauge the amount of local mobilization. For the central officials in Rome and for the local activists, true miracles united diverse people into a social movement. Acolytes had an interest in building mobilization in order to attract Rome's approval, as this would institutionalize their leader's message – and likely result in prominent positions for the acolytes in the religious order that their leader had founded. Therefore, the new institutional environment of modern sainthood thus constructed was not the result of a fight between central officials and local activists, but rather of rules that created greater integration between their interests.[2]

---

[2] Throughout the book I treat a candidate for sainthood as a social movement and acolytes as activists. This breaks in important points with contemporary scholarship. All of the main approaches to collective action – collective behavior, resource mobilization, political process, and new social movements – share one common, albeit unstated, denominator: social movements are features of modernity (Della Porta and Diani 1999). Before modernity, discontent meant two things – violence and repression – not social movements. Without citizens and states, without individuals and rights, subjects made revolutions, crowds assaulted royal palaces, and soldiers plundered the countryside; they did not organize themselves into a movement. Steven Buechler argues that sociology as a discipline and social movements as part of sociology require modernity as precondition (1998). Historically, this is true – sociology as a discipline developed during the later part of the nineteenth century, and with it came sociologists that studied social movements. But this need not imply that sociological phenomena did not exist before the discipline of sociology emerged. During the fifteenth century, people in Florence toppled the Medici under the leadership of Savonarola and organized themselves into a republic before there were scholars of social movements studying them. Yet, a straight application of the theoretical principles of social movements to premodern societies is nevertheless not possible. The organization of the social, political, and economic spheres allowed little room for people to express publicly their grievances and discontent; in most of the times and in the

A MUTUALLY BENEFICIAL EXCHANGE

The events covered in this book occurred during a crucial period of European history, from the mid-sixteenth century to the mid-seventeenth century, when the balance of economic, political, and military powers significantly shifted toward northern Europe. It was during this period that the Europeans forged the links with different parts of the world that would become the basis for a system of global trade (Erikson and Bearman 2006). At the same time, commerce between European countries grew exponentially. The emergence of global trade drove an expansion of the division of labor as well as dramatic increases in industrial production. For the first time in history, better living standards increased life expectancy for millions of people.[3]

This material growth, sustained by increased productivity, differed in important respects from the economic expansions that occurred earlier in other parts of Europe. The occasional burst of economic activity up until the seventeenth century had been part of a cycle of prosperity that either could not keep up with population growth or could not continue after a catastrophe (such as a plague), which was followed by food scarcity, famine, and underdevelopment, before prosperity resumed. These cycles left a territory with almost no lasting progress (De Vries 1974; Mols 1979). But from the seventeenth century onward, economic progress sustained its gains to produce a lasting effect. As a consequence, the population of London increased tenfold during this period. Paris, with a population of

majority of the cases, people remained subjects rather than citizens. This implies that generalizing a social movement perspective to candidates outside of the sample considered in the book will continue to require a case-by-case examination despite the findings this book uncovers. I am thankful to Doug McAdam for forcing me to clarify my interpretation of the social movement scholarship.

[3] The rise was especially pronounced in the Dutch provinces. Due to a good drainage system and efficient labor, Dutch peasants produced a vast range of commercial products – tobacco, cheese, milk, hemp, flax, turnips, etc. – that yielded larger profits on the market than traditional grain. Activities that were ancillary to the development of agriculture grew, funded by the profits of a new class of independent farmers, who now required people to build dykes and polders, perform metallurgy and smith work, and so on. These activities employed the nonfarming members of the rural population (De Vries 1974). By the mid-seventeenth century, foreign grain supplied more than half of the million inhabitants of Holland. "Imported grain," write Rich and Wilson, "not only fed people and supplied raw materials of the intensive brewing and distilling industries of the Republic: it released capital, land and resources ... [that] could thus be more intensively employed" (1977, 24).

two hundred thousand, had been about the size of Naples in 1598; the city had doubled in size by 1656 (Mols 1979).

The sixteenth and the seventeenth centuries were also a period of intense religious turmoil. The Roman Catholic Church came under attack in 1517 with the publication of Martin Luther's *Ninety-Five Theses*, in 1534 with Henry VIII's *Act of Supremacy*, and in 1536 with John Calvin's *Institutes of the Christian Religion*. Helped by the printing press, the ideas of the "protesters" quickly diffused throughout the continent. Their wide publication neutralized the traditional means – force and mass conversions – that the Roman Curia (the government of the Church) and the popes had used to deal with heresies during the thousand years prior. At the dawn of modernity, the Church had to cope with questions and doubts springing up all over Europe, or else risk being displaced, just as local languages were when the army of the Roman Empire carried out the first integration of the Western world (MacMullen 1984). The containment and repression of heresies were no longer options for Rome now that it could not control the diffusion of ideas, and the circulation of goods and people had taken on a truly global scale.

The cults of the saints played a significant role in the controversies among believers. Definitional discrepancies over the concepts of "saint" and "miracle" became obvious to large swathes of European society as never before, straining the Church's credibility on a major doctrinal issue. Believers became skeptical of the authenticity of relics and of the stories that surrounded pilgrimage places such as the Holy House of the Virgin in Central Italy. According to tradition, angels brought the Holy House from Palestine during the thirteenth century for fear of the invading Turks. Along the way from Palestine to Italy, the angels carrying the house stopped, presumably to rest, for a few years in Croatia, where miracles occurred as a result of the presence of the angels and the house. The plausibility of this narrative and of many similar ones came under question. For Rome, maintaining religious legitimacy – or in some cases, such as in northern France, gaining religious legitimacy – meant not only eliminating discrepancies in the definition of saints and miracles but also, most importantly, developing a way to evaluate supernatural events.

The focus of this book is a subset of the supernatural events that occurred during this period – the miracles that charismatic religious leaders performed while alive and after their deaths. Thus crying icons of the Virgin Mary or moving holy statues are not part of my analysis. The development of Rome's method for evaluating miracles was a process of refining evidence and consolidating rules. The by-product of this process was the channeling of religious mobilization into the core of the Church. That is, by establishing new procedures for adjudicating miracles and saints, Rome not only rationalized the miracles at the core of sainthood, but it also produced a positive interaction with local religious activists that enhanced Rome's control over the religious environment and the legitimacy of the Church in the eyes of its believers.

The key to understanding how this process took place is to focus on the work of the Congregatio Sacrorum Rituum, a special commission created in 1588 with the goal of investigating the people who died with a reputation for being a saint and the miracles that they were believed to have performed. This commission transformed sainthood from a dichotomous outcome – somebody is either a saint or is not a saint – into a multistage legal process in which sainthood was only the last step. As I detail later in the book, the Congregatio stipulated that reaching sainthood required moving from the state of venerable to that of blessed to that of saint. These "career moves" are still in use today. The Congregatio made similar procedural reforms to the evaluation of supernatural events, classifying them on a scale of three degrees that followed the suggestions of Saint Augustine as refined by Prospero Lambertini, a member of the Congregatio during the second half of the sixteenth century and later Pope Benedict XIV.

Producing a more rational sainthood served not only the interests of the Church but also those of local religious activists – for different reasons. In an environment lacking the many taken-for-granted beliefs that characterized the preceding centuries, and in which established religious practices were under attack, religious activists and their charismatic leaders began competing for community attention and resources. The countrysides of Catholic countries and the streets of many urban centers were dense with religious movements of all types. A large number of candidates for sainthood during this period started new religious movements, and securing the institutionalization of these orders became the fundamental problem for the candidates' acolytes after the passing of their leaders. Because miracles had attracted donations and generated support for more than a millennium, supernatural events were the ground on which a candidate's acolytes competed locally against other activists.

Finding a way to certify that the miracles their leader performed benefited acolytes not only because Rome's approval would certify their leader's miracles as true and thus generate more support, but also because this support could be used to institutionalize the leader's message. To use Weber's concept, approval from Rome helped routinize the charisma that tied the leader to his staff. This book presents evidence that acolytes used miracles to knit believers into networks that supported the candidacy for sainthood of their deceased leader and that these networks were heterogeneous with respect to gender, status, and kinship affiliation. In the context of highly segmented local societies, the heterogeneity of these mobilizing networks indicates that miracles did not occur randomly in the social fabric but instead resulted from the skilled activism of the acolytes.

Though local activists and Rome had their own reasons for supporting the creation of a mechanism to certify true miracles, they shared a refusal to accept the Protestant claim that miracles, the cults of the saints, and miracle-induced social mobilization were by-products of superstition and trickery. At the individual level, a miracle was a mental frame that reduced uncertainty – something inexplicable occurred, and a miracle explained why. A miracle was the ultimate testimony that nothing happened by chance, or as Albert Einstein would put it a few centuries later, that God does not play dice with the universe.[4] In this light, I define a miracle to be a mental frame, à la Goffman, for explaining unusual events. Empirically, this means that every event that witnesses reported during canonization trials to be a miracle was recorded as such. True miracles were a subset of all the miracles that I collected.

The fact that the canonization rules and procedures that emerged during this period served the common interests of Church officials and local religious activists can lead to the temptation to explain events from their conclusions. One must avoid that trap in order to turn the historical scenario into an analytical case relevant to scholars interested in how organizations can interact positively with activists. This book documents in great detail how the Church and local activists interacted and what were the results of these interactions. There was much happenstance in the creation and enforcement of rules for adjudicating miracles. Factions of cardinals fought for control of the Congregatio during the first part of the seventeenth century. During much of the same period, there was considerable uncertainty as to what a true miracle should look like. However, once the interests of both parties aligned – and to a certain extent that alignment was due to a key change in the larger environment of Europe, a change that was independent of the microinteractions scrutinized here – they locked together to create the field of modern sainthood.

---

[4] From a letter that Albert Einstein wrote to Max Born. David A. Shiang, 2008. *God Does Not Play Dice*. Lexington, MA: Open Sesame Productions.

This institutional arrangement lasted for almost half a millennium, until Pope John Paul II altered canonization procedures during the 1980s.

Modern sainthood originated during the period that this book covers. Its main characteristics are known to causal observers and experts alike. A person dies with a reputation of being a saint, what the Church used to call the *fama sanctitatis* (fame of holiness), and his acolytes petition Rome to open an investigation of this reputation (Papa 2001). Eventually, canonization trials begin, focusing on two aspects of the holy person's behavior: (1) his virtues as a Catholic believer and Christian while he was alive and (2) his supernatural capacities now that, having left this world, he is able to intercede for us with God in the other world. Until the reforms of Pope John Paul II, the number of miracles required for canonization remained the number that was established a few years after the creation of the Congregatio – five at the most, depending on the type of witnesses, as I document in Chapter 1. The required virtues received their coding during the same period. These virtues were faith, hope, charity toward God, charity toward spiritual life, charity toward temporal life, prudence, justice, patience (but during the seventeenth century this was only for French candidates!), and strength, plus the virtue of religious life if the candidate belonged to a religious order.

Throughout the four hundred years that this framework existed, it allowed the Church to incorporate many new religious movements and built enough flexibility into Catholicism to make it capable of penetrating foreign lands such South America, Africa, and Asia. Little historical doubt exists that, since the Schism, the Roman Church has been more successful overall than any particular Protestant sect in amassing believers and support, plotting a trajectory that stands in sharp contrast to the Protestant world's continuous splintering into sects. To think that this success has its roots mostly in the use of repression tools such as the Inquisition is not only wrong, but also it denies the organizational skills of the Church and of its leaders. Scholars of organizations, for example, seem to have ignored a very basic fact for a long time – the Roman Church is the longest-lasting organization in the Western world. This book contends that understanding its extraordinary capacity to adapt and to change its environment can yield fruitful results for other organizations. The process of setting rules for adjudicating miracles is a perfect example by which to analyze the Church's capacity to adapt to and, ultimately, to alter its own environment.

Although organizational scholars have been biased toward underestimating the organizational skills of the Church, it would be an equally grave sin to overestimate the leadership capacities of the people who created the framework for judging miracles and saints. Without question, some were clear thinkers and powerful reformers. Pope Sixtus V, for instance, created the special commission at the center of this book and also masterminded the largest reorganization of the Church before the twentieth century. But also without question, the main characteristics of modern sainthood emerged in large part through a laborious, often-interrupted process of refinement. Equally important, acolytes had trouble understanding the constant stream of changes that characterized the work of the Congregatio from 1588 to 1642.

It took time not just to develop the form that a true miracle had to have, but also for knowledge of that form to become available to religious activists operating in the urban centers of southern Europe and in the countryside. A striking confirmation of this lies in the fact that despite the requirement – adopted early in the process and never changed, that candidates need perform just a handful of postmortem miracles, all of the candidates and their acolytes active during the sixteenth and the seventeenth centuries performed hundreds of miracles, while alive (*in vitam*) and postmortem. The number of miracles began to fall to the minimum only after 1642, when a significant consolidation of procedures occurred. By that time, acolytes had learned the form that true miracles had to have in order to mobilize a community and win the approval of Rome. As a result, they began producing fewer miracles but all of the right form.

The new institutional field of modern sainthood emerged from noncontentious interactions between central officials of the Church and local religious activists. The noncontentious nature of the relationship is an anomaly with respect to current theories of how social movements and organizations interact. Organization scholars have outlined two routes to the creation of a new institutional environment. One route starts with the absence of taken-for-granted beliefs and passes through conflict; the other starts with exogenous regulation that reorganizes taken-for-granted beliefs to produce new ideologies. The first approach emphasizes conflict and considers an institutional environment to be the result of a struggle between competing logics (Greenwood, Suddaby, and Hinings 2002; Lounsbury 2007). Established organizations are at a disadvantage in this struggle because their investment in the status quo becomes a competency trap, reducing their capacity to produce change. The other approach emphasizes rules and sees an institutional environment as the result of exogenous (state) regulations. In this case, rules supply not just a new matrix of acceptable behavior but also new corporate ideologies (Davis, Diekmann, and Tinsley 1994; Davis and Greve 1997) and methods for properly controlling organizations (Fligstein 1990). In this scenario, the greater resources available to established organizations give them an advantage over new organizations (Freeman, Carroll, and Hannan 1983).

This book maps a third route to the creation of a new institutional environment, in which the reduction of uncertainty becomes the common goal of all actors. Change, from this perspective, is the by-product not of conflict but of the recognition of shared interests. Paul DiMaggio shows how a similar process produced change in the field of art museums between World War I and World War II (1991). During the 1920s, DiMaggio argues, many wealthy individuals and foundations began to ask for a reform of the art museum to appeal to the general public rather than just the educated elite. The push produced a new class of professionals whose goal was to change the field of art museums in line with the desires of the foundations. By the 1940s, this change had occurred – without conflict.

The nonconflictive interaction between religious activists and Church officials is also different from the process of co-optation. Charles Tilly has argued extensively that one path that European states traveled toward democratization from the dawn of modernity involved co-opting local centers of power (1978). Similarly, Karen Barkey viewed the expansion of the Ottoman Empire through the lenses of co-optation. In Barkey's work, co-optation was an administrative tool that allowed defeated local elites to remain in charge of administering the newly conquered territory for the Sultan (1994). For Tilly, co-optation neutralized existing threats, while for Barkey, co-optation kept threats from developing. However, the case of the Church and the local activists who mobilized around miracle makers does not fit either of these two interpretations – the Church did not co-opt threatening religious activists. Rather, the Church and local religious activists developed a way to collaborate so that a reformed sainthood could emerge. Two reasons exist for the development of this cooperation.

First, the religious environment of the time was characterized by deep uncertainty, unexpected challenges, and sudden shifts. Neither the Church nor local activists had control of this environment. The Church was a powerful institution that needed to regain legitimacy in the eyes of its own believers; the candidates' acolytes were fervent believers facing steep competition from other activists. Roman officials and local activists had a shared interest in reducing uncertainty: both had an interest in creating a new and more stable institutional environment vis-à-vis the Protestants.

This observation leads me to the second reason why cooperation developed between the Church and candidates' acolytes. As religious activists, acolytes put together movements that were not contentious but instead were vehicles for translating private ideas and goals into a (local) public arena. Activists asked for reforms in the Church; they did not advocate overthrowing the Papacy. When Neri was summoned to the Vatican to explain his suspicious behavior and preaching – Neri would organize thousands-strong "anti-Carnival" walks that visited the seven main basilicas of Rome – he obeyed the pontiff's orders despite the obvious risk of being imprisoned (as it so happened he was for a few days). When Teresa of Avila was sent to confinement for her unusual and fervent preaching, she followed the orders given to her and stayed in confinement for years. Most of the candidates of this period criticized the government of the Church, the Curia, and the Papacy and were reprimanded in various degrees. None of them decided, however, to leave the fold. Dismissing this behavior as inconsistent or as rooted in fear does not square with the evidence that such behavior was very common and that many of the religious orders that deeply reformed the Church originated precisely from the preaching of the same candidates who criticized the Church.

The next three sections develop each of the reasons that cooperation developed between the Church and candidates' acolytes. My goal is to make very explicit the analytical argument that runs through this book and the implications it has for the community of scholars interested in social movements and organizations.

DEALING WITH UNCERTAINTY

The period at the center of my analysis was troubled by deep religious, political, and social uncertainty. This uncertainty characterized northern and southern Europe alike. In Italy, Carlo Ginzburg documented how the circulation of books enabled the diffusion of unorthodox ideas between elites across regions and within a territory across social strata (1970). Sometimes, heterodox ideas created elaborate religious cosmologies (Ginzburg 1976). More common were simplifications of Luther's theses. For example, a witness in the canonization trial of Antonio De Colellis reported that in Naples, a friar had been having visions of the Virgin Mary for quite a long time. His fellow friars doubted the authenticity of these visions and decided to test them by giving the visionary friar a relic of De Colellis (a piece of his shirt) when the Virgin Mary appeared to him. With De Colellis's relic in his hand, the visionary friar began describing the vision and, according to the witness, also "began making mistakes by saying that it was unnecessary to ask the Madonna and the Saints for protection and that only talking to God was necessary" (ASV 1983, folio 167b). Needless to say, everybody agreed that these suspiciously Protestant-sounding visions were the work of the Devil!

Most supernatural events were not so easy to evaluate. For religious activists on the ground as well as for Roman officials in the aftermath of the Protestant Schism, uncertainty about supernatural events created two partially related problems. First, Rome somehow had to make sure that the mobilization surrounding a charismatic religious leader was legitimate. Second, local activists had to reduce the amount of competition that they faced from other activists. Religious competition created havoc in an environment in which taken-for-granted beliefs had broken down. For instance, a priest in a small village near Milan was exasperated by all the attention attracted by a crying image of the Virgin Mary in a nearby parish. During the trial that Church authorities held on the case, he told the judges explicitly that his constituency was diverting prayers and money to the other parish, creating problems for him and his church (Sangalli 1993). Competition was particularly fierce when supernatural results were perceived to be produced by a candidate's relics. For example, the internal organs of Neri were secretly taken from Rome and brought to Naples, where they ended up in the hands of a noblewoman (*Il primo processo*). Similarly, the head of Bernardino of Santa Lucia, another candidate included in this analysis, was stolen from the Franciscan Church in Agrigento, Italy, where the whole body lay exposed (ASV 2209). Such anecdotal examples of relic theft could continue for several pages.

Simultaneously achieving the goals of reducing competition and legitimizing local mobilization would require building a new institutional environment for sainthood. The idiosyncratic sainthood of the Middle Ages, divided as it was between local (low) saints and official (high) saints, could not stand. In the face of local activism and the threat of schism, the new system would have to create the possibility for religious change within the Church, rather than outside of it. Thus reducing uncertainty meant not restricting change but instead creating and controlling the ground on which it would occur.

The difference between uncertainty and change was first noted by Frank Knight during the early twentieth century (1921) and more recently was further elaborated by Ulrich Bech (2004). Change requires the calculation of risks, but uncertainty makes such calculation impossible. An institutional environment therefore is not only a collection of beliefs, practices, and values held in common by the actors (e.g., Catholics during the sixteenth century) but also a system that allows for change, such as changes in which miracles could be considered true and, consequently, a system in which potential religious reformers, that is, candidates to sainthood, could be elevated to the status of saint and their message of change institutionalized. According to Knight, organizations always change in order to increase their profits and fit in better with the environment. Yet not all changes are equally possible, and those that occur either respond to the dominant political logic in the environment (Friedland and Alford 1991) or are by-products of the prevailing cultural beliefs in an industry or among its lead practitioners.

In the case at hand, mastering uncertainty and restoring the possibility of change meant finding a way to incorporate religious activism into the core of Catholicism. Because religious activism at the time meant producing miracles, controlling change meant creating procedures for approving miracles. For this reason, the Church's task also included refining religious activism so that the boundaries of the supernatural became clear to everyone. As later chapters will show, defining the boundaries of the supernatural was precisely the task of the Promotore Fidei (or Devil's Advocate, as the role was familiarly known), the Congregatio's attorney who argued against the candidate. (Like the new procedures for attaining sainthood, this position emerged from the Congregatio's efforts during the first part of the seventeenth century.) The task of the Devil's Advocate was not to deny the existence of miracles but to create space for false miracles – that is, for the occurrence of events or facts that, although inexplicable by science or medicine, were nevertheless not true miracles. Doing so legitimized the claim of the Church to be the guardian of the supernatural. By marking the boundaries of the uncertain, the Promotore Fidei was the institutional figure who, more than others inside the Congregatio, orchestrated change.

A NONCONTENTIOUS MOVEMENT

Immediately after the leader's departure for paradise (the *dies natalis*, in Church terminology), acolytes were faced with the problem of how to ensure that their leader's message of religious reform could continue. In the absence of the leader's charisma, the propagation of the leader's message could occur only by gaining new activists on behalf of the candidate's sanctity. The involvement of newcomers required that acolytes mobilize a community and, given the needs of the sixteenth-century Church, this mobilization translated directly into creating the conditions for the occurrence of more miracles. However, because the candidate was not there in the flesh, the acolytes had to be careful in connecting the occurrence of further supernatural events to the intercession of the candidate, who was now sitting close to God in paradise. Acolytes had to exercise skill in building, and controlling, the networks that generated miracles on behalf of their candidate.

Acolytes also had instrumental reasons for wanting to mobilize a community. Acolytes usually took important positions in the orders that their leaders founded or reformed. Ensuring the continuity of these positions meant ultimately receiving Rome's seal of approval. Thus it is not surprising that, despite the fact that the leader's message was often one of criticism toward Rome, his acolytes looked to the Holy See after his death.

The days immediately after the candidate's death marked a special time in the community in which the candidate and his acolytes were active. It was during this period that the acolytes could potentially capitalize on their skills as activists, because opportunities for miracles multiplied in the days following the *dies natalis*. If the candidate were truly a saint, the general population expected to see postmortem miracles, which could occur only after the *dies natalis*. The days immediately after the candidate's death were also the time when it was easiest to create relics of the saint, which would be the main vehicle of those postmortem miracles. Relics would prove the involvement of the candidate in postmortem miracles, and the candidate's acolytes hoped to control the relics in order to build their network and create more miracles.

Maintaining control of a candidate's relics was a difficult business, however. For instance, when friar Rainiero, one of the candidates examined in this book, died on August 23, 1589, his acolyte and fellow friar, Egidio da Amelia, testified that a mob rushed to the body that lay inside the church and began quite literally to take him apart – taking his hair and pieces of his clothes and punching holes into his body so that tissues could be soaked in his blood. A similar scene happened when friar Pasqual Baylon died in Villa Real, Spain. Egidio's testimony highlights that public fervor was directed mostly toward pieces of the candidate's body, the most common kind of relic.

The public's interest in relics came from the deeply held belief that relics had healing powers. It would be a grave mistake to think that only the lower strata of society held these beliefs. Philip II, the king of Spain from 1556 to 1598, amassed a collection of more than one hundred relics in the palace monastery El Escorial.

Because relics proved the involvement of a given candidate in a postmortem miracle, successfully organizing public fervor into a community mobilization meant maintaining strict control over the candidate's relics. Acolytes who succeeded in maintaining possession of their candidate's relics then organized their control of those relics through the creation of the ritual healing. The ritual helped construct a predictable mental frame – based on popular beliefs about how nature and society worked – around (unpredictable) illnesses and thereby "produced" healings. As an expression of a strict set of guidelines, a ritual reduced uncertainty by removing chance from the equation and instead offered evidence that all forces obeyed God's laws. A healing was a patterned process in time in which the behavior of each actor involved was symbolic (Turner 1967). Acolytes catalyzed postmortem miracles through their role as performers of a ritual at whose center stood the candidate or a piece of his body.

This book therefore treats each candidate for sainthood as akin to a social movement, his acolytes as activists, and the miracles that occurred postmortem and *in vitam* as mobilizing events. The latter type of miracle, performed directly by the living candidate, transformed individuals into activists and created the basis for an organizational structure, based on the candidate's charisma, which became the central force behind the occurrence of postmortem miracles. Candidates for Catholic sainthood during this period represented social movements of a particular type, one that, in contrast to Protestant social movements, intended to remain in the Catholic Church. Although the candidates often expressed deep criticism of Rome, they were also very careful to maintain compliance with the Holy See. Their messages of reform thus remained embedded in Catholicism, and so did the behavior of their acolytes.

Scholars of social movements are instead accustomed to seeing movements as contentious actors (Della Porta and Diani 1999). Thus, for example, Sydney Tarrow writes that social movements are contentious networks capable of sustaining challenges to powerful opponents (1996). For Tilly, social movements are organized, historical actors that use contingent repertoires to protest (necessarily contentiously) against authority (1978, 1985). It is precisely because movements are contentious, that is, change seeking, that the amalgamation of social movement theory and neoinstitutional theory has been theoretically useful. Without social movements, processes such as isomorphism (DiMaggio and Powell 1983), legitimacy (Tolbert and Zucker 1983), and structuration of the environment (Giddens 1984) would quickly lead to a theoretical dead end.

If social movement theory saved neoinstitutional theory from a standstill, it did so at the price of obscuring what institutional scholars showed decades ago – that organizations are powerful actors that shape their social environments, including the movements that arise from those environments (Selznick 1980; Abbott 1988). For example, in describing the interaction between the Tennessee Valley Authority and local organizations, Philip Selznick notes that a procedure that "channels the administration of a program through established local institutions ... tends to reinforce the legitimacy of the existing leadership" (1980: 72). The analytical argument of this book is that uncertainty prompts organizations to seek change, which makes it possible to analyze their positive interactions with social movements. Conditions of uncertainty represent an extreme scenario that is useful for theory building.

Yet positive interactions between movements and organizations do not necessarily require uncertainty in order to develop. For example, Klaus Weber, K. Heinze, and Michele DeSoucey argue that in the case of grass-fed meat and dairy products, organizations and activists created a new economic object through the sharing of cultural codes rather than direct confrontation (2008). Theorizing a positive interaction between organizations and social movements does, however, require a new definition of a social movement that does not assume conflict. I adopt Jeffery Alexander's definition: "Social movements ... can be seen as devices that construct translations between the discourse of civil society and the institution-specific processes of a more particularistic type" (2006: 233). The candidate for sainthood, his acolytes, and the miracles that occurred *in vitam* and postmortem are a social movement to the extent that they represent not just the self-interest of a band of activists but also the claims of the locales where the miracles occurred, the acolytes operated, and the candidate lived. From this perspective, the activism that mobilized around the candidates can be interpreted as an expression of local identities, in the context of the intense rivalries that organized the relationships between cities in several parts of southern Europe. Jean-Micheal Sallmann (1994) makes a similar argument for the case of patron saints in southern Italy.

RULES FOR EXCHANGE

At the dawn of modernity, the medieval version of sainthood presented several complications for the Church. For more than a thousand years, sainthood reflected the beliefs and worship practices of a society so segmented that each social class had its own saints. This not only produced idiosyncratic claims to sainthood but also generated outright abuses of the term, at least from the perspective of Christian dogma. For example, Andre Vauchez documents that one rural community in southern France elevated a dog to the level of a saint (1989). This was not the sainthood that the Papacy promoted. Nevertheless, the coexistence of multiple versions of sainthood was a fact that prominently fueled Protestant claims that Catholicism was rooted in superstitions and sorcery. It was clear to many within the Curia that sainthood had to be reformed. The organizational conundrum that they faced during the second half of the sixteenth century was how to reform it without alienating popular support. People believed in saints because saints performed miracles that reflected the underlying needs of local populations. Thus standardizing sainthood across locales could have created dire consequences for Rome at a time when the Church appeared particularly fragile and needed the support of the people.

The fact that saints incorporated local claims in their displays of supernatural powers made medieval sainthood more similar to magic than to religion. The connection between magic and the local cults of saints was evident during the street processions that characterized life in medieval Europe. Every time a monastery needed to revamp the cult of a saint in order to attract pilgrims, it organized a translation, a process whereby the body of a saint or some part of the saint's body (Vauchez 1989) was transferred from one tomb to a better one. The translation would process through the streets of the village or town and would inevitably generate large crowds. As Church authorities led the procession, first a few people, then increasingly more, would start to experience miracles. If the translation was successful, the snowball effect it set in motion would continue to involve larger numbers of people in increasingly more distant communities, all of whom would become convinced of the reinvigorating power of the saint.

As Weber noted, these beliefs expressed a vision of the sacred that was rooted in exhorting control over supernatural beings, that is, the local saints, in an effort to coerce them to do things beneficial to the believer. The practice of the *ex voto* symbolized perfectly the old arrangement that sustained sainthood and that continued in part into modernity (albeit not in the cults of the saints but in the worship of icons). The worshipper prayed to the local saint by essentially saying: "If you do X for me, I will do Y for you." Y usually meant that the beneficiary of the miracle, the saved, would make donations to a local church, in either money or wax, or would go on a pilgrimage. The relationship between each local saint and each believer was a *do ut des*, an idiosyncratic, irrational exchange rooted in magic.

The rationalization of religion that Protestantism ushered in broke with the beliefs and practices that surrounded the cults of the saints. Protestants turned God into a rational being who organized the functioning of the world, including nature, according to invariant laws. To the extent that miracles expressed local and idiosyncratic demands for salvation, they were simply irrational. Thus, in order to defend the power of the saints, Rome had to develop a system that allowed local demands for supernatural events without incurring the criticism of the Protestants. The solution that Rome devised was to create rules for controlling the magic that produced miracles. That is, instead of eliminating the possibility that individuals could perform miracles, the Congregatio rationalized the form that a miracle had to have and ignored the content of the miracle. A true miracle had an inclusive form, one that crossed kinship and status divisions, across all locales. This form, as we have seen, was beneficial to the Church and the acolytes.

The rules for adjudicating miracles integrated the interests of Rome and those of the local activists who used the supernatural powers of their leaders to create mobilizations. However, scholars of social movements and organizations have largely ignored the fact that rules may integrate various actors' interests, rather than expressing only the power of the dominant actor. When the organization is dominant, its procedures and rules are conceptualized as the instrument through which it directly asserts its power (Fox Piven and Cloward 2005) or interests (Fligstein 1996). When organizations are seen as passive reactors to social mobilization, it is the power of the social movement, not of the organization, that finds its expression through the rules (Van Dyke, Soule, and Taylor 2004; Soule and King 2006). Rules are still conceptualized mainly as an expression of power; what differs is whose power. Thus, for the advocates of the movement-centered path to change as well as for the advocates of the coercive power of organizations, rules are the naked expression of power.

Relaxing the assumption that the interaction between a social movement and an organization is always conflictive (see previous section) implies focusing on rules as instruments for integration. This perspective rediscovers the fact that rules are also a tool for coordinating behavior (Elias 1992) and creating integration (Durkheim 1997). For example, Mitchel Abolafia (2001) shows how the rules of the Chicago Board of Trade created greater integration among its members so that a free market could continue to exist despite the self-interest and opportunism of the traders. Furthermore, seeing rules as a mechanism for greater integration implies looking more carefully at the relationship between a given social movement and a given organization. Because integration can occur only to the extent that both actors – the organization and the social movement – occupy a similar position vis-à-vis each other, it becomes important to historically reconstruct the broader structural conditions that define each relationship. It is only by substantiating this theory with historical contingencies that the risk of abstract theorizing, so common among sociologists (Tilly 1961), can be avoided.

Stating that rules create integration does not mean denying that they also express power. Rather, it implies seeing power as a medium that circulates among actors, similar to money (Parsons 1960), such that, although some actors have more power than others, everybody has some (Schwartz 1976). From this perspective, integration can occur even in cases of power imbalance. Rules and procedures always have an effect, no matter how small, even if they were created for symbolic compliance (Westphal and Zajac 2001). As Robert Dahl points out, the ceremonial apparatus of the American political party – the convention, the caucus, and so forth – serves a symbolic function, but it is also an integrating mechanism for new constituencies (1989). This interpretation is consistent with Lauren Edelman's finding that the equal employment opportunity offices that many organizations created during the 1970s, in symbolic compliance with the law, did have an effect in the long run (1992).

An organization can craft rules to create an institutional process that encodes the interests of a social movement. *Encoding* refers to a process whereby rules are constructed to single out actions that are then encapsulated in a collective structure of meaning that is not related to the context in which the actions originally occurred. Encoding is therefore a dynamic process capable of transforming the environment. Successful encoding makes explicit the interests of both actors, creating a common ideological basis upon which they can continue to interact. This is what happened during the early 1980s, for example, when new rules promoted by FIAT's management made explicit to the established union leadership that the management shared with them the interest of curbing the role of new, independent unions (Locke 1997). The reorganization of the shop floor that resulted reproduced the power of the management and of the established unions on a new terrain.

For the Church, the process of encoding its interests and those of the acolytes into a new structure of meaning meant that true miracles took on the inclusive form previously described, instead of reproducing in content the actions of Jesus, as was the case during the medieval era. Attention to the form of a miracle instead of its content served the interests of the organization because it allowed for a standardization of the practices that produced supernatural events, while still allowing for local variation in content; at the same time, it served the interests of the local activists because it supported the creation of heterogeneous mobilizations capable of attracting local support. The new rules made possible a process that transformed sainthood from the inside out. As the final chapters of this book show, the number of miracles that each candidate performed fell quickly during the second half of the sixteenth century, once it was clear to every actor what a true miracle had to look like.

On the basis of the rules for adjudicating miracles, the Church and the several social movements created lasting interactions. This process is similar to what Tim Bartley observed in two industries, forestry and apparel, during the 1990s (2007). The processes that Bartley considers started from the bottom up, but in the case of the Church, my analysis indicates that new regulations came from the top down and were successful because they solved the competition problems that local activists faced. Rather than creating an equilibrium between conflicting interests – an argument well suited to the context of the liberal democracies that Bartley analyzes but not applicable at the dawn of modernity – the rules of the Congregatio created an interaction similar to a commitment in which legitimacy and control are exchanged (Thompson 1967; Kraatz and Zajac 2001).

For the organization to receive legitimacy from the social movement, the organization has to have the capacity, or be perceived to have the capacity, to increase the social movement's control of the environment. Rules create this capacity if they achieve, or help to achieve, the movement's goals; if they fit with the movement's overall values and practices; or if they are neutral to the (potential) status conflicts among the internal cliques of the movement (Dalton 1964; Gouldner 1965). Because Rome had the power to canonize individuals, activists looked to Rome in order to win their competitions with other activists. Furthermore, receiving Rome's approval could crystallize the structure of the local institution that linked acolytes to their leader and to each other. Rome's approval could create positions for acolytes within the religious orders that many candidates founded or reformed while they were alive.

From a top-down perspective, turning a scenario of uncertainty into an opportunity for institutional change requires that the organization look outside its boundaries and use rules to create a stable exchange with a social movement capable of bringing legitimacy to the organization's core operations. This path to creating institutional stability (Greenwood, Suddaby, and Hinings 2002) transforms the organization and the social movement because it generates an ideology, following Gramsci, that transcends the interests of the dominant actor (Clemens 1997; Rao, Monin, and Durand 2003) and instead serves the common interests of all actors. The experience of the Church teaches us that its rules were successful because they created a version of sainthood that solved the competition problems of local activists and the legitimacy crisis that Rome faced in the aftermath of the Protestant Schism. This exchange constitutes the foundation of modern sainthood. At the core of this exchange were the rules for handling the power of magic that the Congregatio crafted between 1588 and 1642.

THE ORGANIZATION OF THIS BOOK

This book is organized in five chapters, a conclusion, and two technical appendices. The first chapter provides a broad characterization of the historical period in which the main actors at the center of the book operated. The chapter then moves on to the main topic of this book – the establishment of the Congregatio and of the rules for adjudicating miracles during the first half of the century. The next two chapters provide detailed evidence of the social mechanism that produced miracles during the seventeenth century. The second chapter describes the trials of nine candidates to sainthood that took place between 1588 and 1642 and all the miracles that were recounted in these trials. The Congregatio established a series of repeated trials, conducted by different authorities (local or Roman) and treating different subjects (the whole life of the candidate or some segments of it). A candidate for sainthood had to have at least four trials before being considered for canonization, and usually had many more. The analytical focus of the chapter is the miracles that candidates performed while alive. The third chapter examines the role of the acolytes in using miracles to create support for their candidate. From the testimony of more than a thousand witnesses that participated in the nine candidates' trials, a social structure of connected individuals emerges. The candidate's acolytes were those most responsible for holding the structure together. The fourth and fifth chapters move the argument inside the Church and examine the impact that the procedures crafted for dealing with the miracle-induced mobilization had locally and at a more macrolevel. The fourth chapter shows how the Church created the institutional figure of the Devil's Advocate to maintain control of doctors-turned-acolytes that were applying their knowledge in an effort to bypass Rome's approval. Finally, the fifth chapter considers how the Church used procedures for sifting through the amount of local support that the acolytes were building locally. I have also extensively documented the changes that the Congregatio made to the rules for canonization during the middle of the seventeenth century. The switch significantly changed the type of sainthood that predominated during the second part of the century. In the conclusion, I summarize the argument of the book in structural terms and highlight some implications for further research in fields characterized by institutional uncertainty.

I

The Congregatio Sacrorum Rituum

This chapter describes the creation of the Congregatio Sacrorum Rituum, or Congregation of the Sacred Rites, the Vatican's special commission for investigating claims to sainthood. Established in 1588, the Congregatio did not create sainthood but rather adjusted its meaning to preserve the relevance of miracles in modern times. Sanctity has been the object of much scrutiny, mostly historical and anthropological, and primarily focusing on the Middle Ages. This book focuses on the process by which candidates achieved canonization during the first part of the seventeenth century, but a survey of the existing work on sanctity allows us to track the changes in canonization procedures over time before then.

Historians have described the shift in the idea of sainthood that took place during the Catholic Counter-Reformation, specifically with respect to the Church's greater emphasis on virtues rather than on miracles as prerequisites for canonization (Vauchez 1989). Yet despite knowing when the Church transformed sainthood in southern Europe (Bossy 1985; Zarri 1991; Boesch-Gajano and Modica 2000) and why (Gotor 2000; 2004), we know little about how the Church achieved this transformation. This is precisely the puzzle that this book considers. One goal of this chapter is thus to set the stage for the analysis that follows by reviewing the existing literature on sainthood.

In order to develop an analytical model of how sainthood was transformed, it is necessary to explain the impact of an exogenous event, the Peace of Westphalia, on the internal balance of powers of key actors in the religious field of southern Europe – the officials of the Congregatio, bishops, and local religious activists grouped around candidates to sainthood. Concluded in 1648, the Peace of Westphalia marked the end of the bloody Thirty Years War and of the religious turmoil that began more than a century before with the Protestant Schism. The Peace of Westphalia established the notion that a state had absolute sovereignty over a territory, and that intermediate and international bodies had no authority over states' internal affairs. This was the birth of the nation-state and of the international system of nations. Broadly speaking, the Peace of Westphalia became the cornerstone of Europe's enhanced institutional and religious stability, which remained fundamentally unaltered until the first Napoleonic War (Braudel 1992). After 1648, no northern European king seriously considered overthrowing the papacy, and nobles in southern Europe did not do much more to "save England" than to offer masses to that end. A sort of cold war *ante litteram* descended on Europe.

The Thirty Years War was fought, in its various phases, primarily in what is now Germany. The first phase began in 1618, when three counselors of the Catholic King Ferdinand II were thrown out of a window in the Castle of Prague by Protestant Bohemians, who were revolting out of fear that King Ferdinand was poised to revoke their religious autonomy. In 1620 and again in 1623, the Protestants were defeated by the troops of King Ferdinand, who after the death of his cousin Matthias in 1619 had also become the new Habsburg Emperor. Meanwhile, King Christian IV of Denmark hurled himself into the conflict for fear of resurgent Catholicism in northern Germany, thereby beginning the second phase of the war. In 1626, imperial troops under the command of General Wallenstein and General Tilly defeated the Danes.

The third phase began when the king of Sweden joined the Protestant cause. He was more successful against King Ferdinand's troops than either the Bohemians or the Danes had been, in part because of France's financial help and in part because King Ferdinand had dismissed Wallenstein's troops out of fear that the general was becoming too powerful. (Ferdinand had to reinstate Wallenstein in 1631, when the Swedish killed General Tilly; Ferdinand later became suspicious of Wallenstein again and had him killed.) In 1632 and 1634, imperial troops and Swedish soldiers clashed in battles whose overall result favored the former. The Treaty of Prague (1635) ended this phase of the war. Catholicism was on the rise again, and more importantly, the Habsburg family emerged as the dominant royal family of Europe, controlling Spain as well as the Holy Roman Empire.

Seeking to defend French interests, Cardinal Richelieu thrust France
into the war against the Habsburgs, beginning the war's fourth phase.
Richelieu made alliances with the Danes and the Swedes and opened
up hostilities again in Germany. The imperial and Spanish troops were
defeated several times in 1647. On May 15, 1648, a final treaty was
signed in the state of Westphalia in Germany. It was the de facto end of
the Holy Roman Empire.

This book argues that the Peace of Westphalia allowed the new rules
for proclaiming saints that the Church adopted in 1642 (see Chapter 5)
to remain unaltered for almost half a millennium. Yet it is always a risk to
make such a statement without a counterfactual. The Peace of Westphalia
occurred in 1648, while the change in rules happened in 1642: how do we
know that Westphalia caused the permanence of rules adopted six years
before? Although a causal argument is logically impossible on historical
grounds, my interpretation of the changes that the Congregatio introduced in 1642 and the fact that the pace of regulatory change slowed
considerably after 1648 suggest that the larger political, religious, and
cultural equilibrium that the Peace of Westphalia created was in line with
the spirit of the new rules of 1642, which applied only internally to the
religious field of southern Europe. The two events were largely autonomous, but nevertheless they both created institutional arrangements that
favored the centralizing power of the Church and of the state. Had the
Peace of Westphalia not happened, my argument implies, the rules of
1642 would have been just another set of changes, like those of 1634,
1623, and 1600, each quickly overturned by the circumstances that
prompted the next. My approach to this exogenous event is reminiscent
of Max Weber's method of historical analysis; that is, to use theoretical
constructions to explain events, rather than the contrary.

Besides understanding how the Peace of Westphalia allowed the
Congregatio to finalize its rules for granting sainthood, it is also important
to reconstruct the early history of that commission in order to understand
the seventeenth-century transformation of sainthood. We can subdivide
the period of that early history (1588–1642) into three distinct intervals:
(1) 1588 to 1600, when the Church formulated a precise definition of the
presaint title of blessed; (2) 1600 to 1623, when tensions arose between
the Inquisition and the Jesuits over who controlled the Congregatio; and
(3) 1623 to 1642, when the Church tried several times to reform canonization procedures, never quite settling the matter once and for all. This
chapter concentrates mostly on the first two intervals, during which one
can begin to discern a pattern in the commission's decisions. The period

of reform that began after 1623 is described briefly here and examined in greater detail in Chapter 5.

The Congregatio became the Church's main instrument not only for refuting Protestant accusations that the cults of the saints were rooted in superstitious beliefs but also for addressing a more subtle enemy – the rise of a scientific view of the world. The seventeenth century was the century of scientific discoveries. Nikolaus Kopernikus, Johannes Kepler, Isaac Newton, Evangelista Torricelli, Robert Boyle, Blaise Pascal, William Harvey, René Descartes, and several others made their discoveries during the period covered in this book. They contributed to the creation of an image of the natural world as a mechanical entity, in which animals, for example, were considered similar to machines (see the *Principia Philosophia* of Descartes) and the functioning of the universe was compared to that of a clock.

Part of this new interpretation of nature was based on strong empiricism. Members of the Royal Society in London and of the Accademia del Cimento in Florence began engaging in all sorts of experiments in order to discover the laws regulating nature. Yet empiricism was not the sole doctrine that propelled scientific discoveries (Hall 1965). The rational philosophy of Descartes (1596–1650) stood alongside empiricism. More than other thinkers, he put an end to the idea that nature moves toward ultimate ends. Instead, Descartes argued, nature moves mechanically so that everything that changes can be explained by a cause. Contrary to the empiricists, however, he thought that causes could be deduced *a priori* and that every man could access the laws of nature as long as he was able to think. Behind the scientific discoveries of the time, therefore, stood two different perspectives – one based on empirical observation, the other based on rational deduction. The two groups of scientists often entered into intense diatribes (see, e.g., the responses of Thomas Hobbes's *Objections* to Descartes's *Meditations*) about how to see nature properly and, in particular, about the role of observation in the development of theories.[1]

Despite their disagreements, empiricists and rationalists deeply altered the common people's perception of how the natural world functioned (von Leyden 1961). If the forests of Europe still managed to have elves and fairies throughout the Renaissance, the new interpretative grid that scientists began promoting during the seventeenth century quickly plucked them out of this world. Empiricists and rationalists agreed that

---

[1] *Scientist* is a modern term. People doing the work of science were usually identified either as natural philosophers or experimental philosophers.

because nature was fundamentally quantitative (rather than based on qualitative differences, as Aristotle had suggested), the best method for understanding it was to use the precision of mathematics. In the mathematical coordinates of the new scientific grid, elves and fairies had no position.

In this context, Church officials and (Catholic) religious activists faced the common problem of how to reconcile miracles, and the underlying idea that certain people had supernatural capacities, with science. On the one side, miracles required a world dense with magic; on the other, the diffusion of scientific explanations was erasing magic from this world. The solution to maintaining magic and thereby miracles, documented in this book, was to use rationality to control empiricism. In a sense, the Church and Catholic religious activists bet that human beings would never live in a perfectly mechanical world where a cause could always be found for the occurrence of any fact. A rational space for miracles could therefore always exist, as long as religious authorities rather than empirically oriented scientists maintained control of the boundary separating the possible from the impossible.

From the organizational perspective of the Church, the fundamental question became not whether miracles are true, but who decides their authenticity – the Church or the scientists? The Congregatio was instrumental in making sure that, in the Catholic world, this power remained in the hands of Rome. Rather than abdicating control of the supernatural to science, as the Protestant churches did in northern Europe, Rome created an institutional mechanism that, while allowing for the impossible to change depending on the level of scientific knowledge, firmly maintained the power of proclaiming miracles in the hands of religious authorities.

RESEARCH ON MIRACLES

The few sociologists who have studied miracles have done so in connection with studying sanctity. As early as 1902, Henri Hubert underlined the role that "switching" patron saints, the practice whereby towns and cities would periodically update their lists of saints, had in reinvigorating the myths and the miracles at the foundation of a saint's cult. Robert Hertz's analysis of the cult of Saint Besse in Alpine villages across Italy and France (1928) was similarly centered on miracles. Yet this early sociological interest in saints took an unexpected turn with Pitrim Sorokin's work on altruistic love, published during the 1950s. Sorokin looked to sainthood to identify factors that allowed people to live longer and happier lives. Notably, his analysis did not focus on the role of miracles. As a consequence, Sorokin disregarded the sociological intersection of sanctity and miracles, that is, the processes that made certain individuals able to perform supernatural wonders. Given Sorokin's prominence at the time, his work had the positive effect of legitimizing the sociological study of sainthood. Over the long term, however, his decision not to study miracles left a sociologically relevant facet of sainthood almost entirely unexplored.

The study of miracles and those who performed them attracted fresh sociological interest during the early 1990s. Aviad Kleinberg, for example, focuses on the relational aspect of sainthood in describing a saint's behavior as a bargain between the expectations of his audience and the saint's own internal motives. Miracles, from this perspective, become part of a performance that the saint undertakes for his community. Kleinberg illustrates this point by describing the reception given to a miracle Saint Lukardis reputedly performed: "On one occasion ... a certain nun saw Lukardis floating above the ground. She reported this prodigy to her friends; they, however, had seen nothing unusual. Why was this incident recounted as a miracle? On the face of it, there seems to be no reason why it should. The nun saw something, conferred with the others, and found that she was mistaken" (1994: 173). Yet because Lukardis had already achieved the status of a living saint, Kleinberg argues, her behavior was read by the community as that of a saint and thus as that of someone able to perform miracles. This relational perspective inverts the expected causality between miracles and sanctity. It is not the case that someone performs miracles and hence is a saint; rather, someone is first considered a saint and performs miracles as a result.[2] From this perspective, sainthood and miracles could not exist without a community (Delooz 1997).

If sociologists have shied away from the subject of miracles, historians have filled the gap, focusing on the social dimensions of sanctity. Discussing the reputed healing powers of the kings of France and England, Marc Bloch wrote, "The idea that a miracle should have taken place created the faith in miracles. What allowed this faith to survive was that same idea and, with the passing of time, [the accounts] accumulated in generations" (1973: 335). Examining the period of the Counter-Reformation,

---

[2] Pierre Delooz recognizes the importance of the community in establishing sainthood. But though he argues that all sainthood is constructed to a certain degree, he nevertheless maintains that only those saints who never really existed in the first place can be considered entirely constructed (Delooz 1997).

Jean-Michel Sallmann argues that miracles constructed a symbolic good called sanctity. During the Regno delle due Sicilie in southern Italy – the period of Sallmann's analysis – the proliferation of new patron saints reflected the economic organization of the Regno. The economy drove the demand for new miracles as dominant groups shifted within towns or villages and the new power brokers promoted their own favorite saints (Sallmann 1994). Historians have also considered another source of variation in miracles. Francois Lebrun, for instance, noting that saints specialized with respect to the disease they could heal, writes, "some of them are granted the power to provoke a given disease, that often bears the saints' names ... and which, consequently, only they can heal" (1995: 61). During the Middle Ages, miracles became part of verbal contracts in which a man would ask a saint for his intercession with God (Sangalli 1993). If his request was fulfilled, that is, if the miracle occurred, he would bring a gift (the *ex voto*) to the tomb of the saint, often a representation of the body part that received the healing. Bernard Cousin documents that in Southern France, paintings were also used as *ex voto*; believers brought to the tombs of saints small tablets portraying the type of miracle they had received (1983). Because of the cost of commissioning a painting, nobles and the higher strata of society were the first to adopt this new form of worship.

By linking miracles to economic and social forces, the historical research on miracles provides one key to interpreting miracles' persistent legitimacy in the modern religious world. Rather than being random occurrences, miracles address the needs of the recipient population. Although historians and anthropologists have always recognized the social relevance of miracles, sociologists have long ignored miracles as an object of study. One goal of this book is to show that analyzing how certain individuals acquire supernatural capacities in the perception of an audience speaks directly to the core of the discipline of sociology because it can suggest an explanation for a key concept of the discipline, that of social facts.

Emile Durkheim long ago highlighted the importance of studying social facts as a separate category of human facts. In *The Rules of the Sociological Method*, he wrote:

Here, then, is a category of facts which present very special characteristics: they consist of manners of acting, thinking and feeling external to the individual, which are invested with a coercive power by virtue of which they exercise control over him. Consequently, since they consist of representations and actions, they cannot be confused with organic phenomena, nor with psychical phenomena, which have no existence save in and through the individual consciousness. Thus they constitute a new species and to them must be exclusively assigned the term social. (1982: 54)

What gave some people reputations as miracle workers in their communities is the social fact that this book considers.

SAINTHOOD BEFORE THE CONGREGATIO

Given that Christians have worshiped saints since Saint Paul's crucifixion in Rome, it is hardly surprising that the meaning of *sainthood* has changed with the passage of time. Nor is it surprising that different types of sainthood coexisted in the same era. For instance, in documenting the rise of Christianity during the late Roman Empire, Peter Brown suggests that the healings the saints performed were a sign of their ability to intercede with God, and people went to visit the saints' tombs to put themselves at the mercy of these celestial patrons, much as they would do with high-ranking patrons in the mundane world (1981).

Moving closer to the period of considered in this book, Andre Vauchez argues that, during the Middle Ages, a type of sainthood made up of bishops and kings and based on noble kinship stood in contrast to a type of sainthood based on ascetic values and embodied by monks and nuns. Although the former type of sainthood was dominant in France, the latter had its stronghold in Italy. Saint Louis of France and Saint Francis of Assisi embody this regional difference in saintly type (Vauchez 1989; 2000). Although Saint Louis was king of France before reaching the glory of the altars, Saint Francis was the son of a rich merchant who rejected his wealth and privilege. For the most part, the popes canonized candidates who conformed to the Italian model of sainthood.

Models of sainthood did not vary only by region. Because the popes did not have complete control over matters of sainthood until the seventeenth century, Sofia Boesch-Gajano suggests distinguishing types of sanctity based on the authorities that certified them. High sainthood in this model coincides with official sainthood, one that received the approval of the pontiffs (1999). Low sainthood refers to sanctity achieved through popular acclaim and certified by local authorities. The case of a dog worshipped as a saint in the village of Villars-les-Dombles in the Ain region of southern France is a notorious example of this latter type of sanctity. The dog, Guinefort, was (incorrectly, it turned out) accused of having killed a baby and was thrown in a well and killed. After discovering the dog's innocence, the population of the village started to worship the dog, who from that point (and up to the eighteenth century) was known as Saint Guinefort. Vauchez explains: "In the contrast to … harsh punishment and its patent injustice, popular piety was born. This popular emotion is the same which, transposed on the religious sphere, generated devotion. By virtue of a process that we can treat as a 'law of popular affectivity,' popular piety generates religious piety" (1989, 101).

Nevertheless, official sainthood did require the support of people, what the Church called the *fama sanctitatis*, in addition to papal approval of a candidate's sanctity. During the Middle Ages, the support a saint could attract was based largely on his miracles; hence, miracles were a vital instrument for mobilizing the popular support necessary for canonization.

Summarizing the field of sainthood before the Protestant Schism we can say that while low saints had support, high saints had prestige. During the Reformation, Protestants attacked the Church's indulgence of popular devotion of the kind that produced the dog Saint Guinefort. Thus, at the dawn of modernity, the Church was faced with the dual challenge of promoting its own version of sainthood while attracting popular support. To a certain degree, the two goals had the potential to undermine one another: allowing popular devotion was important in ensuring popular support, but allowing too great a variety of popular devotion would seem to prove the Protestants right. The establishment of a central commission to investigate claims to sainthood was part of the Church's effort to reshape the relationship between popularly perceived sainthood and its own official version.

But how did the new commission effect this reshaping? It took considerable organizational skill to reshape the environment from one in which putative saints faced lax scrutiny and were proclaimed locally to one in which Rome asserted close control over sainthood, all the while maintaining popular support. The Church risked alienating its followers during a period when its legitimacy was much in question and when religious wars challenged the authority of Rome. The Congregatio therefore had a double mission with regard to sanctity: reestablish the legitimacy of sainthood and make Rome the owner of this newly legitimate sainthood.

THE CONGREGATIO SACRORUM RITUUM

Pope Sixtus V created the Congregatio Sacrorum Rituum with the January 22, 1588, encyclical *Immensa Aeterni Dei*. The Congregatio was originally tasked with organizing and moderating the Latin liturgy of the Church as well as investigating whether individuals who died with reputations of extreme holiness were saints. The latter function quickly took precedence, so that the work of the Congregatio resembled more that of a tribunal that put candidates to sainthood on trial after their deaths.[3]

The establishment of the Congregatio was the culmination of a long process that began on February 9, 993, at the Church of Saint John in Rome, when the pope officially sanctioned the worship of the bishop of Augsbourg, Saint Udalric. This was Rome's first documented canonization. Interestingly, the *bolla*, that is, the pontiff's communication, issued for the occasion described the twenty miracles that Udalric had performed. Similar canonization *bolla* listing miracles continue to be issued to this day.

Despite this early example, the Roman Curia and the papacy had a very little control over granting the title of saint. Throughout the Middle Ages, Catholic Europe was divided among a myriad of local saints. This state of affairs persisted even though, in order to prevent abuse of the title and to institute some consistency, Pope Alexander III officially took the power of canonization out of the hands of local bishops in 1170. But the new regulations were not enforced, partly because of the difficulty of controlling a territory as vast as Europe and partly because it made little organizational sense to risk alienating popular support. The practice of worshiping local saints continued.

However, in the new social landscape of the Counter-Reformation, the saints and their miracles were a matter of particular importance, and a subject about which Protestants and Catholics fought harshly (Thomas 1997). In this environment, Rome had a direct interest – for the sake of its own credibility – in assuring the quality of the people worshipped as saints. As Rome began to insist more strongly on the importance of its approval, local religious activists found an interest in securing Rome's recognition of their candidate, in order to enhance their reputation and win local competitions. The two demands, one from the top and the other from the bottom, met in the procedures of the Congregatio, which transformed sainthood into a standardized legal procedure (Gotor 2000; 2004). By 1642, a new logic of how to make saints developed in Catholic Europe, a new institutional field emerged, and the role of the Congregatio changed once again. The new rules issued in this period are detailed in Chapter 5.

---

[3] By 1622, e.g., all liturgical questions concerning the Eastern Church were transferred to a newly created office.

The canonized sainthood that the Congregatio instituted was based on a series of trials in which witnesses were called to testify on the miracles and virtues of the candidate. Each trial was divided into sections, and witnesses were called for each. The sections were (1) the early life of the candidate; (2) the sanctity of the candidate in a broad sense; (3) the virtue of faith; (4) the virtue of hope; (5) the virtue of charity toward God; (6) the virtue of charity toward spiritual life; (7) the virtue of charity toward temporal life; (8) the virtue of prudence; (9) the virtue of justice; (10) the virtue of patience (only for French candidates); (11) the virtue of strength; (12) the virtue of the religious life, if the candidate belonged to a religious order; (13) the supernatural gifts of the candidate; (14) the *fama sanctitatis*, or saintly reputation of the candidate; (15) the death of the candidate; (16) the candidate's fame after death; and (17) the candidate's miracles (Veraja 1988, 1992).

Local Church authorities opened the canonization procedure by collecting evidence on the recently deceased holy person and commissioning the writing of *vitae*, or biographies. This first phase was called the Processo Ordinario, because the authority that conducted the investigations was ordinary, or based locally. The evidence gathered in the Processo Ordinario was sent to the Congregatio in Rome, where it received its first scrutiny, based on the way the trial was conducted – whether all the necessary authorities were present, depositions were sealed, minutes recorded, and so forth. Approval during this phase meant that a new trial would be held, this time by the apostolic authorities; therefore the new trial was thus called the Processo Apostolico. The judges in this trial were all selected by Rome. If the Congregatio reached a positive opinion in the Processo Apostolico, it issued the *Lettere Remissoriali*, or permission to gather evidence on specific details (*in partibus*) of the candidate's life and the miracles he performed. Ordinary and apostolic trials were held in multiple locations, multiplying the number of trials, because many candidates were active in more than one parish during their lives.[4]

The trials *in partibus*, often called Remissoriali, were conducted by the Roman authorities. Until the decrees of the period from 1634 to 1642, the Congregatio entrusted a special commission, the Rota, with the task of organizing most of the work related to these trials. The Uditori di Rota,

---

[4] Benedetto XIV wrote that canonization trials could be held not only in the diocesis in which the candidate's body rested but also in the diocesis in which the candidate had spent time during his life ("*non solum erit ille, in cuius diocesi est carpus canonizzandi, sed ille etiam cuius diocesi miracula contigerunt, vel in qua homines degunt, qui super sanctitate et miracula sunt examinandi*" quoted in Papa 2001, 152).

of whom there were three, were the pope's trustworthy advisors. All of them held important positions in the Roman Curia, were usually cardinals, and were often members of the Congregatio. Their predominance during the first decades of the life of the Congregatio shows that the pope intended to maintain close supervision over matters of sainthood (Papa 2001). The *relatio*, or summary of the trials, which the Uditori wrote for the Congregatio and the pope, was the single most important document in a canonization process during this period. This summary of the life of the candidate was divided into two parts: the first addressing the virtues of the candidate and the second his miracles. The miracles discussed in the *relatio* were a selection of all those collected during the trials. Until 1642 the pontiff, the Uditori, and the bishops of the Congregatio conducted several meetings to discuss the validity of the miracles and virtues of each candidate. The reforms of 1642 introduced a new figure to the canonization process that drastically reduced the role of the cardinals of the Congregatio. The Promotore Fidei – a Devil's Advocate with respect to the candidate's position – was charged with the task of dismantling any false claims about the powers and virtues of the candidate. The Promotore Fidei was a lawyer entrusted with representing the interests of the Church on matters of sainthood, and he usually represented the Church several times during his career. The exchange of opinions between the Promotore Fidei and the advocate for the case was based on legal matters; often, the depositions on a miracle contained conflicting accounts, or sometimes the only witnesses to a miracle were women or young children, making the miracle unreliable in the eyes of the Church authorities.

The rules of 1642 produced the lasting form of the process of canonization, but the process of developing modern sainthood was a precarious one that required balancing conflicting interests. This meant that the Congregatio refined and changed its rules many times throughout the years between its founding and 1642. At the beginning of the seventeenth century, the Congregatio instituted one of its first new rules by creating the title of *beato* (blessed). This title had existed informally since Late Antiquity, indicating a cult that the Roman authorities had approved for the purpose of local worship only. After the Congregatio's rule change, the title of blessed in practice became an intermediate step to sainthood. Local authorities carried out the investigations for the title, and this allowed them to assert some autonomy from the Roman Curia. Thus the institution of the title blessed mediated between Rome's desire to assume direct control over sainthood and the prerogatives of local communities that had chosen their own saints for centuries.

The institutionalization of local worship was the crucial step in the transformation of sainthood because it gave local activists a stake in the sainthood that Rome was promoting. Previously, local audiences changed saints by the generation so that each town, city, or village would accumulate many saints throughout the course of history; with the stability of Rome's approval, local activists could now build – and benefit from – lasting institutions. At the same time, the institutionalization of local worship made it easier for Rome to control local efforts by imposing universal requirements. The notable result was that sainthood ceased to be a dichotomous outcome. Candidates for sainthood, though dead, would now have careers, in the sense of being promoted to higher and higher levels of sanctity.

The Paths to Sainthood

Besides creating a new career of sanctity in order to accommodate pressures from local communities, the Congregatio also created separate paths to canonization for candidates who had died recently (contemporary candidates) and for long-dead, or ancient, candidates. Contemporary candidates followed the Per Viam Non Cultum, passing through the statuses of venerable, blessed, and saint. *Venerable* meant for its owner the dedication of a mass in a local church or chapel. A blessed individual could be worshiped in a limited territory, like a parish or a region, whereas a saint could be worshiped universally. Long-dead candidates followed the Per Viam Cultum and could progress through the statuses of ancient blessed or ancient saint to full sainthood. Some of the inconsistencies in the Congregatio's decisions during this period were related to confusion over where to draw the line between contemporary and ancient candidates. It was not until 1642, with the final reorganization of sainthood, that clear guidelines began to be enforced.

The number of miracles a candidate had to perform depended, among other things, on the path he was taking to sainthood. For a contemporary candidate to become venerable – the first step – required neither miracles nor trials; the Congregatio approved venerable status based on indirect evidence and petitions from local authorities. To move from venerable to blessed, a contemporary candidate had to perform two miracles if there were eyewitnesses (*de visu*), or three miracles otherwise. The same applied to moving from blessed to saint. An ancient candidate had to perform four miracles to achieve full sainthood, because none of the witnesses could possibly be firsthand.

Because of the pressures that local communities exerted on the Congregatio, particularly before 1642, few cases moved through all the steps in either process. Of the 348 cases that the Congregatio considered in the period from 1588 to 1751, almost 43 percent remain venerable today, that is, they sit at the lowest rung of the Congregatio's holy ladder (ASV *Fondo Processi*, 1147). More interestingly, 96 percent of all cases during this period moved less than one step. Besides the 108 cases that were made venerable and remain so to this day, there were also eleven contemporary candidates who were declared saints "on the spot." What in theory should have been the most common path to canonization for a contemporary case—venerable to blessed to saint, a path of three positions and two steps—never occurred. Most of the more idiosyncratic paths occurred before 1642, that is, when the pressures that local communities exercised on the Congregatio were at their highest.

With the proliferation of steps and also of trials, the cost of canonization ballooned. The canonization of Carlo Borromeo, for instance, cost 26,000 *julii*. The candidate's promoters had to bear these costs, paying not just for their team of attorneys but also for the services of all the cardinals in the Congregatio and of the pope; they also had to pay most of the servants of those people. The promoters also paid for the copying of documents and, if they succeeded, for the decoration of Saint Peter's Basilica, in Rome, for the mass that led to the canonization. By the end of the seventeenth century, the Congregatio produced a document summing up the expenses of a beatification, which reads like a price list one could find in a service agency today. For a decree proclaiming the blessed or saint, the Church charged 1650 *julii*; for the papal *bolla*, 650 *julii*; for printing the *vitae*, images, and pamphlets, 2,300 *julii*; for the mass in Saint Peter's, 20,400 *julii*; for the clothes of the clergy officiating the rite, 3,602 *julii*; and so forth. By my conservative estimate, at current values Borromeo's canonization expenses would come to 260,000 euros (Ferrero 2002 gives a similar figure).[5] Local activists therefore had to attract a great deal of financial support in order to get Rome's attention.

The Congregatio's Classification of Miracles

The Congregatio began its work by enforcing a classification of miracles in three degrees that had existed since the early Middle Ages (Vauchez

---

[5] "*Ristretto delle spese d'una Canonizzazione cominciando dal Decreto sino alla Bolla*" (ASV 6866 n.13, *folio* 382v). ("Brief summary of the expenditures of a canonization, starting from the decree to the Papal Bull.")

1989; Papa 2001; Gotor 2004). First-degree miracles were those against nature, as when the Red Sea opened to let the Hebrews escape Egypt. Nature, in this case, would have had a disposition against the act of God. Second-degree miracles were exercised over nature, as when Jesus resuscitated Lazarus. In this case, nature by itself could not have produced this outcome. Third-degree miracles, finally, were thought beyond nature, as when Jesus gave sight to a blind man by touching his eyes. In this case, nature could have produced the event, but not in the form and under the circumstances in which it happened. Candidates for sainthood could perform third-degree miracles only after their deaths, with miracles in the other two categories thought to be the exclusive province of God or Jesus.

During the Middle Ages, this classification of miracles was mostly a formality – partly because of the difficulty in translating theology into efficient guidelines and partly because "people's" saints, that is, saints that attracted a great deal of popular support, did not much concern themselves with theological consistency (Vauchez 1989). Whether the saint was high or low, however, miracles were de facto judged true or false on the basis of their content. Although Rome considered true the miracles that imitated those recounted in the Gospels (Boesch-Gajano 1999; Gotor 2000, 2004), the "true" miracles that popular saints performed were those that contradicted common beliefs about how nature worked (Hertz 1928; Delooz 1969; Delumeau 1976). Adjudicating miracles on the basis of their fidelity to the Gospels helped Rome promote its version of sainthood as "high," because the miracles of its saints ultimately imitated those that Jesus had performed. The content of the miracles that people's saints performed answered the needs of their audiences, which assured those saints a large following.

Judging miracles as true or false based on the fidelity of their content to the Gospels created inconsistencies over time, however. What was tolerated in the loosely connected and idiosyncratic religious environment of the Middle Ages became a threat for Rome and for Catholic believers alike once Protestants stood watching and the printing press allowed for a greater circulation of ideas. Candidates' tendency to innovate through original readings of the Gospels only aggravated the problem. For example, Saint Francis of Assisi was the first person to have stigmata (i.e., wounds on his hands and feet in the same places where Jesus was nailed to the cross); after Saint Francis, stigmata became a new type of miracle that was replicated by many candidates. Routinely applying the classification of miracles by degrees was the Congregatio's first solution to the problem of inconsistency. Others, including substituting the form of a miracle for its content in judging it true or false, would follow, as subsequent chapters detail.

STRUCTURE OF THE EVIDENCE EXTRACTED FROM THE CONGREGATIO'S RECORDS

In each case, the Congregatio discussed the validity the candidate's virtues and whether the miracles he performed were true. Between 1588 and 1642, the basis of this discussion was the *relatio* of the Uditori. Sometimes several meetings were necessary, while in other cases, a few meetings did the job; the pope usually participated in all of the meetings, as his was the final word (Papa 2001). For each canonization the pope issued a *bolla* explaining the extraordinary and heroic quality of the new saint's virtues and, more importantly, the list of the saint's approved miracles. The *relatio*, the papal *bolla*, and the recorded depositions of the trials, especially those of the Processo Ordinario, supply my evidence on miracles. I also draw evidence from the list of years and locations where canonization trials occurred during the period from 1588 to 1751. In broad terms, the primary evidence extracted from the Congregatio's records is the following:

- From a sample of canonization trials:
  a. Descriptions of miracles
  b. Information about the witnesses and recipients of miracles
- From a sample of *relatio* and a sample of the papal *bolla*:
  a. Descriptions of the approved miracles
  b. Arguments made in support of or against miracles
- From the registry of the Congregatio:
  a. Information on where and when trials occurred in western Europe

Different pieces of primary evidence are used in each of the next chapters, along with information from secondary sources such as the *vitae* of the candidates. More detailed information about the records I examined and the techniques I used in my analysis is presented in the Appendix.

2

The Living Saint

Where the previous chapter set the historical stage for interpreting the Congregatio's transformation of sainthood, this chapter begins to analyze how that transformation was achieved. The starting point for understanding this transformation is to look at the people who performed miracles – the candidates to sainthood. In this chapter I reconstruct the first stage of the social mechanism that made possible the production of miracles during the seventeenth century. The term *social mechanism* refers to actions that crystallize into a social structure, which in turn channels further action (Hedström 2005). I present evidence that *in vitam* miracles originated from the candidate's charisma and that they created a social structure of acolytes. The charisma of the candidate produced the magic at the root of *in vitam* miracles. Acolytes – people who experienced this magic firsthand – came from different social statuses and families but were joined by their belief in the sanctity of their candidate. After the candidate's death, they used their status and kinship heterogeneity to create an inclusive mobilization in support of the candidate's canonization. I analyze this second stage of the social mechanism that produced miracles in detail in Chapter 3. This chapter focuses on the living candidate and his acolytes.

This chapter begins with a discussion of how I constructed the sample of candidates and a description of the social environments in which the candidates were active. The second section argues that the mobilization power of miracles lay not in their presumed authenticity but in their effectiveness as a tool for reducing uncertainty. The final section explains how living candidates used miracles to create a social structure that sustained the conditions for the production of more miracles after

their deaths. Individuals who experienced, either as recipients or witnesses, an *in vitam* miracle (one performed while the candidate was still
alive) became early believers in the sanctity of the candidate – what I
refer to as acolytes. Through the social structure that acolytes formed,
they became the catalysts for the only miracles that really mattered in
the candidate's trials: postmortem miracles. Although the Congregatio
officially considered only postmortem miracles in deciding sanctity, all
of the candidates to sainthood described in this chapter performed *in
vitam* miracles as well. Charisma made *in vitam* miracles possible and
kept together the heterogeneous social structure of believers that developed around the candidate. The result of *in vitam* miracles was to create
a social structure of acolytes that cut through existing social divisions.
The improbability of this social structure increased the salience of the
candidate's charisma in keeping together his disparate acolytes. Deep
devotion to the candidate as a religious leader was not optional, but
rather was the norm for the everyday operations of the social structure
of acolytes.

In many respects, the magic at the root of *in vitam* miracles resembled the more primitive forms of religion that Carlo Ginzburg argues still
loomed large in Europe during the seventeenth century (1970, 1976). In
Catholic countries, the organic connection between religion and magic –
a common feature of many civilizations (Thomas 1997) – was not severed
at the dawn of modernity. Max Weber argues that in Protestant cultures,
the rationalization of religion meant the expulsion of magical elements
from religious beliefs (Weber 2000). Under Catholicism, it meant instead
a reorganization of magic. Significantly, this reorganization made it possible for the Church to maintain control of the then-emerging boundary separating religion from science. Regardless of the actual events so
described – flying, healing, visions, or prophecies, in Catholic countries
the last word on whether these events could be considered miracles
remained in the hands of the Church.

Given the shared belief in magic, it is hardly surprising that fervent
religious belief in a candidate's sanctity produced *in vitam* miracles. A
feedback loop, in which each miracle reinforced the connection between
the leader and his acolytes, thus creating more miracles, generated a social
space for the supernatural capabilities of the candidate. In this sense, *in
vitam* miracles became the direct expression of an authority structure
based on the candidate's charisma.

After the candidate's death, his believers continued his work and
catalyzed the conditions for the occurrence of postmortem miracles. As

Chapter 3 shows, because the candidate's close followers believed in the sanctity of their leader, his passing away did not open a succession crisis in the charismatic structure. The candidate never really died, but was reborn into paradise; the Church's official term for a saint's day of death is *dies natalis*, literally "day of birth."

Despite their importance, the Congregatio's rules never officially recognized the role of *in vitam* miracles in creating acolytes. Yet because postmortem miracles were essential for canonization and because those miracles depended on the actions of acolytes building a social structure of believers was of fundamental importance for religious charismatic leaders while alive. Without such a structure, they could never become candidates to sainthood after death. Therefore, only someone considered a living saint – that is, someone capable of performing miracles while alive – could become a candidate to sainthood – someone capable of performing miracles after death.

EVIDENCE FROM THE CANONIZATION TRIALS

The scant sociological research on sainthood suggests that saints performed for an audience (Kleinberg 1994) and that the type of miracles they performed varied according to local characteristics (Delooz 1969). I identified two characteristics of candidates that reflect these findings. The first was where the candidate operated – whether in an urban or a rural community. City dwellers were exposed to a wide range of ideas and had more opportunities to encounter foreigners, while tradition governed life in the countryside. The gulf between urban and rural lifestyles widened after the invention of the printing press: large proportions of city dwellers began reading books, while peasants remained rooted in oral tradition (Zemon-Davis 1975). Literacy influenced popular belief in the supernatural powers of candidates and thus the types of miracles people were willing to believe they could perform. In order to sharpen the analytical power of this division, I considered life in small towns similar to life in rural settings.

The second characteristic was the institutional constraints that the candidate faced as a member of the Church – that is, whether he was a member of the secular or the regular clergy. Secular clergy included priests, cardinals, and bishops, who lived in close contact with laypeople and interacted with them frequently (Bonnet 1954). Regular clergy were monks, friars, and nuns, who lived in the seclusion of monasteries or convents. Miracles performed by members of the regular clergy reflected this spatial constraint in that their recipients were, for the most part, members of the institutions that were located where the candidate lived.

These characteristics pair to produce four ideal candidate types:

- *The spiritual priest*, or lay clergy in an urban environment. Characteristic of Italian commercial cities that still retained some of the ferment (and wealth) of previous periods but were headed for decline. This candidate interacted with a large and heterogeneous population whose demands, in terms of spiritual needs and miracles, reflected the disruption caused by changing economic and social forces.
- *The learned monk*, or regular clergy in an urban setting. Typical of the Spanish cities that were still experiencing the boom of the *Siglo de Oro*. The characteristics of his order – for example, Dominican, Augustinian, or Franciscan – played a fundamental role in the candidate's interaction with the population, segmenting his audience and their requests more than those of a spiritual priest.
- *The folksy friar*, regular clergy operating in the countryside or small towns of Italy and Spain and dealing with a mostly peasant population. Some of the pre-Christian beliefs that still informed the culture of these areas emerged clearly in this type of candidate's preaching and miracles. Miracles related to controlling natural elements formed an essential part of the supernatural palette of this candidate.
- *The practical priest*, lay clergy characteristic of impoverished rural areas of southern Europe. This type of candidate was deeply ignorant of Catholic dogma and lacked access to the resources available to rural friars and monks. His audience was mostly impoverished peasants.

This classification by ideal types mitigates the bias produced by limitations in the Vatican archives that I consulted. I provide more detail on how I used this classification to create my sample of candidates in the Appendix. Briefly, I randomly selected some candidates and actively chose others in an effort to maximize the number of miracles for each ideal type.

Table 2.1 shows the contemporary candidates included in my analysis organized according to ideal type. Next to each name, the table reports the candidate's status in 1642 and the number of miracles described in his or her trials. Overall, the trials of these seven candidates include 460 miracles, of which the Congregatio considered thirty-one, or 6.7 percent,

TABLE 2.1. *Contemporary Candidates in the Sample*

	Secular Clergy	Regular Clergy
Urban	*The Spiritual Priest*	*The Learned Monk*
	Carlo Borromeo (saint, 71)	Bernardino of Agrigento
	Filippo Neri (saint, 74)	(venerable, 21)
		Alfonso Orozco (venerable, 82)
		Teresa of Avila (saint, 40)
Rural	*The Practical Priest*	*The Folksy Friar*
		Pasqual Baylon (blessed, 97)
		Rainiero of San Sepolcro
		(venerable, 75)

true. This book considers 511 miracles in total, including those described in the trials of the ancient candidates not listed in this table.[1] For the scope of this work, each candidate's cult was akin to a social movement and each miracle was akin to a mobilizing event.

There are no practical priests, or secular clergy from rural environments, among the candidates (empty cell in Table 2.1). Of the nineteen secular priests the Congregatio considered during the period from 1588 to 1751, none hailed from rural areas. Priests from small villages were not part of the sanctity that the Congregatio promoted. After the Congregatio's establishment, mustering the support necessary to open a case required considerable economic resources, which this type of candidate could not muster. Although some of them had charismatic abilities that likely made them able to perform miracles, their cases never reached Rome, and so their miracles are not represented in this research.[2]

Finally, I also analyzed miracles performed by *ancient candidates*, a term referring to an individual whose death occurred long before the Congregatio approved his first trial. Broadly speaking, the evidence and testimony in ancient candidates' trials revolved around their miracles as written in their hagiographies and depicted in paintings. Only ancient candidates who eventually became saints had trials similar to, albeit shorter than, those of contemporary candidates; that is, trials that contained descriptions of recent miracles. Without the continued ability to

[1] Teresa of Avila is placed in the urban category of Table 2.1 because the majority of her miracles occurred in Salamanca. I placed Baylon in the rural category because despite having defensive walls – a vestige of the Reconquista of the thirteenth century – Villa Real was more a village than a town; life there centered on agricultural work.
[2] Yet, as my analysis later shows, elites' support for a candidate was not the only factor affecting the Congregatio's decisions.

perform miracles, an ancient candidate had no chance of becoming a saint.

The two randomly chosen ancient saints in the sample are Francesca Romana and Raymond de Peñafort, whose trials took place, respectively, in Rome during 1604 and in Barcelona during 1595. Because most of the witnesses offered secondhand accounts of events that occurred centuries before, I include them primarily to demonstrate the miracles' evolution over time.

The Sample of Candidates in Their Contexts

The seven contemporary candidates display the variety of social conditions that characterized seventeenth-century southern Europe. Three of them – Carlo Borromeo, Filippo Neri, and Bernardino of Santa Lucia– came from urban environments in Italy (Milan, Rome, and Agrigento, respectively). Alonzo Orozco and Teresa of Avila were active in Spain, in particular in Madrid and Salamanca. Finally, Pascal Baylon and Rainiero of Borgo San Sepolcro came from the more rural environments of Villa Real, Spain, and central Italy.

Milan was the economic center of the Spanish Empire, the city where bankers financed the wars of the Spanish kings as well as their construction plans for their new capital, Madrid. At the end of the sixteenth century and during the early part of the seventeenth century, piracy drove trade and travelers from the sea and made Milan the center of the route from Spain to Flanders (Vigo 1994). At the heart of a flourishing plain, the Milanese province was known for its industry – arms and clothes were Milan's most famous products. But toward the middle of the seventeenth century, the city experienced precipitous economic and social decline (Braudel 1992). The local bourgeoisie could not cope when England and Germany emerged as competitors in Milan's core industries. The plague of 1576, with a total death toll of seventeen thousand people, left the Milanese economy in a state of disarray for several years and was a destabilizing factor that set the stage for the city's later decline.

Carlo Borromeo (b. 1538, Arona; d. 1584, Milan) became archbishop of Milan on September 23, 1565. Borromeo was of noble origin and his uncle, who became Pope Pius IV, made him a cardinal at age twenty-three. After spending his youth in Rome, Borromeo moved back to Milan and became the first and best exemplar of the spirit of the Post-Tridentine Church. Among his many reforms, Borromeo's new catechism was destined to have great influence, remaining an essential educational tool for thousands of priests until the nineteenth century. In Milan, however, the local authorities of Spanish rule viewed Borromeo's religious zeal with suspicion, seeing him as a dangerous competitor in a territory that was crucial to their entire empire. To many, Borromeo symbolized the opposition against foreign rule that would characterize the Milanese intellectual scene and social life until the *Risorgimento* (Vigo 1994).

The long-standing power struggle between the foreign authorities and the local elite is evident in some of the miracles that Borromeo performed. In October 1601, Count Niccolò Rovelli of Ferrara, a territory under Spanish rule, was in Milan visiting some friends.[3] Rovelli, who was pro-Spanish, saw a painting of the dead archbishop in his friend's house and started making fun of him. Immediately, Rovelli was struck with a high fever (*febbri terzane*) that threatened to kill him. Rovelli's host convinced him to ask Borromeo for grace, and once Rovelli agreed, Borromeo saved him (ACS Storico, *Summarium Miraculorum*).

Borromeo also met resistance from the local Church. In February 1571, a friar of the Order of the Humiliati fired a shot at the archbishop in an attempt to stop Borromeo's reforms. The Humiliati were afterward suppressed and their monasteries given to the Jesuits. Borromeo's premature death, due partly to his gunshot wound and partly to the plague that ravaged Milan in 1576, brought his reforming activities – though not his supernatural ones – to a sudden halt. Yet in the space of few years he left an indelible mark on the Catholic Church, becoming a symbol of the Counter-Reformation.

Rome is the next Italian city in the analysis. The dawn of the seventeenth century seemed auspicious for the Eternal City. During the late sixteenth century, Rome became the model city for Europe's Catholic elites. Beautiful palaces lined streets crowded with pilgrims, who arrived from everywhere in Europe. During the jubilee of 1600, for example, Rome hosted more than a million pilgrims (Petrocchi 1970). A series of reforms introduced by Sixtus V (1585–90) at the end of the sixteenth century and implemented by his successors placed the popes firmly in control of their own state. The popes also wielded a heavy hand against heresy, as Giordano Bruno's burning at the stake on January 17, 1600, testified. Yet the Rome in which Neri (b. 1515, Florence; d. 1595, Rome) lived showed few hints of its future status. He arrived in Rome around 1522,

---

[3] The old school of Milanese intellectuals blamed the Spaniards, who had ruled Milan for more than two centuries, for the city's decline. The works of Piero Verri, Cesare Cantú, and Alessandro Manzoni are examples of this spirit.

five years before a ten thousand–strong army of German and Spanish sacked the city. According to Francesco Guicciardini's *La Historia d'Italia*, blood ran in the gutters as nobles were killed and their bodies dumped on the streets. Pope Clement VII found refuge in the fortress of Castel Sant'Angelo, along with three thousand others – essentially all the extended families of the cardinals of the faction opposed to the Spanish Emperor Charles V.[4] For eight days, the soldiers pillaged the palaces of Rome. In the end, the city had lost half of its population and was economically ruined. The attack ended an era in which the popes were renaissance princes of the Church who concerned themselves chiefly with leisure and arts, holding up classical Greece as a model for Imperial Rome. In the words of sixteenth-century poet Pietro l'Aretino, rather than being the *caput mundi*, Rome became the *coda mundi* – the tail of the world.

It was in the aftermath of this catastrophe that Neri began his activities, which drew wide attention in a city where the spirit of the Counter-Reformation was gaining dominance. He became especially well-known for his Anti-Carnival walk on Fat Tuesday, during which he would conduct a tour of the seven Roman basilicas – San Paolo, Santa Maria Maggiore, San Giovanni, San Pietro, San Lorenzo, Santa Croce, and San Sebastiano. The event attracted such a large following that the Curia became quite suspicious of Neri's peculiar behavior. Slowly, however, Neri convinced the Curia of his orthodoxy. In time his regular meetings, at which friends gathered to talk about religion, play music, and sing, became the basis for a new religious order, the Oratoriani, which would have great influence in France and Italy. With their emphasis on practicality and decentralized organization, the Oratoriani stood in perennial contrast to the spirituality and the hierarchical organization of the Jesuits (Bonnet 1954).

Continuing south through Italy, we arrive finally at Agrigento – the center of agriculture and agricultural trade in Southern Sicily and the last Italian city represented in the sample of candidates. Sicily was under the control of the Spanish crown in this period. Despite the city's large size, its role as a market for agricultural goods, and the fact that the city had been known since the Roman Empire for its vast reserves of potassium and sulfur, Agrigento was impoverished. Much of the land around Agrigento was cultivated with grain and sugar (Bonfiglio 1933), but poor technology made survival difficult for the peasants. Gangs of

---

[4] Francesco Guicciardini (1483–1540) is considered the father of modern history for his use of primary sources in writing *La Historia d'Italia* (the first edition was published in Florece in 1561).

bandits roamed the surrounding countryside and terrorized its residents; they sometimes even threatened the city center. Their ubiquity figures in one of Bernardino's postmortem miracles. As friar Gurlando reported during the trial, bandits stole Bernardino's head from the casket in which he lay exposed. The friars in Bernardino's monastery decided to get another head – complete with bones and hair – and sew it to the body. When the thieves eventually returned Bernardino's head, the friars found themselves in the awkward position of having one body and two heads. Bernardino reportedly solved the problem, making the replacement head dissolve into ashes (ASV 2209).

Two Spanish cities provided the social and economic background for the activities of Orozco and Teresa. The first, Madrid, became the capital of the Spanish Empire in 1561. King Philip II's decision to move the capital from Toledo to the little-known village of Madrid is still a source of curiosity for historians. Madrid had a better location – at the center of the Iberian Peninsula – and a better climate, yet these two factors do not appear sufficient to explain the king's decision. Regardless, the consequences for Madrid were enormous; the town grew from eight thousand inhabitants at the time of the court's arrival to eighty thousand forty years later (Alvar 1994). The kings surrounded themselves with Italian and Dutch artists and architects in order to transform Madrid into a capital city. Rome, with her monumental buildings and churches, was Philip II's inspiration. Monasteries drove some of Madrid's urban expansion by opening new areas to development, but the city's evolution was almost completely dependent on the court – the entourage of counts, dukes, marquis, ambassadors, and high clergy employed nearly half the city. The "elite" Madrid was connected to international commerce and the world system of exchange. The other Madrid was that of the local people; this Madrid depended on the produce of its countryside to survive.

Orozco preached in both Madrids. He was born in Toledo in 1500 and received his religious calling in 1522, while he was studying law with his older brother. He began a successful career in the Augustinian order, and on March 13, 1554, the King of Spain, Charles V, named him a royal preacher. Orozco's oratorical skills drew large crowds and helped the order recover from the stain left by the Augustinian monk Martin Luther. Orozco also wanted to become a missionary. In 1547, he tried to reach Mexico, but his arthritis forced him first to stop at the Canary Islands and then to go back to Toledo. In 1561, he followed the court to Madrid, where he was the leading force in the founding of several monasteries. At the time of his death – September 19, 1591 – Madrid was still undergoing her tumultuous development.

The last city represented in this analysis is Salamanca. When Teresa preached there (1570–74), the Universidad of Salamanca was at its height: one-fifth of the city's residents were students, and Salamanca was one of the great centers of learning in Europe.[5] The city's economy depended on the corps of students and teachers. Furthermore, several students at Salamanca were destined to have great influence and power.[6] Among them, two are particularly relevant in the context of this research: Saint Ignatius of Loyola and Saint John of the Cross. The latter was born in Avila in 1542, some twenty-seven years after Teresa of Jesus. Once in Salamanca, John collaborated with her on the reform of the Carmelite Order and was the first male monk to follow the new rule that Teresa established. It was not by chance that the two greatest Spanish mystics preached in Salamanca: the city had a learned and wealthy public capable of understanding their messages.

Teresa's youth was marked by her father's fierce opposition to her religious calling, but she broke free and joined the Carmelites on November 3, 1537, when she was just twenty-two. The reform of the order became Teresa's self-appointed mission. She began her work on August 24, 1562, establishing a small monastery in Avila where she presided over the ordination of four new sisters. The monastery of Saint Joseph would become the first in a series of reformed monasteries that Teresa founded throughout Spain.

Teresa was animated by a spirit of absolute poverty and had plans to revive stricter rules of conduct. In the constitution she wrote she called for, among other things, the substitution of leather or wooden sandals for shoes.[7] It was the beginning of the Discalced order of Carmelites. Teresa faced resistance from the rest of the Carmelites. She was sent to absolute segregation and forbidden to continue her reforms. The Spanish Inquisition began investigating Teresa and her followers. It was only due

---

[5] Teresa reported that the Jesuits invited her to start a new monastery in Salamanca (*Libro della mia vita*).

[6] Among the first people to attend masses in the new monastery that Teresa founded in Salamanca were Maria Pimentel, Countess of Monte Rey, and Doña Mariana, wife of the governor. Furthermore, the building that would become the monastery of Saint Joseph was a donation from a local knight.

[7] Teresa writes, "*Stavo io molto mal veduta da tutto il mio Monasterio, perche volevo far Monasterio piu' chiuso: dicevano ch'io facevo loro affronto, che ben porevo quivi servire a Dio*" (*Libro della mia vita*, p. 10).

to the pleading of Philip II and the patronage of Pedro de Alcantara that Teresa was allowed to continue her work.[8] She died on October 4, 1582.

Two candidates preached in more rural settings. Friar Rainiero of Borgo San Sepolcro was active in the countryside of Todi, in Central Italy (Umbria) during the sixteenth century. The town of Perugia was the region's economic center, but the region was rent by bitter rivalries between its towns (e.g., Perugia versus Assisi and Todi versus Spoleto). Outside the towns, the legacy of Saint Francis of Assisi – the great saint of the thirteenth century – marked Umbria profoundly. Franciscan monasteries speckled the entirety of the small region; during the sixteenth century there were more than a hundred, divided into several orders. Much of the land was under the control of these monasteries, which served a population of poor peasants.

During the medieval period, the dense population of Franciscan friars was reflected in the frequency and ease of their canonizations in Umbria (Vauchez 1989; Nicolini 1993). For example, citizens of Perugia worshipped a (still) mysterious Saint Bevignate, and those of Gubbio worshipped the elsewhere-unknown Saint Sperandeo. The mountain where one comrade of Saint Francis died was known as Mons Sancti Egidii, or Mount Saint Egidio, although Egidio had not been canonized. It comes as no surprise that the activities of the Congregatio and the decrees of Pope Urban VIII in 1642 – those that regulated matters of canonization once and for all – met with intense protest in Perugia (Nicolini 1993).

The familiarity with saints that characterized people's lives in the Umbrian countryside is well documented in Rainiero's trials. One witness said of him that he performed so many miracles that it appeared that God had personally given him the go-ahead ("*il fiat*," *ACS Storico*, 223). Friar Rainiero was born to a very poor family in Borgo San Sepolcro. When the plague took his family, he was left in the care of the Capuchins – the new Franciscan branch founded in 1525. Never ordained a priest, he remained a lay brother. Even so, he served as a superior in many of the region's monasteries. He died in Todi on August 25, 1589.

Pasqualis Baylon's life had a similar trajectory. He too was born to a very poor family, in Torre Hermosa in the province of Aragona, on May 16, 1540. Orphaned at a young age, he was left in the care of the Franciscans of Saint Mary of Loreto (Alcantarini). He joined the order in 1564 but, like Rainiero, never became a priest. A reputation for sanctity surrounded Baylon from very early in life and, in another striking

---

[8] Pedro de Alcantara was canonized on May 11, 1670.

similarity with the Umbrian friar, he performed many miracles while still alive. He did missionary work in France, where he faced hostility and mockery at the hands of the Huguenots.

Baylon died young, on May 17, 1592, in Villa Real, near Valencia. Despite having defensive walls – a vestige of the Reconquista of the thirteenth century – Villa Real was more a village than a town, and life there centered on agricultural work. It was also a relatively new settlement. In Baylon's time, improved irrigation techniques allowed the farmland around the village to expand, and this is reflected in themes of finding water and saving children who fell into wells that run through his miracles. For instance, on a summer day in 1661, the landowner Domenico Perez decided to search his property for a spring. Ignoring the derision of his neighbors, Perez proceeded to a very dry area of his land and pushed his hoe into the ground, invoking Baylon's name until water sprang out. The Congregatio certified this miracle as true during Baylon's canonization in 1690 (ASV 3043; BAV *Codex Constitutionum*).

The social backgrounds of Rome and Barcelona at the times when the sample's ancient candidates, Francesca Romana and Raymond de Penafort, preached are not relevant for the thread of this research that deals with the birth of modern sainthood. However, these candidates' miracles help show how the content of miracles changed with context, and a few notes on their lives will help explain their miracles' contexts. Romana (b. 1384, Rome; d. 1440, Rome) was born during one of Rome's darkest periods, when the papacy was in Avignon and the city had shrunk to the size of a town. Romana dedicated her life to her husband, the nobleman Lorenzo de' Ponziani, and their six children (only three of whom lived to adulthood) until Lorenzo's death. After that, Romana began taking care of the sick. She transformed her palace in Trastevere into a hospital and quickly became popular for her generosity and piety. She founded the order of the Oblate di Maria which, after her death, was headquartered in the nearby Tor de' Specchi. The order's sisters were not cloistered; they were simply bound by an informal vow to help the sick and the poor. Francesca was worshiped in Rome from the fifteenth century, and masses were dedicated to her on the anniversary of her death, the *die natalis* of March 9. However, her formal canonization trial did not occur until much later – a concrete indicator of the suspicion with which the Curia viewed Romana's independence and that of her followers. As several historians have pointed out, one of the consequences of the Protestant Schism was an increased distrust by the Curia toward female spiritual leaders (Prosperi 1986; Zarri 1991); I come back to this point in Chapter 5.

De Peñafort was a learned thirteenth-century jurist who taught for
several years at the Universitas of Bologna. His legal expertise assisted
in the reorganization of canon law, and his collection of law was the
standard until 1917. He returned to his hometown of Barcelona, where
in 1222 he became a member of the Dominican order and a propelling
force for the conversion of Jews and Muslims. He died in 1275, at the
remarkable age of ninety-five.

The characterization by ideal types (see Table 2.1) suggests a reading
of the candidates' lives and of the contexts in which they operated. We
can already observe that urban candidates met with greater initial resistance from local officials than did rural candidates. Central authorities in
Rome appeared more reluctant ultimately to approve rural candidates.
The power dynamic between three sets of actors – local officials, candidates and their acolytes, and central officials in Rome – that shaped these
outcomes is explored in greater detail in later chapters.

The Witnesses and Recipients of Miracles

The candidate's trial reported the location and date of each miracle, as
well as the disease cured and the way it was cured if the miracle involved a
healing. Sometimes the saved promised the candidate that he or she would
do something in exchange for health; other times the saved went physically
to the tomb of the candidate and received the healing; still other times, the
saved had or borrowed a relic of the candidate which, once applied to that
person's body, healed it.[9] For nonhealing miracles, the trial gave a description of the circumstances under which the miracles occurred. Sometimes the
candidate flew over the sea; at other times a horse-drawn chariot flew over
a river. Also the candidate performed miracles through his own body, such
as lighting candles with his hands or repairing broken objects instantly. For
all miracles, the trials also reported the witnesses, their status and profes-
sion, their relationship to the saved, and their kinship.

More than eight hundred witnesses testified about the 511 miracles that
the nine candidates performed. There were 729 individuals who swore
to witnessing one of the contemporary candidates perform a miraculous
healing or other supernatural act. Overall, more than 70 percent of the
witnesses came from urban environments – Milan, Rome, Agrigento,

---

[9] Miracles performed by a living candidate were coded in the category *in vitam*, regardless
of when they were performed; 34.5% of all the postmortem miracles lack a precise report
regarding when they occurred.

Madrid, and Salamanca. The Church paid particular attention to the witnesses' social status. Nobles and merchants represented the upper class of witnesses. The trial records identify nobles by title, such as duke, count, or prince. Merchants, including wealthy traders or anyone else with a lucrative business, are identified with the title *dominus* or *domina*.[10] I considered commoners or peasants all the witnesses whose names lacked such titles. Doctors were, in many respects, comparable to nobles in wealth and pedigree. I placed them in a separate category, however, to emphasize their role as representatives of medical knowledge. Doctors' testimonies played a unique part in the trials, as Chapter 4 documents, revealing the capabilities of medicine and forcing the judges to define the limits of those capabilities in order to construct their own expertise.[11]

Finally, in a departure from the preceding divisions by class, I divided clerical witnesses into regular versus secular clergy. Secular clergy were individuals such as bishops who lived in close contact with the laity; regular clergy lived secluded lives in monasteries.

Table 2.2 shows that Baylon and Rainiero, representatives of the folksy friar ideal, drew much of their support from the category of commoners and peasants. Bernardino, operating in the urban but agriculturally focused and poverty-stricken setting of Agrigento, also drew most of his witnesses from the lower classes. Neri and Borromeo, both spiritual priests from Rome and Milan, respectively, drew strong support from nobles and merchants, whereas Teresa's and Orozco's witnesses were mostly regular clergy. The columns of Table 2.2 therefore add further dimension to the ideal types previously described. Spiritual priest candidates had support from the upper classes in larger proportion than did

---

[10] In the trial of Orozco, the witness Don Juan Hurtado was introduced with the following titles "Signore dolli Consigli di Stato e di Guerra dol Re Nostro Signore, Suo Maggiordomo Maggiore e Gentil'huomo della Sua Camera, Duca dell'Infantado, Signore dolle Case de Mendoza e de la Vega, Marchese di Cenese, Marchese di Santigliana, Marchese de Argueso, Marchese di Compor, Marchese de la Citta' di Terra Nuova, Conte di Saldana, Conte del Real de Manzanabes, Conte del Cid, Signore della Provincia de Lubante, Signore de Ville di Tor de Humos, San Martino, Menhuda, Arenas e suo territorio, Signore delle Ville del Sexno, de Duran e de Jadiaque, e suo territorio, Barone dolle Ville de Ayora e de la Huna e dolle Baronia de Alberique, Alcozer, Alazquer e Guarda, Signore dolle Ville e Baronia de Castilla, Oriolle, Tibilucheria, Quatroforda, Pinet e Bericolech, Fuente de la Yguera, Picath ... e Marchola nel Regno di Valencia" (ASV 3033, folio 1416r).

[11] Surgeons were included in the same status with doctors. Regardless of the fact that the latter were highly educated people who approached disease mostly from a philosophical perspective, while surgeons were basically like barbers and performed mostly amputations, both had a greater knowledge of medicine than the average population. It was this that made them comparable in the Church's eyes.

TABLE 2.2. *Social Status of Witnesses by Candidate Ideal Type*

	Folksy Friar	Spiritual Priest	Learned Monk
	(proportions)		
Commoners and peasants	.71	.40	.33
Nobility and merchants	.10	.29	.25
Doctors	.05	.05	.07
Secular clergy	.01	.08	.05
Regular clergy	.11	.17	.30
N	199	338	152
Missing status	24	3	13

other types of candidates, while the clergy was overrepresented among witnesses for the learned monk candidates (35%).

Aggregating Table 2.2 by type of community and recoding social status into three macrocategories, by reassigning doctors to the category of nobles and merchants and by combining regular clergy with secular clergy, reveals two key facts. First, regardless of type, candidates and their acolytes received support from members of many social classes. Second, the distribution of this support was not organized by gender. Men and women were equally likely to witness miracles regardless of the type of candidate performing them (Chi square test, p-value = .413). Thus, while Table 2.2 shows that the composition of audiences varies, further evidence indicates that candidates and their acolytes could rally support from all social strata. In the context of the deep class divisions of the seventeenth century, this inclusive behavior stood out. Before exploring in greater detail how candidates were able to construct such broad support in their communities, it is necessary to consider miracles in their singularity: how was it that miracles mobilized people during the seventeenth century?

MIRACLES AS MOBILIZING EVENTS

The material conditions of everyday life during the seventeenth century provide a starting point for understanding why miracles were such a powerful mobilization tool. Uncertainty shaped every aspect of individual life, and people had different strategies for coping with hardships. A miracle was a cultural product that reduced uncertainty – something unusual occurred, and a miracle explained why.[12] Because of their power to explain

[12] Thomas presented evidence of alcohol as a coping mechanism during much the same period in England (Thomas 1997). Astrological beliefs had a similar role.

the inexplicable, miracles brought comfort (Gertz 1966). This definition of a miracle has the advantage of ignoring the question of whether a miracle was "real" and instead highlights what is sociologically relevant about miracles, that is, their function at the dawn of modernity in Catholic countries.

Common acceptance of miracles as reducers of uncertainty constitutes the necessary social context for explaining their mobilizing power. From this perspective, it is not surprising that each generation had its saints to give a sense of meaning to life's hardships and mitigate life's vicissitudes. The rapid succession of saints before 1642 resulted from the inner logic of people striving for stability in an unstable world. Miracles were welcomed as long as people's material conditions continued to be precarious and, generation after generation, charismatic individuals emerged to perform them.

At the root of a miracle was a shared belief that a supernatural event had occurred. Without this shared belief, a miracle was just a personal fantasy. Witnesses were necessary, then, not just to satisfy the Church's official legal requirements but also to make miracles possible in the first place. In the canonization trials, a small fraction of miracles had no witnesses (11.7%); most miracles took place in the presence of several individuals.[13] Yet as a candidate's reputation for sanctity spread in a community, miracles required fewer witnesses. In the case of Baylon in Villa Real, for instance, the odds of a miracle occurring in the presence of two (or fewer) witnesses increased from 1.95 in 1592 to thirteen during the trials of 1603 and 1604, a sixfold increase.

The same trend of progressively fewer witnesses per miracle occurred in Rome in Neri's case. During his 1595 and 1598 trials, the odds of miracles occurring in the presence of two (or fewer) witnesses were 1.63; the same odds increased to two during the trial of 1610. For Borromeo, the odds increased twofold from the trial of 1592 (.14) to the trial of 1605 (.25). Some of the firsthand witnesses of miracles in the first round of trials died before the second trials took place. Yet the short time period between trials for the candidates mentioned in the preceding text – roughly ten years – and the fact that Milan, Rome, and Villa Real did not experience dramatic demographic events during this ten-year period reduce the likelihood that the decreasing number of witnesses per miracle can be attributed to mortality in the population of firsthand witnesses. Thus the Church is expected to have accepted the testimony of a saved

[13] The canonization trials always mention a few cases of people who did not believe in the sanctity of the candidate and were later forced to change their minds and see their mistake. Interestingly, these people were often nobles or members of the high clergy.

individual without witnesses once the idea of a candidate's sanctity was established. The more the idea that someone was a saint diffused in a community, the fewer the risks associated with testifying on behalf of the candidate; thus more miracles occurred with fewer witnesses.[14]

This trend is reflected in the emphasis in canonization trials on people who were initially skeptical of the power and virtues of the candidate. The accounts of these witnesses served as further evidence of the supernatural capacities of the candidate. These witnesses, often nobles, usually experienced miracles later in the candidate's career, after the candidate's power had become or was approaching a social fact.

Despite the mobilizing power of miracles during the seventeenth century, it was in this period that miracles began to encounter a serious competitor for their role as reducers of uncertainty. Scientific explanations of events proliferated in this period and began to challenge people's common assumptions. In Catholic countries, science and miracles entered into a relationship that defined what could be legitimately explained by one instead of the other. Chapter 4 explores the development of this relationship in detail; the next section of this chapter describes the social context that pushed the Church to establish and police the boundaries of that relationship.

Miracles as a Tool for Reducing Uncertainty

At the end of the sixteenth century, science began to flourish autonomously from religion in the northern European countries. Autonomy did not mean opposition, however. Finding the laws of nature was similar to finding the laws of God, and science developed as another realm in which God operated. Its province was the mundane, whereas religion's was the heavenly. The expulsion of God from daily affairs was part of the process of rationalization that Weber identified to be at the core of Protestantism. Science and religion became two independent and separate fields. The process was different in Catholic countries: miracles kept religion and science together in people's daily lives. More importantly, the Church maintained control of the boundary that separated the two institutions.

This was possible not because Catholic believers were more superstitious than Protestants but because miracles offered a process of rationalization not dissimilar to the one that science offered. Like a scientific

---

[14] A similar argument applies for one-witness miracles; i.e., the interpretation of events that led to the miracle is treated not as the fantasy of a pair (saved and witnesses, often related) but resonates with the community's idea of the sanctity of the candidate.

explanation, a miracle creates a chain of cause and effect that explains what seems beyond human control (e.g., healing). The similarity of the two types of explanation was simple to see as long as both created idiosyncratic results. Saintly candidates were thought to heal people by the laying on of hands and the pronunciation of Latin prayers, while doctors prescribed bleeding to balance the humors thought to regulate the health of the human body. Little doubt exists that around the time that the Congregatio was created, miracles had an advantage over medicine; given the poor level of knowledge about the human body at the time, it was better for the sick to pray than to call a doctor.

Random events – whether the success or failure of prayer or medicine, or other inexplicable happenings – are compatible neither with the idea of paradise nor with the idea of finding the laws of nature. In Catholic countries, the possibility that an individual could perform miracles constructed a world in which, in the collective interpretation, nothing happened by chance, not even the wildest of events. In the Protestant world, the same idea came under the control of science (Thomas 1997). In both cases, common people used a rational approach to create a social and natural world in which everything could be accounted for with reference to a higher power.

Weber suggested that this chimera was the inevitable result of the spirit of rationalization that has swept Europe for the last two thousand years. From this perspective, the miracles that candidates performed are seen as irrational beliefs rooted in imperfect knowledge. Miracles were leftover pieces of a world in which magic still existed, destined to be wiped out in the "iron cage" of modernity. Instead, from the perspective that this book develops, miracles and scientific explanations are by-products of institutional arrangements that, in one case, favored the continuation of the Church's control over the production of knowledge and, in the other, favored the autonomy of science from religion. Rather than an external historical force, rationalization was an endogenous process rooted in the political struggles of the early modern era.

Miracles and scientific explanations are thus both perfectly rational, in that they both rule out chance. Thus the miracles candidates performed were viewed as evidence that prayer and patronage were effective for curing diseases, or even for being able to take flight. Faith in miracles additionally offered psychological comfort to many, more than science could and perhaps still can. As Peter Brown has argued in the context of the late Roman Empire, the choice between the doctor and the Christian saint was the choice of the human relationships that people thought could be most effective in the therapeutic process (1981). The effectiveness of patronage in everyday life projected itself into the heavens.

Despite their commonalities, the consequences of using miracles instead of science as a tool for rationalizing the world differed. With miracles, people focus on successful events (see Marc Bloch's explanation of the king's power to heal, mentioned in the preceding text, on this point), whereas with science, people focus on failures. It is precisely by looking at failures that science accumulates its knowledge, allowing it to surpass miracles in capturing progressively broader segments of nature under its rational interpretation of how things (and people) work.

Broadly speaking, there were two momentous consequences of using miracles as a rational tool for reducing uncertainty. First, the fact that what is under human control and what is known of the natural world changes with the advance of science means that the category of miracles must always shift to include new events and exclude others. Any event may therefore be interpreted as a miracle, as long as it is out of the ordinary. For example, Signor Giacomo Lomatio visited Borromeo's tomb in the Cathedral of Milan three years after the candidate's death.[15] For the five years preceding the November 24, 1587, visit, Lomatio endured such intense pain in his legs that walking was difficult for him. So it was with the aid of a cane that he arrived at Borromeo's tomb, where he shouted: "[Carlo] ... if you are the saint that everyone thinks you are ... [you will give me] from God the health of my legs." At the end of the mass, Lomatio threw away his cane and walked firmly on his legs. In 1601, during Borromeo's first canonization trial, seven people testified about this miracle, including Lomatio's wife, Brigida, and one of his servants, Isabella Cernuscola (*folio* 583r, ACS Antico, Borromeo *Summarium Miracolorum*).

Another example occurred in Rome during 1588, when Fulvia de Cavalieri's cousin apparently died. De Cavalieri asked her husband, Francesco della Molara, to bring Neri to visit her cousin in an effort to resuscitate her. Neri came and said to the seemingly dead woman, "You are not going to die today." The woman replied, "Father, I am already dead!" Neri assured her that she would feel better, which subsequently happened. Della Molara mentioned this miracle on August 7, 1595, during Neri's first trial (*Il primo processo*). In both of these situations, something unexpected happened in the lives of the individuals involved. What happened afterward were miracles, because the people involved constructed mental framings that explained how a mortal disease was defeated, or how walking became possible again.

---

[15] By the same token, certain events have never been put under human control and have always been thought of as miracles. Resurrection, e.g., is one such eternal miracle, as death continues to defy human control.

The second consequence of using miracles as a rational tool for reducing uncertainty on an equal footing with science was that the systems of patronage that miracles activated and symbolized made the doctor the subordinate of the priest and placed science under the stewardship of the Church.[16] This had important consequences for scientists in southern Europe. Though it was still rational, the scientific knowledge that developed in these countries remained closed to new explorations and capable only of reproducing the existing balance of power. An example from medicine provides a good illustration. During the sixteenth century, the Bolognese physician Leonardo Fioravanti acquired considerable fame in Sicily for his medical theory, based on data from Europe's new colonies, that cannibalism caused syphilis. Despite the absurdity of the theory, Fioravanti was called to the papal court where he enjoyed a brief period of notoriety (Eamon 1998).

In the meantime, in northern Europe, empiricism was taking root in medicine and in science more broadly, making doctors and scientists more independent of the control of religious experts. At Oxford University in England, for example, a new type of medicine developed that placed barbers, who worked with the human body, above physicians, who theorized about diseases and cures. It would be at least another hundred years before the new *medicina meccanica* (i.e., mechanical medicine), as it was called in Italy, would begin diffusing in southern Europe (Israel 1999). Once on the forefront of scientific innovation, by the end of the seventeenth century Italy and Spain lagged behind the northern countries in scientific discoveries. Furthermore, by that time, the Congregatio had developed an institutional framing capable of handling the challenges of the new, and more independent, *medicina meccanica*, as Chapter 4 illustrates.

MIRACLES

Early on the morning of May 10, 1668, a loud noise shook Valencia, Spain. It sounded like a cannon shot, shattering the silence, and suddenly

[16] Miracles differ from divine punishments in one fundamental aspect: whereas the causal argument for miracles is *post facto*, the causal argument for punishments is *ante facto*, i.e., a miracle explains a healing after a disease; with punishment, transgression explains a sign before it happens. Consider, e.g., the case of Hurricane Katrina's impact on New Orleans. Some considered the storm a punishment for the sins of the city. In contrast to healing miracles, the cause occurred before the event; i.e., no fornication or drinking, no storm. In both cases, a chain of cause and effect eliminates randomness and brings the event into the realm of human understanding and, ultimately, of human control.

everyone was in the streets wondering what had happened. In the mansion of the Comte of Paredes, Don Vespasiano Manrique y Gonzaga, Viceroy of Valencia, the noise shook the walls and caused the portraits to fall off – all except the painting of Baylon, which Don Vespiano's wife, Doña Agnese, noticed still clung firmly to the wall. She informed her husband and the servants present of her theory that the noise was Baylon, knocking from heaven to notify the townspeople of his good humor. Knocking was one of Baylon's most famous miracles.

Vespasiano wanted to believe his wife but remained skeptical – after all, he was the man of law in town and Baylon had yet to be canonized.[17] But when Vespasiano went to mass later that day, he changed his mind. There, he learned that the man who had embezzled money from the monastery in which Baylon rested had finally been caught. The day's noisy beginning, Vespasiano reasoned, was a message from heaven (ASV 3403). This example testifies to the way that miracles reduced uncertainty. Calling the sudden noise a "miracle" was an act of constructing an interpretive frame around an unusual event.

The collective fears and anxieties that miracles addressed changed by location. At a superficial level, this is particularly evident when one compares the miracles performed in Sao Paolo, Brazil, by the Jesuit Father Joseph Anchieta, a contemporary of the European candidates included in this analysis. Father Anchieta's miracles occurred outside the geographical boundaries of this analysis, and the evidence from Brazil includes too few cases to be statistically relevant. Nevertheless, the contrast between Anchieta's miracles and those of the European candidates is so sharp as to warrant comment. Father Anchieta's 1627 canonization trial reports that he was able to talk to animals and that he controlled the rain and the flooding of the rivers. Healing miracles represented only 47 percent of Anchieta's miracles as reported during the trial, versus a minimum of 60 percent for the European candidates. In 1627, São Paulo was far from the urban metropolis of modern times, and its inhabitants were preoccupied with establishing congenial living conditions in an environment not yet domesticated. Anchieta's miracles thus reflected the needs and fears of his environment.

At a deeper level, miracles provide a window into religious beliefs that, even after centuries of Christianity, retained many elements of

---

[17] During the trial of 1648, many witnesses testified to Baylon's knocking. People would go to his tomb to request his aid, and Pasquali answered either with a strong knock or with a lighter one. The latter meant love and good fortune while the former meant sin (ASV 3400).

older, almost primitive religions tied to the cycles of nature – winter and spring, night and day – and to the body. Of the 511 miracles collected for this research, more than two-thirds were miracles of bodily healing. The soul, so central to Christian dogma, was almost completely ignored. In part this is not a surprise, given that much of the uncertainty in people's lives at the time came from diseases and from attempting to cure the human body on the basis of a very imperfect knowledge of it. Yet the centrality of the body was also characteristic of many pre-Christian religions in Europe and thus, as many historians have pointed out, the healings that candidates to sainthood performed can also be interpreted as showing a way in which ancient religious beliefs adapted themselves to the Christian tradition (MacMullen 1984). Examining the types of miracles performed shows this process of adaptation but also highlights the dependence of miracles on the uncertainty that shaped material life. Table 2.3 offers a possible categorization of miracles (Vauchez 2000).[18]

Seven categories are healing miracles, while freedom and protection and religious miracles fall under the broad category of miracles of protection. A miracle of protection is one in which the recipient asks the saint, either personally or by praying, for help in performing a task, assistance in starting a voyage, or, more generally, aid in difficult times (e.g., being incarcerated). Other includes all miracles that do not fall into these categories, such as flying. Finally the category of other disease includes all healings that were missing details that could allow them to be assigned to the other healing categories.[19]

---

[18] The categories of this classification system are self-explanatory. However, in order to have a firmer sense of their meaning, consider that under the category of resurrection fall all cases of children healed after being drawn into rivers, ponds, or wheels. Contagious diseases are mostly fevers, and paralysis includes the broader category of difficulty in movement. The category of wounds includes fractures and other nonfatal injuries, most of which arose during work activities. Mental diseases includes cases of possessed individuals and epileptics. The category of birth includes sterility and difficult childbirth. Finally, the category of miracles of protection includes miracles of liberation from captivity, visions, and punishments for blasphemy. An independent coder assigned the observed cases to the categories. The intercode reliability with my classification was 0.93.

[19] The categorization of miracles suggested in the preceding text highlights the role of healings. Yet miracles that occurred on the body of the saint, of which flying was perhaps the most spectacular, symbolized the body's role as a totem for the community of acolytes. This is analyzed in greater detail in the fourth section of the present chapter. Despite their relative rarity, the miracles that the saints performed on their own bodies had a central role.

TABLE 2.3. *Distribution of Miracles: 1588–1642*

Miracles	%	N
Healing Miracles		
Birth	.068	35
Blind and deaf	.052	27
Mental disease	.06	31
Organic and contagious disease	.242	124
Other disease	.125	64
Paralysis	.197	101
Resurrection	.037	19
Wounds and fractures	.062	32
Miracles of Protection		
Freedom and protection	.017	9
Religious miracle	.064	33
Other	.07	36
N	100%	511

Organic and contagious disease is the most common healing (24.5%). This category includes the general illness of fever, a symptom more than a disease, which was the most common ailment in the data set. The environments in which the candidates operated provide some clues regarding what those fevers may have been. For instance, it is likely that individuals who became sick in the spring in rural communities had allergies.

Examining the descriptions of miracles in the most common categories of Table 2.3, it is evident that many of the miracles could be interpreted in light of the human body's natural tendency toward recovery. Besides fever, other common organic diseases were vomiting, hemorrhaging (*flusso sanguinis*), and colds (*catarri*). In the category of paralysis, one finds headaches and leg pains more often than not (Delooz 1997). Yet even considering that some miracles were trivial events, it is useful to examine whether and how what was viewed as a miracle reflected the characteristics of the population in which it occurred. Doing so will further strengthen the interpretation of miracles as mobilizing events. Figure 2.1 shows the proportion of miracles by ideal candidate type.

Symbols of different shapes represent the types of candidates. Inside each symbol, the proportions of miracles performed by category are reported. At first glance, the absence of a clear pattern seems to deny the hypothesis that the needs of populations for supernatural events varied by their locale. Although each candidate could perform almost the entire

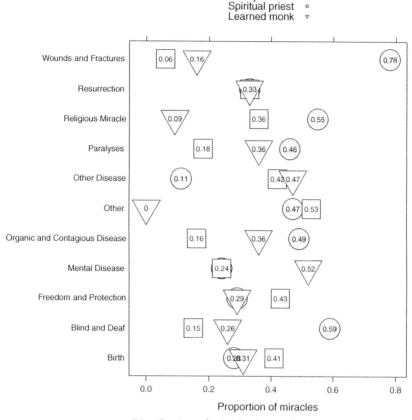

FIGURE 2.1. Distribution of miracles by candidate type.

spectrum of supernatural wonders and there is significant overlap among candidates' abilities, there are some differences among candidate types. The folksy friar type has the greatest degree of specialization, focusing on traditional miracles such as wounds and fractures and blind and deaf. The spiritual priest, by contrast, used the palette of wonders at his disposal in a more balanced way.

This suggests that although the needs of candidates' audiences were defined in part by their locales, within each community candidates were capable of catering to different segments of the population. Tailoring miracles to the needs of subpopulations meant that all candidates were able to perform a vast array of wonders. The contrast between the miracles received by men and women, shown in Figure 2.2, is evidence of such tailoring.

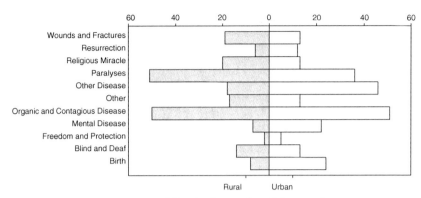

FIGURE 2.2. Miracles by gender of the saved.

Figure 2.2 shows that women received five times more mental health–related healings than did men. Centuries before the invention of psychoanalysis, women were perceived as more mentally fragile. Candidates reacted accordingly. Considered together, these figures indicate that candidates catered to the needs of their communities by catalyzing the capacity of miracles to reduce uncertainty into a shared interpretation of the candidate's sanctity. That is, within each community miracles created an inclusive mobilization.

The Structural Role of Miracles

Magic and superstitious beliefs may be at the root of miracles per se but are not sufficient to explain their mobilizing capacity. As Emile Durkheim (1982) pointed out, religious beliefs are always held by a defined collectivity and "the individuals who make up this … [collectivity] feel bound to one another by their common beliefs" (42); magic, by contrast, does not bind its followers together, and a church of magic does not exist. Because miracles were an essential part of sanctity and saints were an essential part of Catholicism, I present evidence that miracles, like any other religious belief, united people in a community.

The people who received and witnessed miracles believed in the sanctity of the candidate who performed them. In particular, those who testified on behalf of a candidate represented the active group of individuals who sustained the candidate's bid for canonization. I divide the "testifiers" into two groups: recipients of miracles (the saved) and witnesses of miracles. During a trial, each testifier's kinship and social status were recorded, as well as his name. Miracles – performed by

TABLE 2.4. *Three Postmortem Miracles in Milan*

Time Order	Description	Saved	Witnesses
1	*Febre terzana*	Ottaviano	Domina Antea (Ottaviano's wife)
			Dominus Ambrosio Lomazio
			Cureto Francesco
			Emilia De Spadis
2	*Febre quartana*	Emilia De Spadis	Giovanna De Filgeri Laura Coira
3	*Morbum formicalem*	Amrosio Lomazio	Isabella Cernuscola
			Domina Stefania (Lomazio's daughter)

the living or dead candidate – created bonds between the saved and the witnesses that extended beyond kinship[20] and social status.[21] For each miracle, there is at least one saved and, in most cases, at least one witness.

Based on the information about miracles in the trials, I constructed network graphs for all of the contemporary candidates but one. (Bernardino had too few miracles and witnesses to his credit; thus I decided not to construct a network graph for his case.) For each candidate, I pooled both types of relationships across time in order to create networks. For a clearer idea of what this means, consider the descriptions of the following three miracles that Borromeo performed postmortem in Milan. The first two miracles were healings from malaria while the third was a healing from the "disease of the ants." Table 2.4 reports the recipients of the miracles (third column) and lists some of the witnesses (fourth column). The miracles are listed chronologically.

The third column also gives the kinship relationship between (1) the saved and the witnesses and (2) among the witnesses, if there is such a

[20] When they were not reported directly in the books, I reconstructed kinship ties using the witnesses' last names, places of residence, occupations, and the names of the witnesses' parents. Monks, friars, nuns, and their religious sisters and brothers in the same monastery are also treated as being members of the same family. People in the same monastery shared their entire lives together: they ate together and performed all their activities at the same time. Thus their relations resemble kinship in social structure. E.g., most of the witnesses who testified for Teresa were members of the Discalced Carmelites, the religious order she profoundly reformed.

[21] This distinction follows the Church classification of *miracolati*, i.e., the recipients of miracles, and *testimoni*, i.e., the witnesses of miracles that occurred on the *miracolati*.

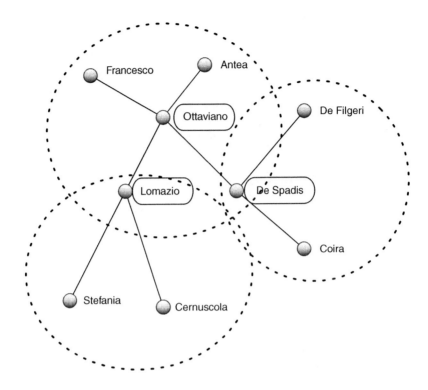

FIGURE 2.3. Network building.

relationship. Because some people experienced more than one miracle, pooling miracles across time results in one component (see Figure 2.3).

For example, De Filgeri, a friend of Emilia De Spadis, testified to only the miracle that saved her friend, while De Spadis testified to two miracles – one that healed her *dominus* in 1584 and one that she received later. Thus De Filgeri has only one tie, while De Spadis has two. Similarly, *dominus* Ambrosio Lomazio witnessed a miracle that *dominus* Ottaviano received in 1584 (*Summarium Miracolorum Borromei*, ACS, folio 583). A few years later, Lomazio also became a recipient of a postmortem miracle (folio 611).

In each network, ties represent either kinship relations between the nodes or the witnessing of a miracle, while nodes represent either the saved or witnesses. More precisely, in each network there are at least as many ties as there were witnesses testifying. In addition to this type of tie, kinship ties join related witnesses in each network.

Cario Borromeo miracles, Milan,
in vitam & 1584–1605

Pasqual Baylon miracles,
Villa Real, in vitam & 1592–1650

Filippo Neri miracle. Roma,
in vitam & 1554–1610

Teresa of Avila miracles.
Salamanca & Avila, in vitam 1582–1610

Friar Rainiero miracles.
Todi,in vitam & 1589–1628

Alfonso Orozco miracles.
Madrid, in vitam & 1570–1620

FIGURE 2.4. Networks.

I repeated the procedure for all of the miracles that the candidates in my data set performed. That is, although the Congregatio's judgments as to whether a miracle was true or false are recorded only for candidates who became saints or blessed, I created networks for all the candidates and miracles in the sample.[22] Figure 2.4 reports the results of these operations. Overall, there are 1,023 testifiers included in the graphs.

Visual inspection shows that in all the networks but one, there is a giant component. Friar Rainiero's graph lacks a giant component despite having smaller clusters, which indicates that his acolytes were less

---

[22] If the saved and the witnesses were related, i.e., if they shared two ties – witnessing of the miracle and kinship – only one tie was retained.

successful than those of other candidates at using postmortem miracles to spread his *fama* to a wider audience. Indirect evidence of this failure exists in Rainero's final status as a venerable – the lowest status among the candidates in this sample. The content of his miracles does not vary notably from those performed by Baylon, now a saint. This is not surprising, because both candidates operated in rural environments and came from the ranks of the regular clergy. Figure 2.4 quite literally shows the difference between the miracles that Rainiero and Baylon performed – Rainiero's miracles had a lower mobilizing capacity.

Direct evidence of this can be found in the narratives of Rainiero's miracles. For twenty years, a spirit possessed Antea d'Antinoro, a woman from a village near the monastery where friar Rainiero lived and preached. One day she ran into the magic friar. Seeing the woman's poor health, Rainiero made the sign of the cross in front of her face. A miracle occurred! The spirit left d'Antinoro's body for good. This experience transformed d'Antinoro into one of Rainero's most fervent believers, making her an active catalyst of postmortem miracles. Yet all of the miracles she propitiated after Rainiero's death were confined to the close circle of her family – her husband, Francesco, who was saved once; her sister's son; and her cousin. Although the details of these miracles are as astonishing as those of any of the other miracles Rainiero performed postmortem, the crucial point for our argument is that d'Antinoro never managed to convince other people besides her own relatives (ASV 3239). A similar narrative applies to several others of the small clusters of miracles in Rainiero's network. The absence of one large component in his network suggests that Rainiero's acolytes failed to mobilize people outside of the original clique of believers.[23]

Note that for all candidates, the majority of miracles occurred in components with other miracles. This finding allows a visual depiction of mobilization capacity and implies that some individuals experienced

[23] A competing explanation for the absence of a large component is that, given that Rainiero had fewer trials than other candidates, his acolytes did not have time to build consensus. This is tantamount to saying that Figure 2.1, panel F shows an early phase of Rainiero's *fama*. However, this argument does not take into account the relative success of other acolytes in building other candidates' *famae*. Comparing the miracles that Rainiero performed during his first trial with those that occurred during the first trials of other candidates shows that Rainiero's miracles involved fewer people. Considering Baylon's miracles – the candidate whose cult most resembles Rainiero's – highlights this; the network extracted from Baylon's first trial in Villa Real had almost 60% of the nodes tangled in a large component. As Figure 2.1, panel F shows, this was not the case for Rainero's.

more than one miracle, whether as a saved or as a witness. By contrast, the typical "isolated miracle" – a cluster of nodes with only one saved at its center – occurs in the form of a network star. A random distribution of miracles in the social fabric of a community would produce such isolated miracles, as well as small clusters of connected miracles, but without a component joining several "stars" together, precisely because the people experiencing miracles would be different each time. Figure 2.4 shows that the distribution of miracles was not random: not only did some miracles occur in components, but five of the six cases include a large component. This demonstrates the existence of people who were involved in multiple miracles. The people holding these large components together are the main focus of Chapter 3.

Yet the fact that certain people experienced more than one miracle is at odds with modern sensibility, which requires that the distribution of miracles in the social fabric look random. If the same group of individuals is involved in many miracles, is it not possible that they all just got together and made up stories? Modern reasoning, however, is rooted in skepticism about miracles and the supernatural more generally, whereas no seventeenth-century Catholic seriously doubted that miracles happened routinely, and that saints performed some (the true miracles) while demons performed others. The individuals who believed in a candidate and recognized him as a leader expected that he would perform miracles. Their expectations constituted the basis for the occurrence of miracles.

People who received or witnessed numerous miracles by virtue of their proximity to the candidate gained credibility in the eyes of outsiders. Such early believers became the direct connection to the candidate – in a sense, spiritual brokers for those facing uncertain situations. This underlying system of beliefs and relationships produced the social structures shown in the preceding text. Miracles were an integral part of Catholicism and, like any other religious belief, bound worshippers together.

Furthermore, considering miracles to be what's left when science has exhausted its explanatory power – with the implication that the more we know about nature, the weaker belief in the supernatural will be – has its uses and its flaws. Such reasoning helps explain the evolution of the types of miracles in isolation from their social and institutional contexts. It is, however, less analytically useful in examining the function that miracles had for individuals. The ability of miracles to bind together people who believed in them gave miracles a secure place in Catholicism well into modern times. Given this, it is perhaps not surprising that the network that best approximates a random distribution of miracles (see bottom left image in Figure 2.4), is that of Rainiero, the candidate with the lowest final status in the sample.

A candidate was more likely to perform *in vitam* miracles of protection and other supernatural events, like flying; postmortem, he performed mostly healings. Friar Rainiero performed a typical *in vitam* miracle over lunch with an acquaintance named Medoro. When Medoro's wife went to get some wine from the barrel, she found that the wine had gone bad. Rainiero insisted that he wanted to drink the bad wine, and begged Medoro not to throw it away. Five days later, the bad wine had become delicious and assumed restorative powers; many people recovered their health after drinking it (*folio* 132v, *ACS Storico*, 223).

Despite this tendency toward different types of miracles *in vitam* versus postmortem, living candidates did perform a large number of healings. For example, when Neri was just another priest in Rome, he encountered Francesco della Molara, who spent the year 1584 wandering around Rome under the impression that he was *belzebu'* (the devil). Neri instructed him to be happy and to start singing, whereupon della Molara started following Neri. At a certain point, Neri grabbed della Molara's head and whispered incomprehensible words to him, perhaps in Latin.[24] By the end of this exchange, della Molara was healed and had stopped thinking of himself as Belzebu'. He told Neri, "I am healed, you are a saint!" From that point on, della Molara was Neri's acolyte and was involved in many miracles that Neri performed. He was also one of the main figures in the canonization trials after Neri's death.

Because of charismatic abilities like those evident in the examples in the preceding text, a candidate could attract followers who admired his virtues and his perfect Christian life. This had its drawbacks. It meant, for one thing, that the candidate was always under his acolytes' close scrutiny while he was still alive. Neri's trials, for instance, report that he never stained his clothes with signs of his temptations, that is, with semen. We also know that several times Father Orozco refused meals sent to his cell

---

[24] The events that put della Molara on the streets of Rome were rather unusual. Della Molara, a nobleman, had fallen from his horse that year. He was brought to a hospital where he met a possessed man, who told della Molara that he too was possessed. Frightened, della Molara started to doubt himself, lost sleep, and began wandering around Rome, asking everyone if they thought he was the devil. Eventually, he became convinced he was the devil, at least until he found Neri (*Il primo processo*).

personally by the king of Spain, thereby showing that his behavior was not motivated by rewards. The people who surrounded the candidate saw this exemplary behavior, which, combined with his charisma, made him a leader.

Seventeenth-century religious leaders were also expected, as part of their role, to have supernatural abilities. Miracles became an expression of leadership; that is, the social position of a religious leader had the effect of producing miracles, and acolytes expected that from them. To the acolytes, the candidate became a living saint before becoming an official saint. No candidate who was not considered a living saint before he died became an official candidate for sainthood. Neither is there a candidate who only performed miracles postmortem.

Acolytes were no different from other people in their assumption that saints performed miracles (Bloch 1973), so once they saw their leader as a saint, they began experiencing miracles. By virtue of his presence merely, the candidate framed any event in which he participated as a potential miracle. When Neri placed his hands on Sister Lucrezia Cotta's chest to expel the devil from her heart, for example, Orsola Marcelli and Giovan Battista Martelli, two witnesses of the scene, did not attribute Neri's actions to prurient intentions. As far as they were concerned, Neri was already a saint, and a saint, by definition, could not behave indecently. They reported actually seeing the devil leaving Cotta's body.[25]

In vitam miracles engaged acolytes, so an acolyte is here defined as an individual who experienced, by receiving or witnessing, a miracle while the candidate was still alive, when his leader had not yet officially become a candidate for sainthood. Becoming a living saint, that is, being able to perform miracles *in vitam*, was the *sine qua non* for becoming a candidate for sainthood and being able to perform miracles after death. The living saint was the leader of a religious group and furthermore occupied a position in its social structure as a connector of acolytes who had no relationship to each other prior their encounter with the candidate.

The social heterogeneity of the people who experienced *in vitam* miracles placed the candidate at the center of multiple simultaneous demands for sanctity, and supernatural activity became the tool for resolving

---

[25] The intention here is not to question Neri's intentions with respect to Sister Cotta. The argument is that the same behavior performed by someone else would have probably made the two witnesses more suspicious, in that a priest touching the chest of a nun might be frowned upon. Further, the same Sister Cotta had already been the recipient of a miracle a few years before: she was exorcised during the exposition of the Felice da Cantalice, an ancient saint (*Il primo processo*).

potential conflicts between a candidate's clients. The extent to which the Church or society at large needed reform, and what kind, was debatable, but that saints could perform miracles was something everyone could agree on. Because acolytes' connections across status and kinship represented a novelty for them and for the community in which they operated, the candidate enjoyed the freedom that comes from occupying a role institutionally undefined.

The more connected the acolytes became, the more the candidate became a hostage of his role. The acolytes' expectations regarding the role of the candidate were projected onto the candidate's behavior at the time of his death. Death was a critical moment for a candidate, as it marked his entrance into paradise. A perfect death was one in which the candidate died peacefully, surrounded by his acolytes. More problematic was a death characterized by a long period of suffering – everyone knew, for instance, that Martin Luther died a horrible death, the just punishment for his heresy (Bossy 1985). By contrast, two days after Baylon died on May 17, 1592, while his body was exposed to the public in Villa Real, he opened his eyes during the celebration of the mass and moved his arms. One of Baylon's most famous miracles was knocking from within his coffin (ACS *Storico*, 123, 345). Perhaps Baylon did not die on May 17, and the events that occurred during the following days had more to do with the expectations connected to the role of living saint than with supernatural events. The road to sainthood was very demanding, and a certain amount of tension between the acolytes and their leader was structurally inevitable.

Table 2.5 shows the distribution of the saved with respect to social status for the candidates in the sample who had the largest number of *in vitam* miracles (more than 20). The table provides preliminary evidence that *in vitam* miracles created a new community of believers united across social status by their faith in the candidate.

The saved display greater heterogeneity with respect to social status than one would expect. Compared to other relevant social structures at the time, acolytes represented an odd bunch. Guilds, for example, were coherently organized along status lines, with the merchant guilds grouping wealthier individuals and the craft guilds grouping smaller, usually family-owned businesses (Richardson 2001). The fact that women also were involved in the nascent cult, as the previous analysis shows, only accentuates the strangeness of the social structures that candidates built using miracles. During much of the same period women were notably banned from joining guilds (Gardner 1986).

TABLE 2.5. *Social Status of the Saved*

	Neri	Orozco	Rainiero
		(proportions)	
Commoners and peasants	.375	.285	.484
Nobles and merchants	.40	.357	.272
Regular and secular clergy	.225	.357	.242
N	40	56	33

Acolytes gathered together at the time of their candidate's death, representing the first moment in the independent life of the new community of believers. One event in this process of community formation had a particular symbolic meaning – the opening of the candidate's body for inspection. In the dramatic hours following Neri's death, for instance, many of the people close to him gathered in the room where his body was being inspected. The bricklayer Giovan Battista Guerra, recipient of one of Neri's *in vitam* miracles, recalled at a canonization trial how he held Neri's body while two doctors and a barber cut him open (*Il primo processo*). Guerra remembered a room full of people – all, like himself, fervent believers in Neri.

Social Structure of Acolytes

In vitam miracles turned those who experienced them into acolytes. By means of his supernatural capacities, the candidate created a social structure of individuals who might have nothing in common otherwise, but who shared faith in the same candidate. I used a standard measure of heterogeneity (Erikson and Bearman 2006) in order to capture the structure that *in vitam* miracles built with respect to status. The measure captures the status heterogeneity of the testifiers to *in vitam* miracles and ranges from 0, perfect homogeneity, to 1, perfect heterogeneity. Because *in vitam* miracles happened early in a candidate's career, they were unlikely to have no witnesses. In this sample, a miracle involves two people at minimum, the saved and a witness, but may extend to more people. Observed values for status heterogeneity were high for all the candidates and very close together regardless of the number of witnesses, ranging between .659 for dyadic *in vitam* miracles and .632 for triadic miracles. *In vitam* miracles created a social structure with members of

The Living Saint

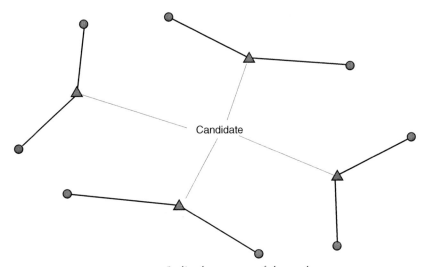

FIGURE 2.5. Stylized structure of the acolytes.

heterogeneous status. This confirms that *in vitam* miracles joined believers from different walks of life into a sparse structure in which the most common structural arrangement was that of isolated miracles.[26]

This type of social structure was well suited for diffusing the candidate's reputation after his death. Yet accounts of the trials and several secondary sources – mainly the *vitae* of the candidates – provide ample evidence that the acolytes formed a close-knit group. The two facts are only superficially contradictory. The result of *in vitam* miracles was a set of unconnected clusters of acolytes held together by the candidate. The result of postmortem miracles was a densely interwoven group of acolytes. After the death of the candidate, acolytes began drawing outsiders into the new cult. Each acolyte, due to his or her role in officiating the ceremonies that produced postmortem miracles, became witness to the salvation of multiple people from multiple families and social statuses. Under this dynamic, *in vitam* miracles formed a social structure more sparse than what would result when all of the candidate's miracles are considered together. The structural dynamic reversed itself after the candidate's death; the unconnected clusters produced by *in vitam* miracles were woven together by the postmortem miracles.

---

[26] The densities of the networks generated using only *in vitam* miracles for the three candidates that performed more than 30 of them was very low. Several isolated network stars made the largest parts of these networks.

In stylized form Figure 2.5 displays the social structure of acolytes that *in vitam* miracles created. The lighter-colored edge represents the symbolic tie to the candidate that united the individuals who experienced a miracle. Ties within an isolated miracle represent a bond of witnessing, and the triangular shape of the central node indicates the recipient of the miracle. All of the trial proceedings and secondary sources reported the renewal that the candidate brought to the lives of the people he touched. Many of them renounced the secular world. This intense communal experience was reinforced by the opposition of contemporary Church leaders to the candidate's preaching. The local Church hierarchy had many reasons to oppose the new religious movements, because many candidates denounced the corruption of the high clergy and called for a public renewal of the spirit. This appeared to be the case particularly for the candidates operating in the urban centers of Italy, that is, the spiritual priest candidates.

Miracles mobilized people not because basic psychological processes were different during the seventeenth century than they are now or because the human mind operated on different principles at the dawn of modernity. Rather, individuals' social and material conditions differed greatly from those of today. As Bloch argues, "we must not leave out of accounts the effects of an astonishing sensibility to what were believed to be supernatural manifestations. It made people's minds constantly and almost morbidly attentive to all manner of signs, dreams, or hallucinations" (1973, 73).

3

The Acolytes

The living candidate used his charisma to unite disparate people into a fluid structure. As Chapter 2 shows, the status, kinship, and gender heterogeneity of the acolytes contrasted with the homogeneity of the members of other associations that shaped people's lives at the dawn of modernity. This meant that the candidate's acolytes had few local institutions from which to draw support for their nascent cult. Consequently, the existence of the acolytes' social structure depended entirely on the charisma of their leader. The death of the candidate therefore posed a unique challenge to that social structure.

The acolytes' first tool in meeting this challenge was their belief that their leader did not die but rather was reborn into paradise. It is a subtle difference, but one that cast the tension that usually follows the death of a charismatic leader into a different light. It framed the challenge facing the acolytes not as one of succession but as one of continuation. It was now their task to transmit the knowledge of their leader's deeds and powers to people who did not directly experience them while the leader was still alive.

A consequence of the acolytes' belief that their leader had not really died was that the routinization crisis that, according to Max Weber follows the death of a charismatic leader, did not occur at the time of the candidate's death. Rather, and to the extent that acolytes managed to involve new people in the nascent cult, a routinization crisis could potentially develop at the time of the death of last individual who experienced the candidate's powers firsthand. From this perspective, the acolytes' rush to win Rome's recognition was a means to ensure that their structure would survive their deaths.

The role of the candidate as the only justification for the acolytes' heterogeneous structure is captured symbolically and materially by the importance that acolytes gave to their leader's body. The candidate's body had a role analogous to that of the totem in aboriginal societies. Like the totem, the body was an object representing a unity that transcended the local divisions organized by kinship, status, and gender. This interpretation explains why every canonization trial began with an inquiry into the current state of the candidate's body.

It was a well-known fact that the acolytes cleaned up the candidate during the hours immediately after his death, and that this allowed the body to withstand the ravages of time. Even so, the uncorrupted state of the body was considered a clear sign of supernatural power. To provide one example out of many, Raymond de Peñafort's tomb was opened for the customary inspection at the beginning of his March 1596 canonization trial in Barcelona, more than three centuries after his death. Church officials wrote that a sweet smell suffused the church, and they inventoried the contents of the tomb: "1. The entire mouth with all the teeth; 2. The lower jaw with the canine tooth; 3. Two clavicles; 4. Two scapulae; 5. Eighteen ribs; 6. Twelve vertebrae; 7. Two bones of the humeros; 8. Two bones of the radius; 9. One elbow; 10. Two bones of the femur; 11. Two tibias; 12 Two bones of the fibula; 13. Two patellas; 14. One sacrum bone in two pieces" (*folio* 272r, ASV 220). The prospect of future inspection motivated acolytes to open up the candidate's body immediately after his death to take inventory. When Filippo Neri's acolytes reported that he had a big heart, they did not mean it only metaphorically.

Keeping the candidate's body well preserved was important given that it represented the unity of the group, but it was not enough to build a local movement in support of the sanctity of the candidate. Postmortem miracles, that is, miracles that occurred after the candidate's death, built the candidate's following – what the Church called the *fama sanctitatis*. Having a *fama* had always been one of the requirements for becoming a saint, but the codification of legal procedures for verifying sanctity after the establishment of the Congregatio in 1588 altered the social mechanism that produced miracles and changed the significance of the *fama*. During the medieval era, having a *fama* did not require organizing support, because Rome made little inquiry into a presumed saint's miracles; acquiring a saintly reputation at that time thus was only a local affair. Without a lasting social structure to support it, however, a *fama* could vanish quickly, and new saints were always in demand. Many saints sprang up all over Europe, and their *famae* were transient phenomena, rather than a series of organized support movements. Although Chapter 2 detailed how the miracles of the living candidate turned the people that experienced them into acolytes, this chapter documents the role of acolytes in constructing a social structure of believers after their candidate's death. The quest for predictability in an uncertain world remained at the root of miracles, but acolytes began tailoring their candidate's *fama* to meet not only the local demands but also the Congregatio's requirements. That is, acolytes used postmortem miracles to reduce uncertainty for individuals whom they united into a community of believers that became a social movement in support of the effort to get the candidate canonized by the Congregatio. The *fama* became the direct representation of the broader appeal of a candidate, the social translation of his sanctity into a community at the hands of the acolytes. In this way, the candidate's *fama* stopped being a transient phenomenon and became part of the identity of the community.

Acolytes propagated postmortem miracles through the tool of the ritual healing. The ritual helped construct a predictable mental frame – based on popular beliefs about how nature and society worked – around (unpredictable) illnesses and thereby "produced" healings. As an expression of a strict set of guidelines, a ritual reduced uncertainty by removing chance from the equation and instead offering evidence that all forces obeyed God's laws. Relics, pieces of the candidate's body thought to have healing power, were central to the healing ritual. Because acolytes alone had access to their candidate's relics, they were thought to be the legitimate presiders over the rituals that produced healings. The second section of this chapter provides evidence of the role of the ritual as a resource in the acolytes' hands.

The third section highlights the roles of miracles as mobilizing events and of acolytes as activists; the distribution of a candidate's miracles over time bears out the idea that the efforts of the acolytes actively built the *fama*. With respect to contemporary theory regarding the diffusion of religious beliefs, this research shows that individual decisions to join the movement, that is, to believe in the candidate's holiness, were brought about by the acolytes' work.

Even so, miracles could occur without acolytes. This kind of miracle was a private exchange between a client and a candidate, rather than a public event that mobilized a community. It was therefore acolytes – not miracles as such – that reached across the social cleavages of the seventeenth century to build social movements in support of canonization efforts. Acolytes' activism was similar to that of bishops at the dawn of

Christianity, who also used relics to give the public a stake in the new faith (Brown 1981).

As with modern religious activists as well as the ancient bishops of Christianity, the means and motifs that acolytes used to create a large base of support for their candidate reflected their time and place. The medium of the ritual healing was born of the uncertainty of material life. The opportunity for its success at creating a social movement came from the seething social unrest that characterized the period. Many of the charismatic leaders who called for reform within Catholicism founded new religious orders and became candidates for sainthood: Ignatio de Loyola, who founded the Jesuits in 1534; Gaetano da Tiene, founder of the Teatini (1524); Teresa of Avila, reformer of the Carmelites; and Angela Merici, founder of the Orsoline (1535). For these leaders and their acolytes canonization meant the institutionalization of the new order and its potential access to donations, new properties, and offices. Acolytes usually took important positions within the religious orders that their leaders started or reformed. The activism of the acolytes should therefore be interpreted within the broader framework of motivations created by the religious turmoil of the century.

As Chapter 2 documented, the *in vitam* miracles that the candidates performed reflected the conditions of the community in which they operated, as did the activities of the acolytes after the candidate's death and the postmortem miracles that they performed. Consequently, the structure and composition of the *fama* varied from place to place. The fourth section of this chapter examines the social status of the people involved in a *fama* in order to highlight the acolytes' role in building a movement that reflected the social environment in which they operated. The *fama* of each candidate varied according to where he fell among the ideal types introduced in Chapter 2: the spiritual priest, the learned monk, the folksy friar; urban or rural, regular or lay clergy.

Despite these tendencies to tailor miracles and the *fama* to local conditions, acolytes' activism was influenced in other directions by the institutional reforms that the Church introduced with the Council of Trent. At the dawn of modernity, the Church found it necessary to promote a new type of worship, more rationally centered on Catholic dogma than on local needs and beliefs. The new instructions for priests that Carlo Borromeo wrote for his dioceses, for instance, were part of this effort. It was as if the Church hoped to introduce a new type of God, one who was less tolerant of idiosyncratic behavior and family-centered expressions of devotion. This rationalization effort promoted religious practices more focused on ritual and external behavior than on internal beliefs (Gotor 2000). Examples of this new emphasis on the external form of worship include the Church's new requirement that the *Credo* be learned by heart (Delumeau 1976) and its new prohibition on prostitutes meeting their clients in the church.

Not all the miracles that candidates and acolytes performed reflected this shift from one God to another. Some candidates continued to mobilize their communities through miracles that reflected a harsh deity involved in daily human activities, rather than a remote God to be invoked through a standardized procedure. Shifting to a more rational God posed a potential problem for Rome in that it might alienate popular support rooted in the idiosyncratic behavior of candidates for sainthood capable of tailoring their miracles to local audiences. Though the ritual healing, with its standard form, ability to build a movement, and amenability to judgment under the Congregatio's new legalistic procedures, fit Church's rationalization efforts, it did not make the Catholic God more appealing to believers. Acolytes operated as a sort of symbolic broker between Rome's new requirements and local demands. It is this brokerage activity that helped bring sainthood into modernity.

THE *FAMA SANCTITATIS* – WHAT IS IT?

Sanctity was a social product sensitive to the cultural and economic context in which the candidate operated. Believers' need for security and stability formed the root of sanctity, creating a market for people capable of reducing uncertainty. Many of these people used their charismatic abilities to produce wonders that built a comprehensible mental frame around unusual events, which allowed people to interpret such events within the standard categories they developed through daily experience and current scientific knowledge. Their miracles allowed charismatic leaders to acquire a reputation for sanctity, a *fama*. Yet from the seventeenth century onward, having a *fama* while alive was not enough to ensure a leader would become a saint. With the establishment of the Congregatio, a successful candidate became one with a large and lasting *fama*, that is, a large "customer base" of believers that continued to use his miracles for a long time after his death. Once the *fama* became an official requirement for canonization, having a reputation was no longer sufficient – a candidate needed followers.

To construct the *fama* – recruit a customer base – acolytes had to spread and organize the knowledge of their candidate's supernatural powers, which they did through postmortem miracles. In the institutional framework that the Congregatio began creating after 1588, postmortem miracles can be thought of as mobilizing events. Without them, the candidate's reputation would be much as *famae* were during the medieval period: confined to the small circle individuals who experienced a charismatic leader's wonders firsthand and were destined to die off quickly after candidate's own death. In a sense, the formula *vox populi vox dei* (i.e., the voice of the people is the voice of God), which characterized the previous conception of sainthood, was codified into a precise institutional meaning during the seventeenth century. In the institutional environment that the Congregatio was creating, acolytes acquired a structural position, transforming the *fama* into a local social movement.

As the introduction to this chapter pointed out, the ritual healing became the acolytes' best instrument for forging and organizing social consensus into a *fama*. There were two reasons for this. First, healings had been part of sainthood since Christianity arrived in Rome; as a type of miracle, healings had a long-standing legitimacy in Europe. Acolytes seem to have stepped up their occurrence. Giulio Sodano noted an increase in the number of healings reported in the three canonization trials that took place in the Kingdom of Naples during the seventeenth century compared to trials of earlier periods (1999). My own research indicates that healings eclipsed the imitation of Jesus's acts, which included a good number of nonhealings, among miracle workers in this period.

The second reason healings became acolytes' main mobilizing tool was that they were easier for the Congregatio to evaluate rationally than were other types of miracles – for instance, visions – and thus became a preferred form of evidence for the supernatural abilities of the candidate. The ritual healing became the prototypical miracle because it could be subjected to the rationalized procedures controlled by the Church. The systematic exploitation of gaps in medical knowledge protected postmortem miracles from the potential skepticism a believer might feel toward the powers of a given candidate. How the Church was able to maintain control of adjudicating miracles vis-à-vis the growing autonomy of medicine is the topic of Chapter 4.

Thus the greater scrutiny that the Church applied to supernatural events and the requirement that candidates have a large and lasting base of followers made acolytes adopt a ritual in order to produce postmortem miracles. In the Catholic world, evaluating miracles did not mean their elimination, but rather a reduction of what could be legitimately considered impossible. Flying across the Mediterranean Sea from the

Balearic Islands to Barcelona on a cape, like Saint Raymond did during the thirteenth century, did not build a social movement, and so was no longer acceptable as a miracle that would build a *fama*. Nor did the multiplication of fish, à la Jesus. The content of miracles became part of the process of rationalization, bringing magic up to speed with modernity. Further, because of their role as presiders over the ritual that created the postmortem miracle, acolytes became the legitimate performers of miracles in the eyes of the community in which the candidate had lived and preached. More succinctly, the ritual healing became the expression of acolytes' activism.

The Social Structure of the Fama

The networks of testifiers (witnessed and saved) presented in Chapter 2 are visual representations of the *fama*. (See Chapter 2 for details of the construction of the networks.) Clusters of saved people are direct evidence that the *fama* united people. The *fama* was a social fact, as a consequence of which the people it united celebrated masses, built churches, started charities, and went on pilgrimages even several decades after the candidate's death. These activities gave concrete consequences to the *fama*.

Figure 3.1 shows the large components of each candidate's network graph. Besides representing the majority of a candidate's miracles, the components isolate the salient structural feature of the *fama*: the fact that people united in the candidate's name.

The panels of Figure 3.1 are snapshots of a candidate's cult in a community. Through time, individuals became socially intertwined in the name of a candidate; that is, the *fama* created a web of relationships that extended beyond kinship relations (represented in the figure by thick edges between nodes). Although family relationships tie together 13 percent of the testifiers in Alonzo Orozco's trial, adding witnessing relationships brings the same proportion of connected people to almost 36 percent—a threefold increase. Neri's graph shows an even more pronounced increase – from 7 percent to almost 40 percent. These individuals built the candidate's *fama*. Who they were and how they were able to catalyze supernatural events is the subject of the remainder of this chapter.

ACOLYTES AND THE RITUAL HEALING

After the death of their leader, acolytes set about creating the *fama*. During a candidate's trials, his or her acolytes greeted people on the streets with

Panel A: Carlo Borromeo   Panel B: Pasqual Baylon

Panel C: Filippo Neri   Panel D: Teresa of Avila

Panel E: Alonzo Orozco   Panel F: Rainiero

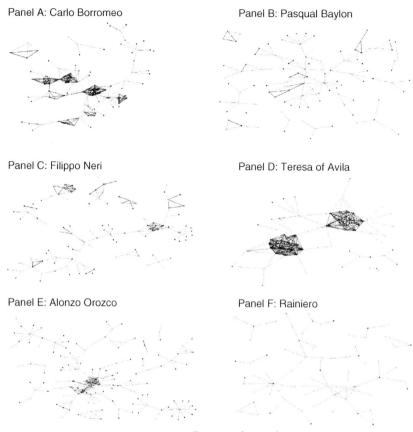

FIGURE 3.1. Connected miracles.

stories of the candidate's past miracles. Based on these stories, acolytes were invited to visit the sick. In contrast to the miracles a candidate performed *in vitam*, postmortem miracles were almost all healings. Acolytes were called upon to attend to the sick because they had direct access to the candidate's relics, which were thought to have healing powers.

During Neri's trial in 1595, Marcello Vitaleschi, one of Neri's acolytes, told the judges that Neri's relics had produced many wonders and that they were in high demand in town (*Il primo processo*). Sometimes, a special event created the opportunity for further miracles. In 1601 a procession in honor of Neri, at that point already a blessed, took place in the narrow alleys of Rome. Several miracles occurred in the following days; Neri's acolytes were called as owners of relics to heal people. Among the more notable miracles was the healing of a boy named Giuseppe Sermei.

According to his mother, Sigismonda, who testified on September 13, 1597, and again on May 3, 1610, Giuseppe got terribly ill and spit a worm from his mouth. He fell into a coma for four days and appeared on the verge of dying. An acolyte arrived with one of Neri's relics that, once applied to Giuseppe's heart, healed him. The next day, Sigismonda said, Giuseppe ate a great deal (*Il primo processo*). Another young boy, named Filippo, experienced a similar miracle in the days following that procession.

Sometimes, acolytes would lend a relic to someone who would use it to heal himself. For example, on a winter day in the town of Amelia in Umbria, four-year-old Venturino Alvi became sick. Venturino, his brother would later report, stopped eating and lay in bed on the verge of death. The entire Alvi family scrambled to gather the resources to get a doctor to come. Meanwhile, fortuitously, a member of the family ran into friar Egidio on the streets of Amelia. The friar had been a member of Rainiero's monastery and was one of his acolytes; he suggested that Rainiero might be of some help in the case. He gave the Alvis a tissue that had belonged to Rainiero and had been placed on the candidate's head at the time of his death. The tissue, placed on Venturino's head by his family members, healed the boy immediately, convincing the Alvis of Rainiero's sanctity (ASV 3239).

Most often, however, acolytes went directly to the sick person's house armed with the candidate's relics to perform the healing themselves. Upon his arrival at the sick person's house, the acolyte would invite everyone present to pray, often instructing them to kneel and pray aloud together. During the prayer, the acolyte asked his candidate for grace for the sick person and at this point usually took out one of the candidate's relics, which he applied to the invalid. Immediately or within the span of a few days, the sick person would be perfectly healed, becoming a saved.[1]

For example, Maria Jaraz de Arraya had almost completed her pregnancy, but on April 28, 1620, she suddenly fell ill. She rolled her eyes backward and began having seizures. Antonio Gutierez, her husband, ran through the streets of Madrid seeking a surgeon to help deliver the baby and a doctor to help his wife. A priest arrived on the scene, and while the doctor and the surgeon went to work, the priest placed several relics on de Arraya's body. Nothing worked, and de Arraya lay there, rigid and

---

[1] This describes most postmortem healings. It is not, however, what Church doctrine required of genuine miracles. The Church mandated an instantaneous healing that in reality seldom occurred.

cold, on the verge of death. Her husband was desperate. Juan de Herrera, Orozco's most active acolyte, learned what was happening at the Gutierez house and rushed over unexpectedly. He requested that all the other relics be removed, inviting everyone to pray while he placed Orozco's belt on the woman's womb. Half an hour later, de Arraya recovered her strength and delivered a stillborn baby. Everyone present proclaimed the event a miracle, though the baby did not survive it (ASV 3033).

Relics operated as specialized medicine, rather than general prescriptions. This specialization suggests that a relic's power was to some degree independent of the final outcome of events in which it was used. Orozco's belt was used only in difficult deliveries; even if the result was a stillbirth, the delivery was still considered a miracle. At first sight this appears paradoxical, but it was an extreme consequence of the specialized power of relics. The belt, after all, performed its function – bringing about delivery, not necessarily ensuring the health of the child delivered. The trials of Orozco and Neri report not only stillborn deliveries as miracles but also scenarios in which both the mother and the baby died after the delivery.

One can interpret relics as objects whose meanings involve two distinct poles (Turner 1967). One pole refers to the principles of social organization and to social structure in general. The other pole represents natural and physiological phenomena. For instance, the trials of Saint Raymond de Peñafort, the thirteenth-century monk, reported that his cape was often used to cure headaches. On the social organization pole, the cape symbolized nobility, because it was generally nobles who wore capes; its ability to cure headaches resonated with the perception of the head as the noblest part of the body. On the natural pole, the cape stood for protection from the cold, which could cause such symptoms as headaches, runny noses, and coughing.

Orozco's belt brings to mind the ideas of a belly, holding on, and power, all concepts loosely related to a woman giving birth. On the social organization pole, the belt stood for male power and male domination. On the physiological pole, it stood for "tying up the belly," or metaphorically squeezing the baby out during the delivery. Thus the belt worked because it reproduced the social order even in a moment of great distress.

Acolytes officiated healings by imitating what the candidate had done before his death. They crossed people on the body part that needed healing and recited the prayers the candidate taught them. A healing was a patterned process in time in which the behavior of each actor involved was symbolic (Turner 1967). The ritual, rather than the powers of the candidate in whose name it was performed, produced the healings, because the ritual offered predictable actions with predictable outcomes (prayer followed by healing). The ritual thereby created a mental frame for reducing uncertainty. Furthermore, by imitating the candidate's behavior, acolytes carried on the achievements their leader performed while alive without risking people seeing them as the ultimate performers instead of the candidate. Acolytes catalyzed postmortem miracles through their role as performers of a ritual, at whose center stood the candidate or a piece of his body.

A successful healing changed the relationship between the saved's family and its community. The saved's family members, having witnessed the healing of one of their own, became supporters of the candidate. Other family members would reach out to the acolytes as a result, thus increasing their own likelihood of receiving or witnessing miracles.

A structural tension therefore arose between the acolytes and a saved's family. Although the acolytes spread their candidate's reputation for sanctity from family to family, each family would claim a special relationship with the candidate, as if he were their personal saint. This tendency was particularly strong in cases in which the saved's family was noble. For instance, the noble De Magistris family in Rome received three miracles through Neri's intercession. The saved were Margherita, who was healed by the touch of Neri's hand; Agostino, who used the same hand to heal his throat; and Epifania Colicchia, a relative, who was healed by a rose from Neri's coffin (ACS Storico, *Relationes Super Vita et Sanctitate*, 223–6; *Il primo processo*). None of the De Magistrises were Neri's acolytes while he was still alive. Their later heavy involvement in his case is an example of powerful families' tendency to assert control, so to speak, over the cults of new candidates, thus taking control away from the acolytes.

However, allowing a particular family to dominate the social movement around a candidate could destroy that social movement. A successful *fama* balanced the competing needs of the acolytes to spread the *fama* widely and the needs of individual families to express their connection to the candidate. Figure 3.2 represents this balance. Thick edges indicate kinship ties while thin edges represent the witnessing of a miracle, and the figure overall shows clusters of miracles within families and clusters of believers joined through miracles.

From this perspective, there are parallels between the role of acolytes at the dawn of modernity and that of Western bishops during the twilight of the Roman Empire. In the empire's later years, the bishops of the new religious elite marked their primacy over local lay elites by exchanging relics and opposing any private and family-based worship in favor of

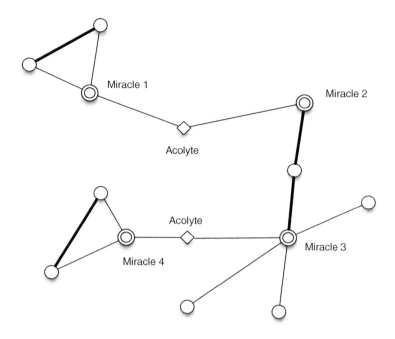

Witnessing a miracle

Kinship tie

FIGURE 3.2. Stylized structure of the building of the *fama*.

public manifestations of faith.[2] The public tombs of the martyrs broke with the Roman tradition of family gods and demons (Brown 1981). Similarly, acolytes directed their activities toward ensuring that the entire community was represented in the new faith.

Church doctrine states that a community rallies behind a candidate through the intervention of the Holy Spirit (Veraja 1992; Papa 2001). The Church viewed the *fama* as the result of divine intervention – the Holy Spirit created a community out of isolated clusters of people. Figure 3.2 suggests a simpler interpretation of how people came together in the faith in the new candidate, however.

In vitam miracles transformed a group of heterogeneous people into a group of acolytes. After a candidate's death, each acolyte officiated many

[2] I am indebted to Sofia Boesch-Gajano for pointing this out to me.

rituals that created miracles for people from multiple families and social classes, convincing them of the sanctity of the candidate. In this way, they built a dense, heterogeneous social network from the previously sparse one composed solely of acolytes and centered on the candidate.

In the context of a segmented society, a candidate's reputation for holiness was bound to fizzle out without the organized effort of the acolytes. The candidate's *fama* might come to appeal only to the poor, merchants, or the De Magistris family, or the candidate's *fama* might be forgotten altogether as the acolytes died. A cult grew through the conscious efforts of a group of fervent believers who were able to involve greater segments of their community in the new faith by using supernatural powers.

Acolytes used postmortem miracles to organize people into a church, in the anthropological sense of a group of people who share a particular belief. Two features of the social world of the seventeenth century help explain why people believed in the miracles catalyzed by groups of religious activists. First, people were for the most part illiterate, especially in the Catholic countries and outside the cities, despite the fact that the printing press had been invented more than a century before. Therefore, although the seventeenth century is usually considered the century of scientific discoveries and progress, this knowledge diffused very slowly in European societies that were still organized orally.[3] Second, popular religion was quite distant from official doctrine. Carlo Ginzburg (1976) documented in detail people's religious beliefs at the time; summarizing the philosophy of Menocchio, a miller living in northern Italy and accused of being an heretic, Ginzburg wrote, "In a terminology imbued with Christianity, neoplatonism, and scholastic philosophy, Menocchio sought to express the basic, instinctive materialism of generations and generations of peasants" (73). Menocchio and others like him lived in a physically precarious and unpredictable world; their needs for magic had more to do with the body than with the Christian soul. In such a world, a great many inexplicable things occurred, and acolytes' use of miracles was seen as bringing some order.[4]

---

[3] On the impact of literacy, Natalie Zemon-Davis argues that, to properly understand the effects of the printing press, one must look at cohesive groups in which some members could read, rather than looking at the population at large (1975).

[4] Something similar sustained the diffusion of Christianity, MacMullen argues. He notes that the majority of new converts were the destitute and poor, not the Roman elites. Miracles convinced the illiterate of the superiority of the Christian God, whereas the very notion of resurrection after death contrasted sharply with what was considered wisdom among the educated (MacMullen 1984).

TABLE 3.1. *The Most In-between Vertices
(largest component)*

Case	Proportion of Acolytes > Average Betweenness
Folksy Friar	
Baylon	.56
Rainerio	.57
Spiritual Priest	
Borromeo	[too few cases]
Neri	.833
Learned Monk	
Teresa	.4
Orozco	.894

Evidence of Acolytes' Activity

With respect to the sample of candidates included in this analysis, clusters of miracles capture the activism of the acolytes – the *fama*. Recall that an acolyte is simply someone who believed in the sanctity of the candidate before anybody else, that is, a person who either received or witnessed an *in vitam* miracle. Table 3.1 shows the proportion, in each candidate's largest component, of acolytes who had a higher than average "betweenness centrality." Betweenness centrality measures how many times a node falls in between pairs of other nodes; it captures the potential that each node has for controlling the flow of communication (De Nooy, Mrvar, and Batagelj 2005).

In four of the five cases I could measure, the majority of the nodes in the giant component with the highest betweenness correspond to individuals who experienced a miracle performed by the living candidate. In Orozco's graph, for instance, almost 90 percent of the nodes with above average betweenness represent people who interacted personally with the candidate.[5] Table 3.1 provides evidence that the acolytes were those most responsible for connecting others in the cult of the candidate.

---

[5] The proportion for Borromeo could not be calculated because there were fewer than five *in vitam* miracles included in his trials. Such a small number would produce unreliable calculations. This does not mean that Borromeo performed only five miracles *in vitam*. Rather, it shows that the local authorities where Borromeo operated complied more fully than others with the rule stating that only postmortem miracles were valid evidence for canonization. Given that his trials did not otherwise differ from those of the other candidates, the impossibility of calculating a proportion for his case does not undermine the reasoning on the importance of acolytes.

Acolytes appear to have played a different role in Teresa's case – for her, only 40 percent of the nodes with high betweenness centrality were acolytes. Teresa's cult diffused mostly within the boundaries of the monasteries and convents that she founded. Opening a new convent was a very intense experience for those who participated; convents were often started in very poor areas, yet the women there relied on charity and donations for their survival (*Libro della mia vita*). In a sense, fewer miracles were necessary to convince Teresa's spiritual sisters of her sanctity, because surviving the most adverse circumstances with Teresa's guidance was a miracle. Few ritual healings were needed to convince the members of Teresa's spiritual family of her sanctity; they had proof enough without them. The monasteries furthermore provided the institutional setting for the preservation of her charisma in the form of memories of Teresa's innumerable achievements.[6] This type of sainthood, removed from popular devotion and physically centered within the walls of monasteries and convents, would become dominant after 1642.

Relics

Between the founding of the Congregatio in 1588 and the promogulation of its final rules for canonization in 1642, however, a candidate needed the support of a strong social movement in order to become a saint, and ritual healings, mediated through acolytes and their use of relics, were the most effective tool for building such a movement. The transformation of the *fama* from unorganized consensus into a social movement displaced nonhealing miracles, not only because they were more difficult to evaluate (see Chapter 4) but also because they did not strictly require the presence of acolytes. Furthermore, because of the heterogeneity of their social structure, the healings that acolytes officiated were more likely to cut across kinship lines and join different families together. The two types of miracles, healing versus nonhealing, therefore differed with respect to the social structures they produced. Although healings created clusters of testifiers, nonhealing miracles remained more isolated.

---

[6] This is not to say that Teresa did not perform miracles. She did, but her miracles had a different role in terms of engaging acolytes. Teresa's miracles eased the lives of a previously established community of women, but did not create a new community of believers by e.g., knitting together families in a town. One of Teresa's miracles occurred in 1580; while Teresa was in Villanova starting a new convent, she multiplied flour for her sisters so that everyone could have enough food (ACS, *Storico, Relatio Uditori di Rota*).

With some notable exceptions, after the establishment of the Congregatio, nonhealing miracles became more part of the realm of magic than of religion; religion binds people together by their common beliefs, whereas magic does not (Durkheim 1982). The seventeenth-century updating of what a miracle could do was therefore the direct result of a process, quite different from the one identified by Weber, that rationalized their magic.

Relics were central to acolytes' power to create social movements, but acolytes did not create the power of relics. For instance, in 1608, Gregorio Maro, an accountant for the Inquisition in the Kingdom of Sardinia, then under Spanish control, visited the cloister of the Augustinian sisters in Madrid. During his stay, a noblewoman sent some donations wrapped in a shirt that had belonged to the Augustinian candidate Orozco. The shirt, apparently, was responsible for having assured the noblewoman a safe delivery. Maro, interested in the shirt, took it back to Sardinia with him over the nuns' protests. Even in Sardinia, away from the sisters who first believed in its power, the relic's reputation diffused throughout the community, and all the women started asking for it during deliveries. Every time the shirt was sent back to Maro, donations were wrapped in it.

Anything that belonged to the candidate could become a relic: a cane, some hair, a nail, a tooth, a piece of tissue soaked with blood, a piece of his finger, or even his internal organs. When Rainero's body was opened in search of evidence of his saintly status, his followers discovered three kidney stones that they eventually brought to Rome, where the pope inspected them; they had the images of the Virgin Mary and of Baby Jesus carved in them (ASV 3239). (Despite the papacy's initial attention to Rainiero's relics, his acolytes' brand of activism failed to engage new people in the nascent cult, and he remains a venerable.)

The relic's magical power even extended to the building in which it was kept. After his canonization, for instance, Borromeo's heart was taken to Rome, to the newly built church of Saint Carlo along Via del Corso. When it arrived, the Romans cheered for it on the streets and followed it, symbolically as well as physically, to the new church. Borromeo's heart is still on display in the church today and is an object of popular devotion.

Capitalizing on the power of the candidate's relics was one of the acolytes' primary tasks, and this meant maintaining control of the relics. It was a fundamentally difficult task because believers wanted to gain access to the relics – in a sense, to cut out the middleman. Pieces of the candidate's body were thus highly sought-after items, jealously guarded by the acolytes. Relics gave acolytes an official role in the ritual of healing; thus it was only by restricting access to the magic embodied in these objects that acolytes could construct the *fama* as a social movement, knitting together families of different social status.

Believers' direct access to the relics would have decreased the chances that the candidate's *fama* could become a local social movement, because each family would keep the relics for itself. For instance, after they opened his body for inspection, Neri's acolytes put his insides in a bucket that they buried for safekeeping in an undisclosed location near a church. Even so, when acolytes went to retrieve the bucket a year later, their fears were confirmed: Neri's heart was missing. It turned out that the precious relic was in the hands of a noblewoman in Naples (*Il primo processo*).

The Congregatio required large and organized consensus around a candidate if he was to be approved, and acolytes were structurally necessary for building this organization. Structural considerations were not evidently on the minds of many believers when, on August 23, 1589, a large crowd gathered outside the monastery in Borgo San Sepolcro where friar Rainiero had died that day. The crowd broke down the barriers that the friars put up and rushed to the body that lay inside the church. "The crowd cut five or six [of his] uniforms and a cape that I myself had thrown on [Brother Rainiero] because he had ended up almost naked. Three scissors were brought in ... his hair was cut along with his beard and the hair of his eyelashes. His nails were removed along with the flesh; the crowd removed one of his teeth" (ASV 3239 *folio* 81). Controlling the power of relics was a rather complicated task.

Besides their healing power, relics also testified to the triumph of life over death in their role as pieces of a mysterious but very real paradise. They also exemplified the hierarchy of relations among the acolytes, being distributed based on how close a given acolyte was to the candidate. Prominent acolytes owned prominent relics; though a given relic's importance was related not only to its size but its availability (e.g., a heart was better than a finger, which was better than hair).

PUBLIC WORSHIP

Acolytes had a direct interest in spreading the cult of their leader. Of the three saints included in the sample, two started new religious orders and one was a powerful reformer. The acolytes of Neri, Borromeo, and Teresa of Avila took on important roles in the new orders and in the organization of the reformed local church. Among Neri's first followers, Cesare Baronio became a very active member of the Oratorio, the religious movement that Neri founded; Baronio would go on to become a cardinal and a venerable, and he is currently up for beatification. Giovanni Francesco Bascapè was a devotee of Borromeo and authored one of the most well-known of Borromeo's *vitae*. He was appointed a bishop and was also a secretary of the Barnabiti, the religious order that Borromeo directed for some time. When he entered the Barnabiti, Bascapè changed his name to Carlo in honor of his spiritual father. Perhaps the most successful of the acolytes included in the present analysis is Ana Garcia, the first spiritual sister that Teresa ordained in the monastery of Saint Joseph in Avila. Garcia became Teresa's faithful companion and was beatified in 1917 with her religious name, Ana of Saint Bartolomeo. Other acolytes took on important roles in the new orders or within the local Church hierarchy.

Miracles were, in a sense, the arguments acolytes used to convince people to support their request to the Roman authorities for the canonization of their leader. Acolytes' material interest in the canonization of their leader explains their behavior but does not call into doubt the authenticity of their convictions. Postmortem miracles in this sense functioned in a similar fashion to events used by the leaders of social movements, and acolytes were similar to leaders who fight for causes today. The legal procedures that the Congregatio established constructed a matrix of incentives and payoffs for the emergence of social movements. Miracles catalyzed these movements.

Viewing the ritual healing as a mobilizing resource suggests a process of social contagion that made people return to acolytes over and over in order to reduce uncertainty. Believers could always use the relics of already established saints to get their healing, or they could go on pilgrimages to saintly tombs. But the more the rumor of a new candidate's powers spread, the more people sought out his relics and by extension the acolytes who owned them. Trials triggered acolytes' activism and thus the mobilization of the community where the candidate's trial was taking place. The stage was set for miracles. For instance, on November 1, 1619, in Madrid, a doctor named Alfonso Lopez ran into Giacomo de Herrera, the mastermind behind Orozco's canonization efforts. Being longtime acquaintances, the two got to talking, and during the course of the conversation Herrera showed Lopez the documentation he had with him proving the sanctity of Orozco. Herrera went on to tell the doctor of the many miracles Orozco was performing postmortem. Lopez, meanwhile, was astounded that he could read the documents Herrera was showing

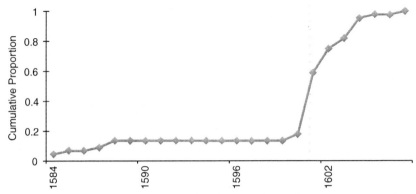

FIGURE 3.3. Cumulative percentage distribution of miracles occurring in Milan, 1584–1607.

him without the help of his glasses and asked, "Isn't this another miracle?" Herrera invited him to come to the stand the next day because, without question, this was a miracle.[7]

The occurrence of miracles fueled more rumors about the power of the candidate, fostering yet more miracles. This process is reflected in the timing of miracles. For instance, consider the postmortem miracles that occurred in Milan in the period from 1584 to 1607.

Figure 3.3 gives the relative cumulative distribution of the forty-four postmortem miracles performed in Milan, by any saint or candidate, for which it was possible to assign a year. The opening of the first of Borromeo's ordinary trials (*processo ordinario*) on February 26, 1601, marks the beginning of a climb in postmortem healings. This trial lasted until December 11, 1603, and was followed by an apostolic trial that started in August 1605. The curve presented in Figure 3.3 has the characteristic sigmoid shape that suggests a process of contagion in which knowledge of recent miracles triggers more miracles. The more people in Milan knew about Borromeo's powers, the more they invoked him in times of need. Early commentators on Borromeo's canonization noticed how quickly the Congregatio processed his case, and the considerable economic resources of Borromeo's acolytes have been cited as an explanation. Here, I suggest another element: the activism of Borromeo's acolytes

[7] Two witnesses corroborated Lopez's and Herrera's story: Caterina Carta and Giovanni de Orimonte, both servants of the doctor.

successfully claimed for their candidate every miracle that occurred in Milan between 1601 and 1607.

Neri's first trial in Rome displays a similar temporal dynamic. Because the trial took place very shortly after Neri's death, the time distribution of miracles has an immediate sharp increase followed by a plateau and then further increases as each of his subsequent trials opened. Of the forty-three postmortem miracles in Rome that have a clear date, Filippo performed two in 1590, one each in 1592 and 1593, six in 1594, and fifteen in 1595, the year of his first trial. His healings resumed in 1603 when a new trial began.

Acolytes' capacity to recruit outsiders into the nascent cult depended greatly on their abilities as religious activists. Neither relics nor miracles were by themselves enough to reach canonization; skillful religious activists were also essential. The remainder of this section discusses the private forms of worship that stood as alternatives to belief in a candidate during the seventeenth century; and the ways, both effective and ineffective, in which acolytes used their activism skills.

Private Worship

Though I have demonstrated acolytes' central role in building a candidate's *fama* through miracles, it is also true that healings occurred without acolytes. Healings that occurred without acolytes took the general form of private exchanges between two individuals, a client (the saved) and a patron (the dead candidate). At the end of the seventeenth century, for instance, Maria Nicolecia, originally from Ragusa (now Dubrovnik) but living in Milan, made a promise (*voto*) on the tomb of Geremia da Valecchia, a candidate to sainthood. If da Valecchia would heal her lame daughter, Caterina, Nicolecia would bring her daughter's hair to the tomb. Five days later, Nicolecia's daughter, who lived in Apulia in the village of Tripuzzi, was healed. True to her word, Nicolecia then embarked on the trip from Milan to Apulia to get her daughter's hair to bring to the tomb (Sangalli 1993).

The exchange between Nicolecia and da Valecchia resembled a contract between two individuals (with the caveat that one of the individuals was dead). This private agreement, commonly known as the *ex voto* (Cousin 1983), did not organize consensus into a social movement. The *ex voto* bound only the two individuals included in the exchange; it remained a private relationship rather than a public one. For da Valecchia, as for other candidates who engaged individuals mostly in private exchanges, the consequence was a lack of social support.[8] Da Valecchia died in Naples on March 25, 1625, but reached the status of blessed only three and a half centuries later, in 1983.[9]

Private exchanges within the frame of the *ex voto* were common in Catholic countries during the seventeenth century. These exchanges produced miracles similar to those that acolytes produced. All candidates to sainthood engaged in private exchanges of this sort after their death.[10] Sometimes a detailed list of *ex voto* was included as extra evidence in the canonization trials. For example, a list of every *ex voto* that occurred from Borromeo's death to the time of his first trial was brought in to support the claim of his long-lasting *fama*. Private exchanges helped a candidate's reputation but were not by themselves sufficient to create a lasting *fama*.

Although the new regulations imposed by the Congregatio made performing miracles more complicated for candidates (see Chapter 1), they had the complementary effect of an increase in statues of the Virgin Mary and Baby Jesus moving on their own. From this period onward, statues and icons performed miracles similar to those of candidates and acolytes.[11] For instance, in 1619 in Colturano, a village north of Milan, an icon of the Virgin began crying. The chaplain of the local church, Prospero Castiglioni, also started crying.[12] He also recovered his voice after having been mute for a long period (Sangalli 1993). This miracle

---

[8]   *Ex voto* means "from the promise." The expression refers to the object brought to the tomb or shrine of a candidate, established saint, relic, or holy statue in return for the received miracle. Thus, a collection of *ex voto* is simply a list of objects left at the holy site. Sometimes, the *ex voto* could take the form of a plaque with the name of the saved inscribed in it, a sort of thank-you note. This latter version of the *ex voto* became more popular as literacy rates rose.

[9]   Da Valecchia had an ordinary trial in Naples in 1679. Boesch-Gajano and Modica report on several miracles recounted during this trial (2000). They were mostly old miracles, which occurred during da Valecchia's life. His postmortem miracles occurred in distant places; acolytes thus had a very small role in them. Finally, the requirements for reaching the status of blessed, which da Valecchia attained in 1983, cannot be directly compared with those explained in this work, as Pope John Paul II changed most of the rules for establishing sainthood (Woodward 1990; Papa 2001).

[10] Although it was during the Counter-Reformation that the *ex voto* became widely used, its existence dates back much further, and it originated in Greece.

[11] The Curia saw the worship of statues and icons as less threatening than popular support for candidates to sainthood.

[12] Evidence of the humanization of statues and icons can be found in the fact that people began worshiping the Madonna of Mount X, or the Baby Jesus of Y, as if there existed multiple Virgin Marys and multiple Jesuses. This process of humanization relates directly to the new role that images acquired as substitutes for candidates.

was the result of Castiglioni's *ex voto* with the Madonna. An unintended by-product of the rationalization of the magic of the candidate's miracles was that icons and statues acquired a life of their own, so to speak.

Between 1569 and 1704, there were forty-three documented active icons and statues in Milan. These holy images engaged in many private exchanges within the general frame of the *ex voto* and performed miracles similar to those performed by candidates for sainthood. In Milan, their frequency – new holy images appeared about every three years on average – and the fact that none of them is currently remembered are indirect evidence that the *ex voto* was largely private and that the Church authorities were quite tolerant toward this form of popular piety.[13]

Thus during the seventeenth century, miracles occurred as a result of two different social mechanisms. One rested on private exchanges (*ex voto*) that increasingly involved images and icons instead of candidates; the other rested on charismatic candidates and the activism of their acolytes. In the social and political landscape of the Counter-Reformation, controlling statues posed less of a challenge to the Church than controlling social movements that were built around charismatic leaders.

Brands of Activism

Constructing a social movement required the active participation of acolytes, but not all had equal success in building movements. Simply put, some acolytes were better activists than others. It was not the case that one candidate was less powerful than another, but rather that postmortem miracles often failed to engage new members in a cult. In keeping with the metaphor of social activism, the miracles that acolytes performed often failed to convince their intended audience.

Much of the historical literature points out that, without the support of the higher classes, a candidate was unlikely to become a saint during the seventeenth century (Prosperi 1986; Rouselle 1999), but even with their support some activists were not sufficiently skillful in mobilizing a community. Nobles in Todi supported the candidacy of friar Rainiero; some actually commissioned paintings of him (ASV 3239). But this narrow, albeit high-status, support was not sufficient to achieve Rainiero's canonization. Similarly for Antonio de Colellis, a Neapolitan priest of the

[13] What occurred in Milan was no different from what occurred in other parts of Catholic Europe. Every monastery has its share of *ex voto* that testify to the supernatural powers of its statues, paintings, and icons.

Confraternity of the Pius who lived and preached during the first half of the seventeenth century. During his life he did everything right; he was a virtuous man, held in high esteem by the local elites, who performed all the wonders that other candidates did.[14] Some of his *in vitam* miracles were strikingly similar to those of Neri, reflecting commonalities that the two men's shared social environment (urban) and institutional constraint (secular) gave them.[15]

De Colellis's acolytes, however, catalyzed the wrong kind of postmortem miracles. The visions that a lay brother in de Colellis's confraternity began to have are one example. How could one evaluate whether these visions were real, that is, the work of God, rather than of the devil? This was a difficult question to answer – and one that Girolamo Sparano, another of de Colellis's brothers and one of his acolytes, asked (ASV 1983). Because any evidence about a vision relies on the word of the person experiencing the vision, it is complicated to subject this type of miracle to rational evaluation. Most of de Colellis's eighteen postmortem miracles were visions of this type and occurred without any ritual. In the institutional environment that the Congregatio created, de Colellis could not achieve sainthood; his acolytes were performing miracles that were hard to verify independently and had little binding power.

Figure 3.1 gives direct evidence of the relative skill as activists of the various candidates' acolytes. As noted, acolytes were the people most responsible for holding the large component of each candidate's network together. The larger the component, the more successful acolytes were in proving their candidate's sanctity through healings.

Interestingly, Church officials seemed to employ similar reasoning. The candidates with the largest components saw their cases advance faster within the Congregatio, controlling for the number of witnesses and miracles. For instance, friar Rainiero had the smallest large component, and his case took the longest time to advance.[16] A ranking of candidates according

---

[14] He is currently a venerable. His first and only trial occurred in Naples between 1728 and 1730.

[15] Like Filippo Neri, Antonio de Colellis also licked wounds and people to produce healings. A man who was suffering from *male gallico* (i.e., syphilis) in consequence of his libertine lifestyle was scared of the painful medicines that a doctor prescribed. The man went to see de Colellis, who spit on him and then began licking his hands. The man was healed (ASV 1983).

[16] E.g., Teresa of Jesus had only 40 witnesses but was canonized at the same time as Filippo Neri, who had 119 people testifying about his miracles. Orozco, by contrast, had almost the same number of witnesses as Baylon, 125 to Baylon's 126. Yet while Baylon became a blessed in 1618, Orozco remained a venerable for 250 years more.

to the time elapsed between their death and their advancement to the title of blessed puts friar Rainiero in first place (longest lapse), followed by Orozco, Pasqual Baylon, Borromeo, Teresa of Jesus, and Neri. This rank-ing highly correlates with the ranking of the candidates according to the size of their largest component – the observed Spearman coefficient (φ) is .78 and is greater than ninety-seven out of a hundred φ generated between two random permutations of rankings based on six elements.[17]

The organization of community support through the work of acolytes met the requirements of the Church. Being able to catalyze postmortem miracles was necessary but no longer sufficient for canonization. The rationalization of procedures and the creation of formal rules for estab-lishing true miracles required skillful acolytes who were able to create the conditions for the occurrence of miracles of the correct type.

TYPES OF *FAMA*

In the medieval era, a broad *fama* sufficed to make someone a saint. With the Reformation came the requirement that the *fama* must also be durable. Historians have argued that the new requirements for reach-ing canonization created greater emphasis on having elite-status wit-nesses. The Congregatio considered nobles more reliable witnesses than the common people, a belief that was broadly shared among people in a community. Because of their better access to education, nobles were perceived as less prone to superstitious beliefs; furthermore, because of their greater means, nobles were also perceived to be less susceptible to influence. Jean-Michel Sallmann showed, for instance, that the support of Neapolitan nobles was the sole difference between the cases of Orosola Benincasa and Alfonsina Rispoli, the latter of whom was denounced to the Inquisition while the former was beatified (1994). This would sug-gest that acolytes spent more energy on recruiting nobles as testifiers, if Rome's approval was their goal.

Looking at the composition of the *fama* thus becomes a useful exer-cise for illuminating the type of consensus that acolytes organized. Because acolytes were fundamental in connecting miracles, it is on the large components of the networks shown in Figure 3.1 that my analysis

---

[17] The ranking of candidates according to the size of the largest component is, from small-est to largest: Rainiero, Borromeo, Orozco, Baylon, Neri, and Teresa. The ratio is calcu-lated as the nodes in the largest component over the total number of nodes in the graph. The rankings of the candidates from the day of their death to the achievement of the status of blessed are measured in years.

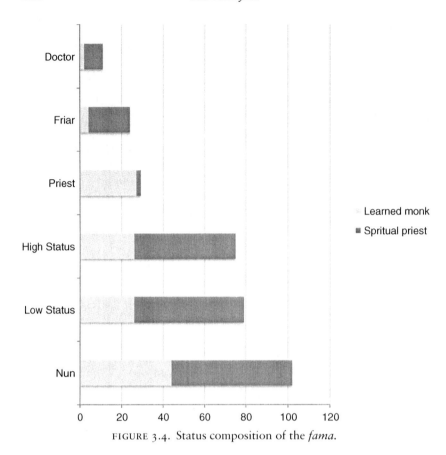

FIGURE 3.4. Status composition of the *fama*.

concentrates. I compared the status of the testifiers in the largest component for the spiritual priest and the learned monk cases. (Because Rainiero did not have a largest component, I considered the status of testifiers for Baylon and Rainiero separately, rather than combining the two cases into the folksy friar type.) Figure 3.4 plots the number of testifiers by status for the spiritual priest and the learned monk types.

   The acolytes of the spiritual priest candidates (solid bars) included a higher proportion of high-status individuals than the acolytes of the learned monk cases. Instead of finding refuge within the walls of monasteries, the spiritual priest candidates (Neri and Borromeo) intended to directly address the problems in the social environments in which they operated – the city or town – by maintaining close contact with believers. Because of that, the spiritual priest often displayed unorthodox behavior, with respect to other priests and to the regular clergy.

This meant that the spiritual priest's acolytes had not only to defeat the typical skepticism about the power of their candidate but also had to overcome strong internal resistance within the local Church hierarchy. Because people of higher status were considered better witnesses, the acolytes of the spiritual priests sought to involve them in their nascent religious movements.

Doctors too made up a larger proportion of testifiers for spiritual priests than for learned monks. Like nobles, doctors lent credence to the miracles described during the trial and therefore helped justify the spiritual priests' unorthodox behavior. Obviously, Neri and Borromeo were not the only two candidates to attract resistance from the Church hierarchy. A similar fate befell other spiritual priest reformers such as Gaetano da Tiene and Giampietro Carafa, founders of the Teatini (in 1524); Girolamo Miani, founder of the Somaschi (1528); and Antonio Zaccaria, founder of the Barnabiti (1530). This analysis suggests that the acolytes of these candidates had to defend themselves strongly from a broad range of critics, and that one way to do so was to attract the support of the higher classes and of doctors, that is, of witnesses thought to be highly reliable.

Acolytes built the *fama* of the learned monk by attracting testifiers mostly from the ranks of the clergy, regular and secular. Priests and nuns formed a large share of the testifiers for this type of candidate. Both Teresa and Orozco were examples of Spanish mystics, adhering to a type of religious fervor that found the road to sanctity in a constant dialogue with God and an eschewal of secular activities. Their miracles reflect this distance from more mundane concerns. For example, in the hours after Teresa's death, in October 1582, the tree in front of her cell blossomed as if it were spring while a bright light emanated from her bed (*folio* 343v–348r, ACS *Relazione Uditori di Rota*, vol. 1). In many regards, the structure of the learned monk's *fama* contrasts with that of the spiritual priest, who preached in close contact with the laity and made their mission within secular life (Zarri 1991).

Baylon's acolytes adopted a different strategy compared to the acolytes of the two types of candidates described in the preceding text: 70 percent of the testifiers in Baylon's largest component were from the lower classes. Baylon's acolytes were in part constrained by the fact that fewer people of high social status lived in rural areas. We can confirm this indirectly by examining the status of the testifiers in Rainiero's components, as his acolytes operated in rural areas as well. For Rainiero, 52 percent of the testifiers whom acolytes connected came from the lower strata of society.

Nevertheless, Baylon's case is striking for the comparatively large share of priests and doctors in his network's largest component. Baylon's acolytes evidently knitted more doctors into the nascent cult than did the acolytes of Teresa or Orozco, as well as an almost equal number of priests. The key to interpreting Baylon's acolytes' pursuit of priests and doctors again emerges from a comparison of their behavior to that of Rainiero's acolytes. Rainiero's acolytes did not involve doctors in any of the components and recruited very few priests. Combining this information with the fact that Rainiero's acolytes persuaded very few other high-status individuals to join the cult, we can see a clearer picture of why Rainiero's candidacy did not advance further: his acolytes failed to attract credible witnesses.

Postponing Routinization

Acolytes tried to engage entire communities in their religious reform projects, and successful acolytes catered to all segments of society with a wide variety of miracles. Neri's acolytes had to heal the gout of *dominus* Claudio by using one of Neri's hats; they also had to use some of Neri's internal organs to help the servant Sebastiani deliver her baby (*Il primo processo*). Baylon's acolytes had to bring the candidate's hair to heal Catarina Ramirez, the wife of a peasant, from her three-week headache; they also used a piece of Baylon's body (it is not clear which part) to cure the asthma of the Honorable Salvador Sola (ASV 3393).

Besides the difficulty of performing miracles that catered to the needs of a heterogeneous community, keeping the movement together also represented an organizational challenge. The problem was not so much in gaining strong support through miracles, but rather in building and maintaining a broad support despite the segmentation of society along status lines. The social institutions around which individual life revolved – the guilds, neighborhood church, extended family, festivities, work in the field, manor, and so forth – were all organized by status. The inclusive mobilization that acolytes built could not, therefore, rely on the support of other community institutions. The movement required acolytes' constant building and organizing efforts to survive.

The lack of established institutions capable of supporting the candidate's acolytes exposed them to competition from believers in the other charismatic leaders, religious reformers, and zealous friars of which the seventeenth century was full. Sometimes the acolytes had the upper hand, as in the previously described difficult labor suffered by de Amaya; an acolyte of Orozco ordered aside the doctor, surgeon, and priest attending to the woman and placed Orozco's belt on her belly, which proved effective in its way (ASV 3033). Nothing, however, protected Orozco's acolytes from being displaced in the same way by other, more powerful, relics the next time.

The fluidity of the religious world after the Protestant Schism and the uniquely heterogeneous type of mobilization that acolytes built required that they gain some source of external legitimacy in order to consolidate their social structure into a durable organization. The Church was the only institution in a position to provide this legitimacy and routinize the acolytes' charisma-based structures.

With their belief in the candidate's death as his ascension into paradise, the acolytes pushed forward in time the problem of routinization, which usually occurs with the death of a charismatic leader. The candidate's charisma continued in the words and gestures that acolytes used to catalyze postmortem miracles.[18] The real challenge for the acolytes was to make sure that the structure that they created would survive the death of the last person with direct experience of the candidate. Recognition from Rome could achieve this goal, because it institutionalized the message of the candidate and produced a flow of resources toward the new local structure (often, a new religious order). At the same time, Rome benefited from granting recognition, but only if the mobilization was large, diverse, and well organized, maximizing the local support that the Church could thereby channel into its core.

A God with Many Faces

After the Council of Trent, the Church embarked on an ambitious plan of reform. The germs of this reform predated the Protestant Schism, but it was the fracture of the religious unity of Europe that gave Rome an opportunity to intervene against local, idiosyncratic, and family-based worship (Evennett 1968). The new Catholicism that the Church imposed was based on attendance at rituals and public ceremonies (Le Bras 1955). The Jesuits became the army that, more than other religious orders, enforced compliance with the new rules, and the local parish became the territorial unit through which such control was organized (Bossy 1985). Often the Jesuits forced groups of peasants in the Italian countryside to take part in religious processions or public worship (Rusconi 1992).

---

[18] Small businesses, e.g., family-run firms, often face a similar problem of routinization at the time of the founder's death or departure.

The new catechism that emerged from the Council of Trent (published in 1566), of which Borromeo was the main author, became the instrument that local priests used to enforce obedience through participation in Church ceremonies. The Church's attempts to reform individual religious beliefs through ritual produced the result of detaching external behavior from internal beliefs – a kind of paradox, at least from the perspective of the religious rejuvenation that was envisioned in the Council of Trent (Bossy 1976). In the territories where the presence of the Church was stronger, particularly in Italy, a long-lasting anthropological effect of the Church's efforts was a discrepancy between appearances and reality, between form and substance (Gotor 2004).

The more ritualistic religion that the Church promoted had a precise extrareligious goal – the Church saw itself as the sole legitimate community, or aggregator of consensus, and standard religious rituals would aid the Church's efforts to convince its followers of its legitimacy. Most of the policies that the Church adopted during the Counter-Reformation, John Bossy argues, were aimed at reducing the role of families or clans in order to enhance the role of religious organizations centered on the parish. A direct consequence of these changes was that, in the realm of everyday worship, the Church gave God a new idealized face.[19] God ceased to be construed as the arbiter of a truce between factions organized along kinship lines and became instead the remote observer of an order between individuals (Evennett 1968) whose loyalties were expected to belong to Church before kin. Religious activists were called to organize popular piety into acceptable forms: for example, Easter banquets in which participants ate lamb to evoke the Lamb of God were expelled from churches (Bossy 1985). "Eating the lamb" became more a symbolic reference than an actual practice. The new ideal God had a more peaceful face than in previous periods, when revenge and fear, more than other sentiments, motivated people.

Creating a new face for God was a complicated task even for the pope. The Church accomplished it in part through the use of force (e.g., the Inquisition and mass conversions) and in part by convincing believers of

---

[19] Bossy writes, "what made the Church during the medieval period a true popular community was, essentially, the acceptance of the parental group, natural and artificial, as the fundamental element of its life despite the ignorance and deviance that this acceptance caused" (1985, 30). This preeminence of the family *tout court* in all its manifestations, nuclear or extended, real or artificial, was precisely what the Counter-Reformed Church rejected. As a result, weddings ceased to be an agreement between families, baptism ceased to include multiple godfathers, confession became private, etc.

the legitimacy of the new face.[20] Acolytes' activism must be interpreted within this broad framework, independent of the different contexts in which they operated. The intent to build consensus through ritual, that is, to attach believers to a nascent religious movement using postmortem miracles, was common to acolytes' activism. However, the sensitivity of the composition of the *fama* to local conditions indicates that the ritual by itself could not displace the outdated versions of God. Acolytes became brokers not only across divisions in their communities, as the networks of Figure 3.1 suggest, but also on a symbolic plane between Rome and local religious demands.

Popular religiosity remained anchored to centuries-old traditions based on fear and punishment. Traces of the old God could be found easily in some of the rural candidates' miracles. Friar Rainiero once told a woman who had a violent fight with her son Rubino that the son would soon die. Rubino was shot to death twelve days later (ASV 3239). Miracles of this kind treated fear and hostility as the basic human emotions. They embodied a social world fractured into rivalries and clans in which the vendetta was a tool for maintaining order (Dickens 1968). Punishment was the almost certain outcome of interacting with such a harsh, unforgiving God. Consider the miracle that Baylon performed on April 9, 1591, for Elisabeth Pallares, when her son fell from a seventeen-rung ladder and hit his head. Baylon happened to be in the neighborhood, and Pallares asked him to intercede with God to spare the life of her son for one more year. A short time later, Baylon died, and on April 9 of the next year, Pallares's son died too. Her husband was furious because he could not understand why she had not asked Baylon to prolong their son's life even more (*folio* 73v, ASV 3393).

The old God was not present just in the countryside, though He survived longer there. Neri in Rome was so upset to have saved Prospero Cribelli – an early acolyte who turned his back on Neri – that he shouted "never more do I want to pray for someone's life!" (*Il primo processo*). Italy and Spain, historians have shown, never really lacked the type of wandering friar and priest that preached divine punishment and disaster (Ponnelle and Bordet 1932).

The Counter-Reformed Church, however, had little tolerance for the idiosyncratic aspects of this God and for the miracles that expressed

---

[20] In the new catechism, e.g., the seven deadly sins were barely mentioned, though they were of fundamental importance for the entire history of Christianity up to that point (Bossy 1976).

The Acolytes

them. Acolytes learned that. Thus just as it is easy to spot the outdated
version of God in the miracles, it is also easy to trace the acceptance of
the Church's ideal conception of a God removed from daily life. Sister
Maria of San Miguel, the first woman whom brother Orozco ordained in
the new Augustinian convent of Madrid, once said that in Orozco's cell
lived a rose that never died (ASV 3033). Yet given the centrality of the
body in the belief system of many, pure spiritual miracles generated little
mobilization. Acolytes operated here as brokers, connecting the demands
from Rome with the local demands of their audiences. As the networks
shown in the preceding text illustrate, miracles that crossed social cleavages were particularly relevant in building mobilization.

   The key question for the Church was how to incorporate the consensus embodied in the heterogeneous *fama* as a part of sainthood while
establishing that God could only have one face. From an organizational
standpoint this question is equivalent to asking how the Church could
incorporate local practices and still enforce standardization across locales.
From the standpoint of the acolytes, the question regarded how to maintain support from a broad range of followers in a society segmented by
status and kinship.

4

The Devil's Advocate and the Doctor

Relics were at the center of the ritual that acolytes officiated and that catalyzed the occurrence of postmortem miracles. Postmortem miracles built the *fama* of a candidate in a community by attracting new people to the candidate's nascent cult.[1]

Relics, therefore, were one of the main mobilizing tools in the hands of acolytes, and maintaining control over the circulation of relics was, as Chapter 3 indicates, a challenging task. Whoever controlled the candidate's relics largely controlled the production of postmortem miracles.

A by-product of the centrality of bodily relics and local activists' focus on addressing the needs of a wide array of potential believers was that the healing of the body became the dominant type of miracle. This preference in favor of the body has characterized religious beliefs in Europe since the fall of the Roman Empire, despite the fact that Christian dogma has always emphasized the soul and the healing of the spirit. The acolytes of the seventeenth century therefore did not change believers' preferences; instead, they skewed them even more. In medieval Europe, miracles also included visions, flight, and imitations of the nonhealing acts of Jesus, such as walking on water. These types of miracles fell out of favor as acolytes found that miraculous healings attracted the wider networks of believers that the Church required to certify their candidates' sanctity. By the end of the period under study, the postmortem miracles that acolytes catalyzed by using relics were almost exclusively healings of the body.

[1] Bice Peruzzi helped me translating into Italian quotes from primary sources reported in Antonelli 1962 (see bibliography).

Doctors became key figures in acolytes' mobilizing efforts. This seems obvious from a modern perspective because, after all, we would expect doctors to be involved in the process of certifying healings of the body. However, the fact that doctors became central to the canonization process only after the establishment of the Congregatio points toward a more complex picture. Understanding the complex role that doctors played in local mobilizations requires looking at medical knowledge from a broader perspective and understanding the position of medicine in the system of scientific knowledge prior to the establishment of the Congregatio.

For centuries, physicians struggled to have their expertise recognized as a science rather than as a technique. Physicians aspired to develop a complete philosophical system capable of explaining the ultimate causes of diseases. During the medieval period, when medicine first gained scientific status, what separated a science from a technique was the philosophical approach of the Scholastica. Scholastic sciences relied on the axioms of canonical texts, from which scientists reasoned out the answers to questions. Consequently, the empirical activity of opening, exploring, and repairing body parts, what we would now identify as mainly the task of surgeons, was seen as less relevant and was left to barbers, that is, technicians not versed in philosophical knowledge and often ignorant of Latin. The rest of this chapter gives more details about the Scholastica, but it is important to highlight that becoming a branch of this system gave medicine prestige and elevated the status of physicians. A deep barrier developed that separated the physicians from the barbers, the theorists from the technicians.

As part of the Scholastica, medicine shared its body of knowledge with other sciences, such as philosophy, theology, and astrology. We would not recognize these disciplines as sciences today, but at the time, the humanities were considered sciences, and medicine was part of the same philosophical system. Sharing its axioms and approach to knowledge, medicine had very little independence from other medieval sciences. Things began to change during the sixteenth century when medicine began to take a more empirical direction. This opened up a process of knowledge accumulation that would eventually lead medicine to separate from the humanities. This process presented a unique challenge for Rome in that it created a knowledge base that activists could mobilize locally and that was difficult to subject to centralized control. It is this autonomy, more than any increase in the accuracy of medical knowledge at the time, that made doctors more relevant for the mobilization of communities and that created a challenge to Rome's control of the process of certifying miracles.

By the first decades of the seventeenth century, a doctor could already certify a true healing without deferring to the expertise of Roman theologians, who were well versed in the truths of the philosophical texts that had governed medicine during previous periods but who were largely ignorant of the experimental approaches of the new medicine, as it was initially known. In the first part of this chapter, I briefly describe medicine's transformation from an ancillary science into a discipline of increasing autonomy and power. I focus in particular on the increasing inclusion of medical experts in canonization trials, which in turn prompted the Church to adopt new regulations designed to handle the power of medicine.

As discussed in the previous chapters, the new procedures that the Congregatio introduced piecemeal between 1588 and 1642 served two goals. The first was to project an external image of accuracy to counter the Protestant accusation that supernatural wonders were the result of superstition and sorcery. The second goal was internal, to secure centralized control of the process of miracle adjudication so that allocating saints to (Catholic) territories would remain the exclusive prerogative of Rome. The Congregatio's procedures for controlling the role and power of doctors as acolytes mainly addressed this second goal.

This chapter documents how and why the Congregatio secured institutional control over the process of verifying miracles against the growing autonomy of medicine. Although the previous chapters analyzed the mobilization that each candidate and his acolytes built locally and how in many cases this mobilization included doctors, this chapter examines the procedures for adjudicating miracles that the Church developed in order to neutralize the opinions of local doctors. The empirical focus of the chapter is on the role of doctors (particularly on doctors who became acolytes) and on Rome's procedures for handling them.

The most prominent of those procedures was the Church's creation of a new institutional role, the Devil's Advocate, to counter the medical claims of religious activists. Instituted in the reforms of 1634 through 1642, the Devil's Advocate was charged with trying to discredit most of the deeds of the candidates under trial. The Devil's Advocate used the tools of logic to question medical claims, not because he was skeptical that miracles could occur, but to create a space in which religious expertise remained relevant for adjudicating miracles. The middle section of this chapter discusses how the Church tried to control the boundaries of the supernatural and focuses on two central figures who significantly shaped the operations of the Congregatio: the Roman doctor Paolo Zacchia (1584–1673) and the Devil's Advocate Prospero Lambertini (1675–1758).

The legal category of a false miracle was the basis for the Devil's Advocate's authority. It allowed him space to scrutinize reports of individual miracles without undermining the idea of a sainthood based on supernatural abilities. The material conditions of the seventeenth century made it clearer than it is now that unpredictable and unexplainable phenomena are constant features of human life. Consequently, there will always be space for supernatural explanations of unusual events. By establishing the possibility of a false miracle, that is, of something that medicine could not explain but was nevertheless not a miracle, the Church claimed for itself the control of the boundaries of the supernatural, leaving the explanation of the natural world to medicine and to science more broadly. False miracles, this chapter demonstrates, were a key aspect of the process of the rationalization of magic.

Writing at the beginning of the period analyzed in this book, Francis Bacon argued that *scientia est potentia*, that is, science generates power. Medicine's seventeenth-century transformation from philosophy into empirical science substantiates this claim, as evidenced by doctors' growing importance as acolytes and by the Church's moves to mitigate their power. The institutional creation of the role of the Devil's Advocate suggests that the reverse of Bacon's argument is also true, that power generates science, or *potentia est scientia*. In his historical analysis of the relationship between mental illness and civilization, Michel Foucault argued that once the mentally ill began to be moved into institutions, they fell under the scrutiny of a power that began distinguishing between different types of psychological malady (e.g., alcoholism and depression). Different types of mental illness became the objects of analysis of a new discipline, psychology. Thus, according to Foucault, the exercise of power creates knowledge (2001). The category of a false miracle can be seen as new knowledge that the Devil's Advocate administered through the procedures of the Congregatio, that is, through the exercise of its power in order to neutralize medicine's new knowledge.

On a local level, false miracles legitimized the Congregatio's prerogative to intervene in community affairs far outside of Rome and to override doctors' opinions. By the second half of the seventeenth century, only authorities sent from Rome could claim to have the requisite knowledge to evaluate the miracles of local candidates. Perversely, in every investigation of miracles, Church authorities aimed to identify false miracles, not true ones, because it was false miracles that justified their role. This effort, in turn, forced the Church to specify the characteristics of true miracles that Chapter 5 analyzes.

Both sides of the relationship between science and power are covered in this chapter: the mobilizing power of medicine and the use of false miracles at the hands of the Devil's Advocate. An underlying process of rationalization links these two sides of the argument and indicates the limits of the common perception that science displaced the power of miracles in northern Europe but not in the Catholic countries of the south. As Max Weber noted, Puritanism was the result of an irrational impulse, the idea of a calling that expelled the possibility of miracles from religion. This expulsion did not mean that miracles could not occur, but that it was the task of scientists, not theologians, to certify them. The Catholic Church never abdicated its role of arbiter of miracles. As long as miracles remained part of the institutional landscape of the Church, they rationalized things that medicine could not explain. In Catholic countries the symbolic fight between the priest and the doctor (and later the scientist) focused not on where to place the boundaries between science and religion, but on who had the authority to oversee those boundaries.

DOCTORS AS ACOLYTES

As Chapter 3 shows, doctors were often part of a candidate's circle of acolytes. This was particularly true for spiritual priest candidates, whose missions took place in urban areas where they had ample opportunity to interact with doctors, but doctors were also important acolytes in nonurban settings. Chapter 3 argued that having doctors as acolytes was instrumental in creating credible miracles amidst the many, varied requests of a heterogeneous crowd of potential believers. Because doctors had access to medical knowledge, their testimonies about miracles during the trials were that much more credible. However, medicine's increasingly specialized knowledge and the fact that medicine could be used to mobilize communities represented a challenge to Rome's claims to jurisdiction over supernatural activity. Many of the institutional innovations that the Congregatio introduced during the first half of the seventeenth century can be interpreted as ways of handling the power of doctors as acolytes.

As Figure 4.1 shows, Doctor Francisco Benet was a central figure in the network of acolytes around the rural candidate Pasqualis Baylon. Darker nodes, regardless of shape, are Baylon's acolytes. They have an above-average betweenness centrality, meaning that they are more likely than others to fall between any two other nodes in the connected network.

As expected from the analysis of the candidate's *fama* in Chapter 3, removing the acolytes severs the connectedness of the network. That is,

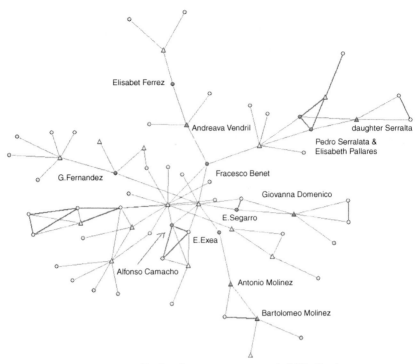

FIGURE 4.1. Baylon largest component in Villa Real.

acolytes are more likely than nonacolytes to be cut points, so that a network without them will have more components. Benet was one of the early believers in Baylon's sanctity, having been present both for *in vitam* miracles that Baylon performed and at the opening of Baylon's body nineteen years after his death. Benet was very active during Baylon's first trial. Another doctor, Angelo Vittori, played an equally central role in the network of acolytes around Filippo Neri. Vittori testified to Neri's *in vitam* miracle of saving the life of a bricklayer who fell to the ground during construction on the Chiesa Nova, as well as to Neri's postmortem miracles. In the role of acolyte, these doctors mobilized their medical knowledge to certify that the supernatural events their leaders produced were genuine.

As acolytes began to use doctors' new empirical knowledge to verify their candidates' miracles and to pressure Rome to do the same, the types of miracles that acolytes put forward postmortem changed significantly. An entire set of supernatural powers slowly disappeared from the candidate's palette. Visions, for example, were central to the medieval idea of sainthood, but during the period under study they became suspicious supernatural events mostly associated with trickery. This was largely because medical expertise did not extend to determining the legitimacy of visions. Doctors could not certify visions independently of the opinions of Rome's experts, so this type of miracle was of little use to acolytes who wished to speed their candidate's progress through the canonization procedure. Visions had the added disadvantage of attracting few new believers, compared to bodily miracles, and putting forward postmortem miracles of this type resulted in weak local mobilizations, as the case of Antonio de Colellis, described in Chapter 3, illustrates. Thus, of the eighty-nine candidates who reached the state of blessed or saint between 1588 and 1751, none produced a postmortem miracle of the vision type. The four miracles most closely related to visions all dealt with psychological problems, giving them a medical tinge. Three of these miracles saved recipients from madness, while one saved a person from insomnia.

This latter miracle was performed by a female candidate, the Discalced Carmelite nun Barbara Avrillot (1566–1618), who reached the status of blessed in 1791. The recipient of the miracle was also a woman. The gender of the candidate and of the saved is important because they highlight a notable by-product of the new palette of miraculous powers. Historians have pointed out that the modern version of sainthood was primarily a male-dominated world (Prosperi 1986). The success rate of female candidates declined starting during the second half of the seventeenth century and remained low into the twentieth century. The miracles that characterized female sainthood during the medieval period, prior to that decline, were of the types that doctors could not certify as genuine: prophecies, visions, transcendent physical states, and so on. As the historian Adriano Prosperi wrote, a female candidate who experienced visions at the beginning of the sixteenth century could legitimately be considered a viable candidate to sainthood, while the same woman performing the same type of miracle a century later was likely to be considered with suspicion and referred to the Inquisition (Scaraffia and Zarri 1994). What historians have not explored are the microlevel mechanisms that led to the exclusion of certain types of miracles from the range of supernatural wonders. I claim that the changing roles of doctors as acolytes and the increasing use of medical knowledge in canonization trials disproportionally penalized the types of miracles that female candidates performed, resulting in a predominantly male modern sainthood.

The importance of doctors as acolytes rested only partially, however, on the increasing accuracy of their knowledge. The empirical methods that expanded their knowledge differed sharply from prior practice (to which the Church still held), making medical knowledge independent of Church experts and officials and turning it into knowledge that could be mobilized locally. It was because of this independence that doctors acquired a prominent role among acolytes. The next section explores how medicine became an independent science and how the Church changed canonization procedures in response.

The Mobilization of Medicine

During the period under study, medicine developed from a science based on logic, similar to philosophy, to a science based on empirical observation. As long as doctors continued to derive their recommendations from canonical medical texts that the Church also accepted as true, Rome faced no challenge in controlling the production of medical knowledge. The Church's theologians, logicians, and attorneys had access to the same canonical texts and could reason from them as well as any medical doctor. Thus, for example, during the early sixteenth century the doctor Paul of Middleburg (also bishop of Fossombrone from 1494 to 1533) could prescribe the following cure for a disease of the skin known as *lupus* (from Thorndike 1951):

To kill the *lupum* [i.e., the wolf] a proved experiment which I had from a master of Canterbury. Take a partridge and pluck it and cast it into wax and prepare it as if to be eaten. On the other hand take a toad and skin it and put it inside the partridge and roast on a spit. And when the partridge is well roasted, take it off the fire and throw the toad away and slit the partridge down the middle and bind half of it tightly on the wolf [i.e., on the part of the skin that has *lupum*]. And straightway he [presumably, the patient] will cry *pa* and will be in pain for six hours. Then remove the first half and bind on the other half, and know that the wolf will die within six hours, and when it is dead, the pain will cease. (151)

A doctor like Paul of Middleburg had little mobilizing power not because of the obvious absurdity of his recipes (everyone believed in those medical recipes!), but because he, and the knowledge on which his advice was based, were not independent from the Church. Such a doctor had no special authority that the Church could not also summon to verify a miraculous healing. From the perspective of local religious activists, having doctors in a circle of acolytes was similar to having nobles: their credibility was based on their social status rather than on their medical knowledge. Medical knowledge began to produce power, as Bacon would have it, only once medicine adopted empiricism and separated itself from the other philosophical sciences that remained under the control of the Church. Only then could the independence of doctors' knowledge be mobilized in the interest of local candidates. This separation and independence were the results of a long process, rather than a sudden shift.

In the medieval period, medicine was a branch of knowledge in the philosophical approach known as Scholastica. Scholasticism had many ramifications outside of medicine, but two characteristics are relevant for understanding how doctors became part of the canonization process during the seventeenth century. The first is the importance of authority, as it was to be found in the ancient texts of Aristotle, Galen, Hippocrates, and Avicenna. These texts gave physicians of the time a set of axioms on which to base their speculations about the ultimate causes of diseases. The goal of the scholastic doctor was to connect observed symptoms to the truth contained in the texts.

The method for connecting the empirical evidence to the ultimate truth was logic – the second major element of scholasticism. Most of the physician's logical reasoning was inductive, but unfamiliar diseases were instead subjected to deduction. A famous example of the latter is the treatment that Gentile da Foligno, the celebrated physician of the fourteenth century, suggested against the plague of 1348 based on his research about snakebites. As in the case of poison, Gentile reasoned, the plague was an *occulta*, whose biological mechanism (i.e., the ultimate cause) could not be discerned. Despite that lack of knowledge, placing the plague in the same logical category as snakebite gave Gentile some insight into how to handle the epidemic. Like other then-mysterious diseases, the plague seemed to feed off the body's own moisture to enlarge itself and spread quickly. "It was then exhaled as a poisonous quality ... and taken by other people, where the cycle started again" (French 2001: 285). Gentile advised fleeing the city or, for those who could not leave, fumigating their homes with a mix of oak bark and vine cuttings (French 2001).

The fact that Gentile succumbed to the plague is beside the point. Because medicine was the application of logical reasoning to a series of axioms, failed cures were believed to be the result of logical error rather than wrong theory. Both characteristics – the authority of the texts and the logical method – were instrumental in giving medicine legitimacy despite its evident failures. Scholasticism, therefore, was instrumental in making medicine a science in its own right. More importantly, scholasticism (medicine included) was a philosophical system that Rome's own experts had mastered and that Rome could easily control.[2] Doctors could not mobilize medical knowledge as distinct from the Church's knowledge, even if they did happen to be part of the circle of a candidate's supporters.

Thus when doctors participated in medieval canonization trials, they did so as high-status witnesses, rather than as medical experts. Doctor Jean de Tournemire, for example, was expert and witness in Pierre de Luxembourg's trial in 1390. De Tournemire first gave an expert opinion about the incredible state of de Luxembourg's body after his death – the body was not stiff but seemed relaxed, as if sleeping. Then de Tournemire testified as a witness regarding a miracle de Luxembourg performed on his eighteen-year-old daughter, who was healed from breast cancer when a relic – a strand from a rope that had belonged to de Luxembourg – was applied to her breast. In both testimonies, de Tournemire's credibility rested ultimately not on his medical knowledge but on his status as a doctor (Ziegler 1999).

If the preceding testimony describes the role that doctors played in canonization trials before the Protestant Schism, it also serves as a bench-mark against which one can measure the changes in medical knowledge that began during the sixteenth century. At that time, doctors began to rely on systematic observation, particularly of their failures, to advance their art. Failures provided the space for learning that pushed medicine farther away from philosophy and into what was previously the territory of the unknown. Before documenting the key characteristics of these changes, I broadly survey the historical contours of how the Church involved doctors in its canonization procedures.

The Inclusion of Medicine in the Canonization Procedures

From the fourteenth century onward, lawyers and courts began seeking doctors' written advice, called a *consilium* (plural: *consilia*), on matters mostly related to paternity and inheritance. Notwithstanding the increasing use of doctors' opinions in lay courts, the Church did not adopt this practice until after the Protestant Schism, not even for the canonizations that Rome directly supervised (see Chapter 1 for a description of the difference between low and high sainthood). As long as doctors remained

---

[2] This state of affairs makes scholastic medicine very similar to contemporary sociology. The endless debate about some key texts and authors simply masks the lack of engagement of the discipline as a whole with social reality. Furthermore, in a more striking similarity with scholastic medicine, sociology too is a discipline that is in between philosophy and technical knowledge.

a branch of philosophers, the Church had no reason to include them and their particular knowledge in its evaluation procedures, given that it could already include the opinions of its own experts: theologians, philosophers, logicians, and various other thinkers.

Church practice began to change only after the establishment of the Congregatio and after medicine began its separation from the Scholastica. Some historical doubt exists regarding precisely when the Congregatio requested its very first *consilium*, though it appears that the Uditori began seeking *consilia* about miracles from doctors in the very first cases that reached them in Rome. Documents relating to the case of Francesca Romana at the beginning of the seventeenth century (Papa 2001) seem to suggest that a *consilium* was requested in that trial (Antonelli 1962). Clear evidence of doctors' more formal role in the canonization process appears in the records of one of the miracles that Carlo Borromeo performed postmortem. In Milan at the beginning of November 1604, the twenty-four-day-old infant Carlo Nava recovered his sight after his parents prayed to Borromeo (ASV 1681). Doctors certified the event as a miracle, and it was then recognized as such in the canonization process.

Despite the greater use of *consilia* in the following years, the involvement of doctors in canonization trials was not strictly required until 1642. The first case in which a doctor's advice was sought for all the miracles that a candidate performed was that of the Jesuit Luigi Gonzaga, whose trial took place ten years or so after Borromeo's trial. Scholars of the Congregatio have always considered this case particularly interesting because it illuminates more than others the extent to which the procedures of the Congregatio remained in flux before the final reforms of 1642. The high social status of the candidate and his membership in the Jesuits exerted considerable pressure on the Roman Curia for a quick outcome, despite the more stringent requirements for sainthood that the Congregatio was developing at the time (see Chapter 5). It is therefore interesting to see, at the beginning of the systematic incorporation of medicine into canonization procedures, such a clear example of the tensions between local activists' mobilization of medicine and the central officials of the Curia.

In sum, the Congregatio inserted the *consilia* into canonization procedures first as a matter of practice and then, with the reforms of 1634 and 1642, by rule. While these institutional developments were taking place, medicine was in the midst of a great transformation, as established axiomatic truths were challenged and the empirical method based on factual evidence began replacing induction from those truths. Medicine's shift toward empiricism posed a new, multifaceted challenge to Rome. Empiricism generated a new type of science that was separate from the Church's philosophical expertise and was therefore more difficult for the Church to control centrally. Yet by 1642 the Congregatio had successfully created a frame for incorporating this new type of medicine into canonization trials. The Congregatio's ability to create that frame relied in part on the medical *concilium*, particularly the *concilia* of Paolo Zacchia, whose medical texts provided the new axioms to which the Church's experts referred in countering the new power of the outside medical expert.

The Evolution of Medical Advice

Examining two lay court *consilia* about the same topic, pregnancy, written three centuries apart highlights the challenge that medicine posed to the Congregatio and provides context for the institutional solution Rome forged.

The first *consilium* was written by Doctor Gentile for his friend, the lawyer Cino dei Sinibuldi da Pistoia, regarding a case of paternity attribution between two brothers. Because the time of delivery was used to identify the father, Cino wanted to know if all pregnancies lasted for a fixed time, or if they varied in length. Gentile's answer was characteristic of the scholastic approach. Gentile began with Aristotle's axiom that although animal pregnancies last for a fixed time, human pregnancies do not. Gentile gave two theories explaining this variation. The first was the work of Italian philosophers who doubled the number of days between conception and the formation of the fetus (35 or 45 days, according to Aristotle) to obtain the baby's first movement at seventy or ninety days. The date of birth was calculated by tripling whichever of these numbers applied, putting it at 210 or 290 days (7 or 9 months) from conception. The other way Gentile purported to explain human pregnancy's variable duration was by considering which of the seven planets dominated the growth of the fetus. Because each planet was thought to have different effects – Venus for instance made the skin beautiful, while Mars bequeathed a short temper – the lengths of pregnancies varied, depending on the positions of the planets in the sky.

Such was medical theory during the fourteenth century. The following *consilium* similarly reflects medical knowledge three centuries later, but it points in a radically different and, at least for Rome, wholly more problematic direction – the use of evidence instead of philosophical theories to support reasoning. Paolo Zacchia (1584–1673), a famous seventeenth-century Roman doctor widely considered the father of legal medicine, was called upon by the court in a murder case. The neighbours of a woman named Matthia accused her of killing her own newborn baby and disposing of the body to conceal an illegal relationship. The surgeon and the two midwives whom the prosecutor sent to inspect Matthia's house found blood everywhere, evidence in their eyes that the woman had delivered a baby (De Renzi 2002).

In his *consilium*, Zacchia took the opposite position. But instead of basing his advice on the canonical texts of antiquity, Zacchia used empirical facts to show the prosecutor's error. For example, Silvia de Renzi reports, "in their internal examination of Matthia's body [the midwives and the surgeon] failed to appreciate the presence of those pieces of flesh which are normally in a woman's womb, but which tend to disappear after she gives birth" (2002: 230). Similarly, Zacchia continued, the midwives and the surgeon did not notice the absence of a fundamental clue: lactation. Matthia was ultimately acquitted.

To a modern reader, Zacchia's empirical objections sound more familiar than Gentile's learned disquisition. For the officials of the Congregatio, however, Zacchia's empiricism was a worrisome new development. Although the medical theories of antiquity fit easily under the umbrella of Christianity because of the fixed and immovable status of the truths on which they were based, empiricism implied an open-ended process of knowledge accumulation over which Rome could not guarantee its control.

From Rome's perspective, the fundamental issue was not the evolving accuracy of doctors' opinions. The analogy of Zeno's Paradox is instructive in this regard. The Greek hero Achilles is racing against a turtle. Achilles is ten times faster than the turtle, so he gives the turtle a head start of ten spatial units. Will Achilles ever reach the turtle? If the distance the two have to run is infinite, the answer is no, because the turtle will always be ten units ahead of Achilles, no matter how infinitesimal the units are. Similarly, if we think that making life completely predictable is like running an infinite distance, miracles will always occur in the space of things that science cannot explain. Thus establishing the authenticity of a miracle was not mainly a question of truth, but of authority: should scientists or priests have the power to declare an event a miracle? This was a particularly relevant question at the dawn of modernity, as Church officials struggled to answer this question in their own favor – at the same time that the schismatic Protestants were deciding in favor of the scientists.

It is important to note that "certifying" miracles did not mean establishing the existence of miracles per se, but rather controlling the boundaries of the unknowable. This meant creating the category of the false miracle, or an event seemingly explicable only as a miracle but that was nevertheless not a true miracle. Excluding chicanery and tricks, the category of the false miracle had the most explanatory power in the limiting cases. It was precisely in the category of the false miracle that the expertise of the Church officials would dominate the expertise of doctors.

The Congregatio created a new institutional figure in the canonization trial that presided over the establishment of false miracles. This figure was, quite literally, the Devil's Advocate.

Pope Sixtus V saw the task of canonizing candidates as similar to other ritual procedures of the Church. At the time of its creation, the Congregatio was charged with two main operational tasks – maintaining and developing ritual procedures and making sure that canonizations were treated with the "necessary care" ("*Diligentem quoque curam adhibeant circa sanctorum canonizationem,*" in Papa 2001). Cardinals were placed in charge of the Congregatio, but because of the commission's broad portfolio, they could also hire experts to assist their work. To Pope Sixtus V, "experts" for the most part meant theologians and lawyers ("*viros sacrae theologiae, pontificii caeserique iuris peritos, et rerum gerendarum pollentes,*" Papa 2001).

This arrangement reflected the Curia's skepticism about many of the candidates who reached the attention of the Congregatio during its first years of operation. As Chapter 1 highlighted, Rome had always been aware that many local cults had very weak religious foundations, but before the Protestant Schism, the Curia had no real interest in intervening to correct this state of things. There was no outside pressure on the Church to do so, and the deep segmentation of society allowed Rome to be content that the saints it promoted enjoyed higher prestige and more universal recognition than local saints. The Church's need to establish a coherent new frame to counter the threat of the Protestant Schism together with its skepticism toward local cults gave birth to a complex and very slow set of procedures. The canonization of Raymond de Peñafort, for example, was Rome's recognition of a preexisting local cult rather than the formal authorization of new worship; the candidate died during the thirteenth century. Nevertheless, the Congregatio met three times to debate his canonization, and the case took four years to be resolved. The duration of the proceedings surrounding even this relatively straightforward case was a direct manifestation of the caution with which Rome approached candidates, regardless of how long they had already been worshiped.

Rome could, and tried to, use lengthy procedures as a way to regulate contemporary candidates' access to canonization, but this created its own problems. First, local activists, often supported by local authorities, pressed the cardinals of the Congregatio and even the pope to have their candidates canonized. The pressure intensified particularly after the candidate reached the status of blessed. In the presence of such pressure, the duration of the process made it difficult for the Congregatio to create consistent rules and procedures. (Chapter 5 discusses this phenomenon in detail.)

Second, the newly empirical doctors' opinions that acolytes used as a tool to apply that pressure were not as amenable to being overturned by stalling as were the previous scholastic *concilia*. Because Scholastic science meant logical reasoning on the basis of canonical texts, giving Church officials more time to "reason through" things was a viable strategy for slowing the canonization process. Under the more empirical approach that began developing during the sixteenth century, medicine produced autonomous knowledge that activists could mobilize quickly and outside of Rome's control. That knowledge also accumulated infinitely, which meant that stalling put the Church's experts at a disadvantage, as it made it more difficult to attack evolving, interrelated pieces of medical truth. Finally, experimental science opened the door to different types of expertise, making centralized control more difficult.

The aforementioned case of Luigi Gonzaga is a perfect example of the challenges that Rome faced. The Jesuits used medicine to advance their candidate quickly through the Congregatio's procedures. Furthermore, the Gonzagas used their political clout to pressure the pope for a speedy and favorable resolution of Gonzaga's candidacy. The end result was that his path to canonization shattered the procedures that the Congregatio was slowly developing and opened the door to more "exceptions." Rome could no longer use redundant procedures to enhance its institutional control of local (and powerful) activists. The Church would need new instruments to protect access to sainthood from local pressure, the new medicine, and the coalition of the two.

From the Congregatio's creation until 1634, the importance of the Uditori declined relative to that of a new institutional figure – the

Curia's attorney, or the *promotore fiscales*. The use of legal experts on religious matters was a long-standing tradition in the Church, but the extent of their involvement in canonization procedures was one of Congregatio's many institutional innovations. The first attorney nominated to defend the interests of Rome during a canonization trial was Giovanni Giacomo Nerotti, for the de Peñafort case. However, Nerotti's task remained confined to the traditional role of the Curia's attorney – that is, establishing that local trials followed proper procedures. Nerotti and his counterpart on de Penafort's behalf, the Dominican priest Michele Llot, did not address the merits of de Penafort's purported miracles.

As local activists made greater use of doctors' opinions, the *promotore*'s role expanded beyond procedural supervision to resemble that of a prosecutor attacking the evidence offered by the defense attorney. This required the creation of a legal-theological frame for handling medical knowledge. With the *promotore*'s changing role came a new title – Promotore Fidei, or protector of the faith. Although several documents from the first decades of the seventeenth century mention the new title, the job was not officially created until the reforms of 1634. Key to the Promotore Fidei's job was authoring opinions (*animadversiones*) about the candidate's miracles. These documents, which outlined the *promotore*'s doubts about the miracles, would circulate among the members of the Congregatio and the pope.

In describing his "doubts," the *promotore* used the best medical authority accessible to him in order to poke holes in the evidence collected about miracles by the candidate's attorney, the *postulatore*. During the seventeenth century, the writings of the doctor Paolo Zacchia became the *promotore*'s main weapon. Zacchia wrote a voluminous book, *Questiones Medico-Legalis*, that systematized the empirical knowledge he had accumulated and that distilled the existing *consilia*. On one hand, Zacchia's writings became the foundation of legal medicine and can be considered an integral part of the new medicine. On the other, Rome incorporated his writings into the canonization procedures precisely in order to neutralize the empiricism of the new medicine. For Rome, Zacchia became a sort of new authority to which to apply the scholastic tools of logical reasoning. For example, in the *animadversiones* for the case of Baylon, the *promotore* wrote that in the presence of other medicines administered by a doctor, it was not possible to establish if a miracle had occurred, "according to Zacchia, *Questiones Medico-Legalis*, lib. 4 tit. I, Queast. IV" (ASV 3407).

Zacchia's importance can hardly be exaggerated. It was from his *consilia* that the *promotore* constructed the framework used to dispute the *postulatore*'s claims that the miracles the candidate performed were true. It was through the application of this framework that the *promotore*, and hence the Congregatio, enhanced its control of canonization trials despite local activists' mobilization of medicine. For example, Zacchia's book argues that a true miracle requires curing a disease that is considered hard or impossible to cure and that the healing must occur instantly and completely. The *promotore* incorporated these two suggestions into a classification of miracles by degrees. This produced a new, more refined list of the characteristics of a true miracle, and knowledge of and the ability to judge those characteristics belonged to the Church, not to doctors.

The *promotore* used legal reasoning to weave Zacchia's *consilia* into Church regulations. In this way, the Congregatio was able to create a legal framework to control the boundaries of the supernatural and to protect it from the potential further claims of medicine. The countermobilization of medicine at the hands of the *promotore* implied the creation of the legal category of the false miracle, that is, of something that doctors and laypeople would consider unusual, but that was not a miracle according to the Church. This was of crucial importance.

A False Miracle

The *promotore*'s incorporation of medicine to serve the goals of the Church is best represented in the writings of the Congregatio's most famous Devil's Advocate, Prospero Lambertini (1675–1758), the future pope Benedict XIV (Siraisi 2007). Lambertini wrote the tome *De servorum dei*, summarizing canonization procedures and listing the cases that had reached the Congregatio since its foundation. He also wrote about how to handle the adjudication of miracles. His writings became the Devil's Advocate's manual of operation for the next several centuries.

Lambertini placed medical expertise firmly under religious control. With respect to instant healings, for example, he argued that it was the judge, that is, the Congregatio, that could establish whether time or the candidate had produced the healing – the doctor could not make this determination, as Zacchia had pointed out. Lambertini reasoned that because nobody could know exactly how long a natural healing would take ("*quanto iuxta naturae vires contingere numquam potuisset*" in Antonelli 1962: 35), "moral and ethical instantaneity" was sufficient to produce a true healing. But how to proceed if the symptoms of the disease reappeared later in the healed person? Zacchia considered such a case in an empirically based *consilium* and suggested that the healing had to be perfect, that is, without the reappearance of the disease. Lambertini used scholastic reasoning to refine Zacchia's *consilium* and bring the issue under the expertise of the Church. First, he distinguished between people who had only one disease (e.g., blindness) and those with multiple diseases (e.g., blindness and muteness). For people with only one disease, Zacchia's *consilium* applies, but for people with multiple diseases, it is important to establish if the symptoms that remained or reappeared after the miracle were related to the disease that was healed. If a candidate healed somebody from blindness, the fact that the saved remained mute did not argue against the perfection of the healing (Antonelli 1962). Lambertini used scholastic reasoning to refine Zacchia's empirical opinions on many other issues: for example, the use of medicines; the transformation of one disease into another; and the presence of bodily fluids such as blood, vomit, urine, and sweat, before and after the healing. Using this technique, Lambertini developed a legal edifice that allowed for medical mysteries that only the *promotore*, the expert capable of understanding the full implications of a true miracle, could explain fully. The *promotore* now had the option of declaring a miracle false without having to rely solely on medical opinion. Within the legal edifice that Lambertini created, a false miracle would now reinforce the control of the Church, in the same way that the commission of a crime can seem to justify the law that bans it. In a reversal of the formulation that knowledge generates power, the work of Lambertini in his position as *promotore* shows that power generates knowledge.

Consider the following example reported by Fernando Vidal (2007). The candidate Joseph of Cupertino (1603–63) had extraordinary supernatural powers, including the ability to fly. Lambertini reviewed the case, including testimony from doctors and medical opinions regarding some of the witnesses. He had two objections about Joseph's flying abilities, Vidal reports, "The first one was that, since Joseph went into ecstasy on non-religious occasions," particularly when listening to music, it was not clear to Lambertini what produced the wonders (491). Second, Lambertini wondered if the candidate had the necessary humility and reserve and if his flights "had been followed by positive spiritual consequences" (491). Lambertini did not, therefore, question that Joseph had supernatural powers and could fly. But a true miracle, Lambertini argued, required more.

A false miracle justified the role of the Roman judges in local proceedings and created the legal framework necessary to neutralize the power of the autonomous new medicine in the hands of local activists. Only authorities sent from Rome could claim to be impartial and to have the expertise to evaluate the miracles of local candidates. Because Rome's authority manifested itself in the category of the false miracle, it was on this type of miracle that much of the *promotore*'s attention focused. By incorporating the early empiricism of Zacchia's writing into his "doubts," the Devil's Advocate created a new knowledge that securely defended Rome's control over the boundaries of the supernatural. Perversely, then, in every investigation of miracles, Church authorities aimed to identify false miracles, because it was on false miracles that their authority relied. The magic that was at the core of the local relationships between the candidate and his acolytes was not eliminated but rationalized. The Devil's Advocate was the main institutional figure presiding over this process of rationalization.

5

Manufacturing True Miracles

Chapter 4 looked at the procedures that the Church developed in order to regulate the relationship between religious expertise and medicine. By creating the figure of the Devil's Advocate, the Congregatio was able to neutralize the autonomy of local doctors-turned-acolytes and thereby maintain control of the boundaries of the supernatural. This did not mean that medical opinions were excluded from canonization trials or, more broadly, from sainthood, but instead that doctors' opinions were incorporated so as to be subject to the control of religious experts. The main tool in the Devil's Advocate's arsenal for exercising control over doctors was the false miracle. Although hoaxes and swindles populated the category of the false miracle and part of the task of the Promotore Fidei was to reveal candidates (and acolytes) who used tricks to advance their cases, the real importance of identifying a miracle as false was the creation of a space for things that medicine considered inexplicable but that were not true miracles for the Church.

The category of the false miracle and the role of the Devil's Advocate made the rules for adjudicating miracles into a code. As Niklas Luhman highlights in the case of the code of romantic love that developed during the modern period, a code originates at discontinuous points in time from a continuous and increasing need to make sense of heterogeneous social worlds (1993). The code serves the process of sense making by creating closure. It is a self-referential process that, by labeling certain actions or events as deviant (or "false," for the case at hand), produces outcomes that reinforce the code. In this respect, every false miracle augmented the authority of the Congregatio's experts vis-à-vis doctors, acolytes, and local Church officials.

Looking at the rules and procedures of the Congregatio not from a historical perspective (as Chapter 4 largely does) but from an institutional vantage point reveals that the rules encoded the heterogeneity of local demands for miracles into a coherent set of categories that would become the Congregatio's basis for judgment. In large part, miracles varied in content because they catered to different segments of local society. As described in Chapter 1, before the Protestant Schism, segmentation produced different models of sainthood – one high (or learned), based on formal procedures promulgated by Rome; the other low, based on popular support (Ginzburg 1976; Duby 1980; Boesch-Gajano 1999). The status divisions of this world were projected into the sky (Brown 1981) so that people of different status worshipped different saints (Vauchez 1989). The Protestant Schism, however, labeled religious practices that continued the projection of this world's status divisions to the other world as superstitious (Dickens 1968; Evennett 1968). At the dawn of modernity, a saint was such to the extent that he was universal, that is, capable of attracting support across social cleavages. In local Catholic communities, producing modern saints meant that acolytes faced stronger competition to attract support across status. The result was that the miracles of the same candidate became more heterogeneous because acolytes' religious activism took place mostly in between the status and kinship cleavages of their community.

The process of encoding gave the Congregatio a way to deal with the heterogeneity of miracles. Encoding made judgments legal in nature; that is, they were based on the consistency between the actions of the candidate and his acolytes and the categories of the code, rather than on the content of the miracle. The code made possible the adjudication of miracles because it gave a unique form to supernatural events. Irrespective of its content, the Congregatio declared a miracle true if it crossed kinship and social cleavages and united believers from different walks of life. Rome's recognition transformed this unlikely social structure into a local institution. It was this external seal of approval that made the reputation of a candidate's holiness a symbolic good that lasted beyond the lives of the acolytes. Acolytes learned the form of a true miracle through the public display of the Congregatio's decisions, and they applied this external (i.e., nonlocal) model for correct behavior (Durkheim 1982) in order to ensure the success of their mobilizations. Over time, acolytes presented fewer miracles at canonization trials, but all of the correct form.[1]

---

[1] In the original French version of *The Rules of the Sociological Method*, Durkheim uses the word *régle*, which I think better conveys the sense of "being regulated" than the English word *rules* that instead emphasizes the hierarchical aspect of the process.

A miracle's content – the actual event reported as a miracle – remained relevant locally, however, because Catholics' ideas of what constituted a supernatural event varied according to local circumstance. That is, the postmortem miracles that acolytes catalyzed had local mobilization power precisely because of their content. Paradoxically, the Church's separation of form from content may have created a space for miracles to change, and it certainly represented a clear break with medieval modes of approving miracles. What the high and low versions of sainthood had in common during the medieval era was an emphasis on miracles that imitated those performed by Jesus. When the Congregatio was established, it began to enforce the classification of miracles in degrees (see Chapter 1; Veraja 1988, 1992; Papa 2001), with the result that the imitation of Jesus stopped being a criterion for the adjudication of true miracles.

This decline in the relevance of Jesus's acts did not occur all at once. During the period from 1588 to 1642, for instance, a large number of approved miracles continued to consist of healing the blind or deaf (10 miracles total), two of the most common miracles recounted in the Gospels. After 1642, however, approved miracles showed few similarities to those of Jesus. Healing people from cancer became the most common approved miracle in the century after the year 1642 (Delooz 1997).

Baylon performed miracles at the beginning of the seventeenth century, a few years after the Congregatio's establishment, and also around 1660, several decades after the Congregatio began operating. Some of Baylon's early Church-approved miracles were healings from blindness and lameness (ASV 3393; 3399), resembling the miracles described in the Gospels. By contrast, Baylon's approved miracle in the later part of the seventeenth century involved a poor peasant, Domenico Perez, who lived in a small village in the diocese of Valencia in Spain and desperately needed water for his land. The property he owned was arid and had no value. On a summer day in 1661, the exasperated Perez set off to look for a water spring in the name of candidate Baylon. Ignoring his neighbors' derision, he began shoveling at random in the hard soil. Water suddenly started pouring out (ASV 3403). The description of this miracle in the 1669 proceedings of Baylon's canonization trial includes detailed maps and calculations showing that the river that bordered Perez's property had to be ruled out as an explanation for the new water spring. Besides the fact that these maps are a fascinating study, what is most relevant is that the Gospels contain no mathematical calculations.

By adjudicating the truth or falsehood of a miracle based on the form that mattered to the Church, while ignoring the locally significant content of the miracle, the Congregatio encoded local practices into the fabric of Catholicism without any need to confront the content at the base of a local mobilization. Whatever their content, miracles acquired collective significance for all Catholics when they followed the form that the rules established. General and abstract rules gave meaning to local and concrete actions. It was still magic, but with a spirit of rationality.

The process of encoding that the Congregatio's rules created is the reverse of the neoinstitutionalist process of decoupling.[2] Neoinstitutionalists argue that organizations resist change by using rules to decouple internal practices from external pressures (Edelman, Uggen, and Erlanger 1999) or as tools of symbolic compliance in the hands of organization leaders (Westphal and Zajac 2001). Yet rules can also provide symbols for coordinating behavior (see the introduction to this book for a fuller articulation of this point). For example, Mitchel Abolafia shows how the rules of the Chicago Board of Trade created greater integration among its members so that a free market in futures transactions could continue to exist despite the self-interest and opportunism of the traders (2001).

The integration of actors through encoding does not mean compliance with rules (Elias 1992). Compliance means that certain practices become illegitimate and are replaced by others, while encoding means that rules select established practices and provide them with new meaning (White 1992). Instead of rules governing behavior, encoding turns the process inside out, so that an organization selects acceptable actions first and afterward produces a code of rules to insulate those actions from future changes in practice. It is a process by which an organization increases its fit to an environment by incorporating the elements of the environment that best suit the organization's goals and then using them to promote change.

The Protestant Schism gave the Church of the late sixteenth and early seventeenth centuries an incentive to listen to local acolytes and incorporate their mobilizing power into the core of Catholicism, lest they split from Rome. This meant that between its founding in 1588 and the middle of the seventeenth century, the Congregatio's enforcement of its rules was regularly influenced by pressure from acolytes. The application of the process of encoding, although originating from the top down, did

---

[2] Encoding provides legitimacy insofar as it provides action with any collective meaning. This argument resonates with Weber's point about instrumental rationality – that rational action is simply action that follows general and abstract rules (Merelman 1998; Weber 2000). For this reason, he noted, bureaucracies are terrible political instruments (Collins 1986).

not proceed smoothly but more by happenstance, through the different interests of the individuals who occupied key roles in the Roman Curia or the Congregatio. Only when the threat of further religious schisms in southern Europe faded during the middle of the seventeenth century was the Church finally able to systematically enforce its new code to govern acolytes' behavior.

In Chapter 3, I discussed the havoc created by competition between the acolytes of different candidates for the finite resources of a community. Encoding not only had the potential to regulate this competition but also to exacerbate it. Rome's commitment to the acolytes of one candidate came at the expense of those of other candidates who were also active in the community at roughly the same period. The authority of the Congregatio rested in part on channeling local religious practices but also on limiting how many practices could be channeled. A systematic enforcement of the rules required that the Church pursue the process of encoding with only one charismatic structure at a time. Otherwise, encoding would create more competition between the acolytes of different candidates to enter into a commitment with the Church. Not until the second part of the seventeenth century was the Congregatio able to fully resist local pressures and use its power to consistently control its allocation of commitments to charismatic structures.

Documenting the process of encoding and how the Church coordinated local religious activism requires the top-down, Rome's-eye view that this chapter takes. The first section details the Congregatio's process of encoding the beliefs of local activists and how this incorporated them into the centralized Church. The next section discusses the threat that uncontrolled local activism posed to the Church and how the Church controlled the timing of canonization trials to minimize that threat. The chapter then analyzes the tensions in the Congregatio between those more inclined to centralization and those in favor of greater local autonomy. A detailed discussion of the centralizing rules of 1642 and the reasons they persisted for so long (Pope John Paul II made the first changes to them more than three centuries later) is followed by an analysis of their effects, making a dynamic structural argument that captures the birth of an institutional environment.

THE PROCESS OF ENCODING

Formal rules are a tool that organizations can use to incorporate fragmented belief systems into their core (Selznick 1980; Zhou 1993). For this to occur, rules must highlight the common interests of local activists and the central authority that promotes the rules. A successful alignment creates (1) a stable relationship between an organization's central authority and its environment and (2) an attendant reduction in potential threats. The Congregatio developed highly detailed rules for adjudicating miracles, that is, for channeling consensus (Veraja 1988; Gotor 2000). The Church left the initial administration of these rules in the hands of local bishops (Chapter 1) as a means to secure local support. At the same time, the rules reduced competition among local activists in two ways. First, the rules clearly marked which religious behaviors were no longer allowed. Second, external recognition made the acolytes who gained it the clear winners in their local competition for resources. Such recognition was an essential tool in crystallizing a candidate's *fama* into a durable local institution. Thus local activists had an interest in attracting the Church's recognition, just as Rome had an interest in extending it through the local bishop.

Though it was miracles that inspired popular devotion and local mobilization, the Congregatio was less concerned with the actual deeds of saintly candidates than with ensuring that all reported miracles were channeled through the proper approval procedures. The Congregatio's rules thus addressed not the content of miracles but the form of social support that miracles built. The Congregatio approved miracles with high mobilizing power across kinship and status; that is, miracles that involved acolytes and the networks they built. Meanwhile, acolytes used miracles' content to achieve this mobilization. Decoupling miracles' content from their form therefore lay at the heart of the Church's strategy for incorporating local consensus and subsuming local interests into the global Church.

The recognition of miracles on the basis of their form ensured that everybody, not just acolytes, could access a candidate's supernatural powers. In this way, the codification of aspects of popular religiosity within the formal laws of Catholicism benefited local activists. The candidate's *fama* became part of the landscape of a community, as Robert Hertz highlighted in a study of five Alpine villages in France and Italy – Cogne, Campiglio, Ronco, Valprato, and Ingria. Hertz noted that the people living there gathered during the summertime only because of the *fama* of the local patron, Saint Besse. Saint Besse's reputation symbolized the old unity of the mountain community at a time when political and national divisions had pulled the villages apart (Hertz 1928). Similarly, Rome's approval crystallized a candidate's *fama*, rendering it independent of its

original context and of the people who built it. Rome's approval transformed the candidate's reputation for performing wonders into a social
fact in the Durkheimian sense. Modern travelers can still experience this
phenomenon, particularly during the summertime, when people of different European towns gather on the streets without knowing much about
the saints they are celebrating.

From religious turmoil, the Church forged a new ideology that reorganized – rather than eliminated – the magic at the heart of miracles. The
Church channeled local legitimacy into the core of Catholicism, religious
activists received recognition of the diffusion of their practices, which
routinized a candidate's charisma, and local religious authorities shared
with Rome the role of judges. The needs of all these stakeholders found
expression in the rules for adjudicating miracles that the Congregatio
forged between 1588 and 1642.

However, identifying true miracles was not in itself sufficient to elimi-
nate competition between acolytes. The Congregatio had an evident
interest in closely monitoring the number of saints in each community,
as an unchecked profusion of candidates would have undermined the
Congregatio's authority. Encoding added another level of competition
among groups of acolytes. Instead of competing only for a share of local
resources, they now also competed for recognition from the Congregatio,
which would lead to the routinization of their charismatic structure.
Recognition was a resource that the Congregatio controlled, and it used
this control to regulate the timing and the location of religious activism.
In the next sections, I analyze the Congregatio's concerns in adjudicating
true miracles, then consider the dyadic relationship between Rome and
a local charismatic structure (i.e., the process of encoding), after which I
look at how the Church managed commitments in one city. I leave a more
comprehensive spatial and temporal analysis to the end of the chapter.

True Miracles

During the final phases of a canonization trial, the Congregatio, in con-
junction with the pope, decided which miracles were to be declared true.
Historians have argued that miracles were judged according to the status of their witnesses – nobles were considered more reliable witnesses
than commoners, men more reliable than women. For example, in the
1648 canonization trial of Blessed Pasqualis Baylon in Valencia, Spain,
witnesses testified about the following miracles: Baylon's knocking
from within his coffin, which had been occurring since his beatification

in 1618; the resurrection of a drowned five-year-old boy, Pedro Blasco; Claudia Sobias's healing from paralysis; and another resurrection of a drowned boy, the four-year-old Miguel Juan Agremont. None of these miracles were judged true. The Promotore Fidei argued that witnesses did not agree on the number of knocks they had heard from the coffin. As for the miracles involving drowned children, some of the witnesses were children at the time of the accidents and thus considered unreliable. Further, the *promotore* continued, Blasco's resurrection did not happen right away but later, at home, violating the "instant healing" requirement of true miracles. Finally, medicine rather than a miracle was thought to be at the root of Sobias's healing (ASV 3400).

Very few of the witnesses to these miracles came from the ranks of the nobility, which would seem to confirm that the Church based its decisions on witness status. Yet if one examines in the aggregate the decisions that the Congregatio actually made about miracles, this trend is less clear. In considering the miracles performed by the candidates who reached either beatification or canonization and whose trials I examined in greater detail, I reassigned clergy members to either high or low social status. This new classification treats abbots, bishops, and prioresses as high-status individuals, as well as nobles, considering that the high clergy very often came from the nobility. Low-status clergy were priests, monks, friars, or nuns.

In Table 5.1, the ratio between the odds of approval for a miracle with low-status witnesses to that for a miracle with high-status witnesses is .611. The 95 percent confidence interval includes 1, however, suggesting that status by itself cannot explain the Church's approval of miracles. Examining the aggregate decisions of the Congregatio therefore does not confirm the status hypothesis, which leaves the question: if the social status of witnesses is not sufficient to explain which miracles received approval and which did not, how did the Congregatio adjudicate miracles?

For comparison's sake, consider the following miracles, also performed by Baylon and both judged to be true. Cecilia Sordi was a poor woman from the village of Benicarlo whose arm and hand were paralyzed for several months. After Baylon's death, she decided to try the new candidate and applied one of Baylon's relics first to her hand, which instantly healed, and then to her arm, which healed only later (ACS, *Relationes, Storico*). Another case is Ursula, an eight-year-old girl with an ulcer, who was healed by a liquid that dripped from Baylon's body (ASV 3400). Were these two approved miracles somehow better than the rejected miracles? The status of the witnesses cannot explain the difference in the

TABLE 5.1. *Proportions of Approved Miracles*

	High Social Status (nobles and merchants, doctors, and high-status clergy)	Low Social Status (commoners and peasants and low-status clergy)
Approved	.11	.17
Rejected	.89	.83

Congregatio's decisions – there was just one noble among the witnesses for both of the approved miracles, but there were many women. These miracles were similar in content to those that were not approved, leaving unanswered the question of how the Congregatio reached its decisions.

In order to interpret the Congregatio's decisions, it is necessary to examine in greater detail the committee's motivations for accepting or rejecting miracles. If one views the canonization procedures of the Counter-Reformation as a tool Rome could use to incorporate consensus, then Rome analyzed miracles to scrutinize the mobilizations that acolytes built and to evaluate the strength of the movement around a candidacy. A closer examination of the miracles that Baylon performed reveals an important feature – the approved miracles involved the use of relics, and relics, as Chapter 3 made clear, were for the most part under the control of acolytes. The approved miracles showed the strength of the acolytes' mobilization, while the rejected miracles did not.

In 1618 Giovanni Coccino, titular archbishop of Damascus and a member of the Congregatio, wrote that achieving canonization required being written into the book of the Church according to "present justice, just as those who are … promoted by [their] works and helped by the instructions and examples of the Church" (*Relatio*, in Papa 2001, 247). According to the archbishop, a mobilization centered on "works" (*opera* in the original Latin) had to be blended with the instructions coming from the Church, that is, "present justice" (not divine!) in order for the candidate to achieve sainthood. The fact that Coccino wrote this explanation in a *relatio* about a candidate (see Chapter 2) is significant because it makes explicit that although the Congregatio might not support all aspects of a specific local mobilization, neither did it intend to crush all local mobilizations. Within the mobilizations that the Congregatio chose to engage, it had an interest in channeling the parts that followed the "instructions" of Rome. These instructions were what gave local mobilization the correct form.

TABLE 5.2. *Likelihood of Miracles' Approval (N = 220)*

	Coefficient (odds ratios)	Robust clst.s.e.	Robust clst.z.	$p > |z|$
(Intercept)	.013	1.29	−3.37	.00
Saved Female	.86	.45	−.33	.74
Saved Noble	.571	.20	2.80	.01
Saved Clergy	.618	.43	−1.12	.26
No. Witnesses	1.462	.11	3.31	.00
Relic	2.61	.28	3.44	.00
Connected Miracle	3.12	.61	1.87	.06

One can comprehensively test the importance Rome placed on the form of mobilization by evaluating the likelihood of a miracle's approval with respect to the structural position of the saved: was the event she experienced brought about by acolytes or was it the result of isolated prayers? Structurally, acolytes connected people into a social movement. If their presence mattered, connected miracles would be more likely to be approved than isolated ones. Table 5.2 presents the results of a logit model that predicts the likelihood of a miracle's approval. The technical appendix provides further detail about this model. The coefficients refer to the odds ratio.

The connected miracle variable tests the hypothesis that the structure of local mobilization mattered for a miracle's approval. This variable is significant at more than the 90 percent confidence level and just a bit less than the 95 percent confidence level ($p = .06$). The odds that a connected miracle would receive approval were greater by a factor of more than three than were the odds of those of an isolated miracle, controlling for other factors. Because acolytes were the ones responsible for connecting miracles, this suggests that the Congregatio's officials paid particular attention to the structure of local mobilization. The importance of acolytes is reinforced by the significance of the effect of relics in increasing the likelihood of approval.

The model also supports the idea that the Congregatio paid attention to the amount of local mobilization: each additional witness increased the odds of miracle's approval by a factor of almost 1.5. In all, Table 5.2 suggests that a large and structured mobilization increased the chances of a miracle's approval and thus of the candidate's eventual sainthood. This statement can be further refined by considering the status of the miracle's recipient. The likelihood of the miracle's approval decreased if the saved was a commoner (the reference category in the model). If the saved was a

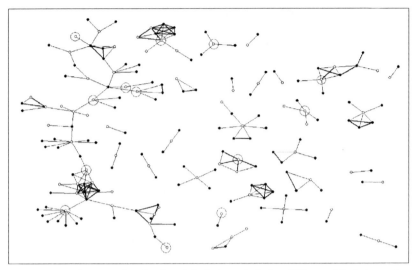

FIGURE 5.1. Approved miracles (circled nodes) for Filippo Neri (complete network).

nobleman, by contrast, the likelihood of approval increased. Considering the historical argument that during the Counter-Reformation sainthood increasingly excluded women (Zarri 1991), the nonsignificant effect of the saved being female indirectly reinforces the argument that structured mobilization is what interested Rome the most.

A network analysis of the complete set of miracles that Filippo Neri performed in Rome during his candidacy provides further evidence that the Church rewarded strong, structured mobilizations (see Fig. 5.1).

Approved miracles, the circled nodes in the network, disproportionately occur in the largest component or in a component of at least two miracles. This is further evidence that Rome took into account the mobilization surrounding a candidate when making decisions about miracles. Recognizing the sanctity of a candidate implied the institutionalization of the candidate's message in a religious order; if the mobilization around the candidate was strong, it also implied an endless supply of new believers.

The Church certified the following as true miracles of a certain form: miracles that that bridged cleavages and united people across differences of status and kinship. Yet it was because of their content that miracles mobilized communities. What was perceived as supernatural varied according to the characteristics of the venue in which the candidate and his acolytes operated. The cornerstone of the Congregatio's rules for distinguishing true from false miracles was a process of encoding that separated the content of miracles from their form. For Rome, the channeling of mobilization meant that not all miracles could be considered true. Local activists meanwhile were concerned with securing recognition for their leader's supernatural powers, something that required the mobilization of a community through miracles. By approving miracles regardless of their content, the Church institutionalized the inclusiveness of the religious movement that acolytes built. The process of encoding turned local beliefs into a social fact because by focusing on the form of miracles, it guaranteed that everybody in the community believed the same thing.

Regulating Activism: From a Dyadic Relationship to the Coordination of Relationships

Encoding implied a two-party commitment between Rome and a specific movement in a community, which further implied that other candidates operating in the same community would not engage with Rome as the same time. This meant that instead of competing directly for local resources, candidates and their acolytes now competed to attract Rome's attention. If the process of encoding addressed the former competition, it did nothing to reduce the latter.

Given the precarious living conditions of many witnesses and the fundamental social and political uncertainty of the first part of the seventeenth century, the passing of time weakened acolytes' chances of building a large and inclusive mobilization. This gave acolytes a direct interest in receiving Rome's approval quickly, and they did not restrain themselves from pressuring Rome. (See Chapter 4 for a discussion of how they deployed medical knowledge to this end.) It was part and parcel of the Congregatio's daily routine to resist the pressures streaming from the bottom up (Gotor 2000). One way that acolytes of powerful candidates tried to expedite procedures was by "artificially" augmenting the number of miracles, de facto reducing the time needed to mobilize a community.

Thus although Catholic canon law clearly established that only post-mortem miracles could be considered for judgment (Veraja 1988), there were several famous exceptions to this rule. One was Neri's *in vitam* resuscitation of the fourteen-year-old Paolo Massimo, which occurred in 1583 in Rome. Paolo was the son of Fabrizio Massimo, who had been exiled from Rome in 1558 for stabbing his sister, Plautilla, for her suspected betrayal of her husband, a member of the prominent Lante family. Massimo returned to Rome in 1561 as a faithful follower of Neri and married Lavinia de' Rustici in 1562. Massimo's wealth and rank made the miracle that Neri performed on their first son significant not only for their household but also for the entire town.

Massimo gave his first deposition in Neri's trial on September 13, 1595. In it, he said that when Neri arrived at his house, Paolo was already dead. Nevertheless, Neri put his hand on the forehead of the boy, who suddenly opened his eyes and asked for a place to urinate. Fifteen minutes later, Paolo died. During this deposition, Paolo's brief resurrection played a small role in Massimo's account of Neri's powers and virtues. During his second deposition, on February 20, 1596, Massimo gave more details about Paolo's fifteen-minute return from the dead. He said that after Paolo was resuscitated, he began talking with Neri (*ragionare*), who asked the boy if he would prefer to die and go to see his sister, who had died a few days before, and his mother, who also was dead. Paolo, Massimo explained, said that he would, and Neri let him die. A few months after this second deposition, Massimo commissioned the painter Cristoforo Roncalli, known as Pomarancio, to depict Paolo's salvation. The painting portrayed the scene as Massimo described it the second time: Neri resuscitates the boy and lets him die only after Paolo expresses his wish to go to see his sister and mother.[3] Pomerancio reproduced the scene in two paintings, one of which was lost in a fire; the other is a fresco, still visible today in the Chiesa Nova in Rome.[4]

If artificially inflating the number of miracles by including miracles *in vitam* was one way to exert pressure on the Congregatio, a more common tool in the acolytes' arsenal was petitioning the Congregatio to open a trial. The opening of a trial marked the beginning of the process of encoding – and the movement's exclusive relationship with Rome. It is through the decision whether to open a trial that the Church controlled the movements' competition for its attention.[5]

---

[3] On December 24, 1596, Fabrizio, gave 25 coins (*scudi*) to Roncalli for the paintings.

[4] The visual reproduction of the facts surrounding Paolo's death augmented Neri's reputation for sanctity and helped shape accounts of the miracle. Germanico Fedeli, a priest and another of Neri's acolytes, mentioned Paolo's resuscitation in his last deposition in 1610. In his prior five depositions, however – between September 5, 1595, and September 28, 1600 – Fedeli did not mention Paolo's resurrection. This temporal dynamic highlights the role of collective memory in shaping individual accounts of miracles. Further, this miracle was included in Neri's first *vita*, which was written by Gallonio, one of Neri's acolytes. It was then repeated in all subsequent biographies of Neri and became the subject of a commemorative publication in 1883, three centuries after the event.

[5] Clearly this did not imply that all trials ended in a positive outcome, i.e., canonization. Rather, it means that the process of encoding always started with the first trial.

Giving a tempo to religious mobilization protected the process of encoding from competition and kept outbursts of popular religiosity from creating an autonomous market for supernatural powers. Although direct evidence of the Congregatio's efforts to regulate local religious competition does not exist, I looked at the timing of permission to open trials in one small yet fundamental city, Rome, in order to gauge the extent to which the Congregatio worked to regulate competition among acolytes.

The Eternal City is ideal for this analysis because of its high level of religious activism during the period under study. Between 1588 and 1751, the Congregatio gave permission to open seventy-nine canonization trials in Rome.[6] This number was very high compared to other southern European capitals, such as Madrid, Milan, Valencia, Naples, and Florence. It reflected the centrality of Rome in Catholicism – even candidates who operated largely elsewhere often had followers in the city. Although it is the case that a large number of these trials dealt with the same candidates, as each candidate went through several steps in his path toward sainthood, it is also the case that each trial activated acolytes. Thus, independent of how many trials a candidate had already had, each one meant a new burst of activism and supernatural activity.

Evidence of the Congregatio's goal of regulating the timing of supernatural activity can be constructed from the time distribution of the trials. I identify three general conditions for analyzing the timing of trials:

(1) There is a constant (λ) that describes the propensity for trials in a particular community. Although this propensity refers indirectly to the underlying potential for religious mobilization in a community, it relates more directly to changes over time in how the Congregatio interpreted the mobilizations that the acolytes of different candidates built in the community. It captures how the officials of the Congregatio interpreted the structure of the local religious field, an interpretation that changed as the Congregatio's own rules changed.

(2) Within a given community, λ is constant throughout the period. As long as the Congregatio's interpretation of the characteristics of the local religious field did not change, the propensity for religious activism of a given community remained constant. Changes in the

---

[6] I took this latter year as the end of the analysis because it symbolically marked the beginning of a new period in European history – the Enlightenment. It was during 1751 that the first volume of the *Encyclopédie* was published.

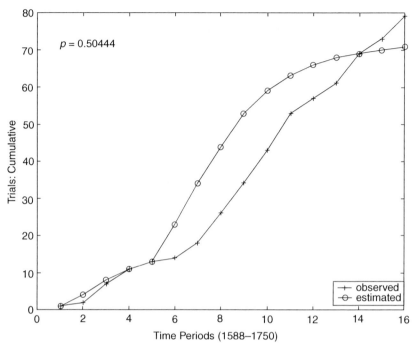

FIGURE 5.2. Distribution of trials for public miracles in Rome.

Congregatio's rules for adjudicating miracles and trials were likely to alter the Congregatio's interpretation of local characteristics, generating a new propensity. In contrast, changes in local characteristics did not necessarily produce changes in the community's propensity. Because the Congregatio changed its rules in 1642, my assumption is that two propensities existed, one before 1642 and one after.

(3) The occurrence of a trial is independent of previous trials in the same location. This means that permission to open a trial at time t is not related to permission at time t-1 but only to effects of the Congregatio's rules, either before or after 1642.

To what extent do these three conditions describe the time series of permission to open trials? Figure 5.2 provides an answer to this question, while the technical appendix describes in more detail the fitting procedure that I followed. The figure plots the observed number of trials per decade in Rome and fits the estimated curve under the previous three assumptions. Time is measured in decades and is reported in the x-axis.

To account for the change in Church rules that occurred in 1642, I calculated two propensities: one for the period from 1588 to 1642 and the other for the period from 1643 to 1751. Each propensity is calculated as the expected value of the number of trials in the period and is used to calculate the estimated curve (round points). The change in propensity occurred during the fifth decade of the Congregatio's existence. Twenty years after the establishment of the Congregatio, in 1608, five trials had taken place in Rome. By 1650, thirteen trials had taken place altogether. The changing rules are reflected in the steeper slope of the observed curve starting in 1660 (7th decade). A rank and sum test was used to test the likelihood that the two curves were identical. The high p-value (.504) indicates a failure to reject the null hypothesis: the observed number of trials in Rome follows a stochastic process described by the three assumptions discussed in the preceding text. Therefore Figure 5.2 does more than simply fit two curves: it validates the idea that the Congregatio acted to control the amount of religious competition occurring in Rome by giving a tempo to the activism of acolytes. This subordinated local religious activism to the Church's approval. Rather than allow a market for supernatural beliefs to form, the Church reinforced its hierarchy by controlling the timing of trials to protect the dyadic nature of encoding.

To what extent can this argument be generalized to other communities? The latter part of the chapter presents more evidence that the Congregatio paid keen attention to the distribution of trials in time and space throughout Italy during the same period. Thus, although Rome occupied a special place for the Catholic Church, the decisions of the Congregatio for this city appear consistent with the idea of a general institutional attempt to curb local competition between religious activists.

Modern Sainthood

From the perspective of the Congregatio, unsupervised competition could create a market for supernatural forces in which acolytes of different candidates would use their skills to produce postmortem miracles in an effort to attract more followers. This locally based process would in turn undermine the centralizing role of the Church. In the north, the expulsion of magic from religion had the effect of flattening the hierarchical structure of religious institutions and turning religion into a market. It was in the Church's interest to prevent such a market from forming in the south, and the Church created a vertically integrated structure that prevented the formation of a competitive field of religion. This required a mechanism for the centralized coordination of acolytes' activism, that is, for protecting the dyadic process of encoding from competition.

In sum, creating modern sainthood meant two things. First, it meant selecting true miracles independent of their content; second, it meant controlling the activism of acolytes so that competition would not escalate out of control. In practice, Rome began selecting miracles on the basis of their form and dictating the tempo of religious activism. During the first part of the seventeenth century, the authority structure that supervised this process was a shared arrangement between Rome and the local bishop. As the next section shows, this arrangement was not without problems. As Rome strengthened its position with respect to local bishops during the second part of the century, it moved toward assuming complete control of the process. Nevertheless, the two elements at the core of modern sainthood remained unaltered until the reforms of Pope John Paul II.

The procedures that the Congregatio crafted during the early part of the seventeenth century made sainthood modern because they made it more rational. According to Max Weber, rationalization was a historical process that subjected practices to measurement, calculation, and control. In the field of religion, rationalization meant breaking the connection between religious practices and locales, creating a disenchanted world that was empty of magic. Miracles appear quite the opposite of rationalization because, as the previous sections show, at their core stood religious practices that addressed local demands. Miracles worked in the eyes of the many precisely because they were heterogeneous; miracles worked (and still work today) precisely because they contained magic. Yet, although magic is a fundamental part of miracles, the supernatural actions of modern saints are completely different from those of prior historical periods. Before the seventeenth century, saints flew, brought light to dark buildings, and controlled the natural elements (Delooz 1969; Klaniczay 1997); after the seventeenth century (and still today), saints cure specific diseases. Why? The naïve answer follows Weber, saying that rationalization did not happen in the religious field of southern Europe and that Catholicism created miracles out of things that science could not explain. My argument is instead that, with its rules, the Church created an institutional environment that allowed the expression of magic in a religious world that rationalization had deeply penetrated. The miracles of the modern saint are still not rational events, in the meaning that Weber gave to the word, but they are more rational than they ever were before.

Not everything that looked inexplicable could be considered a miracle, not even in southern Europe.

THE BISHOPS AND THE BLESSED: A SHARED GOVERNING STRUCTURE

In the aftermath of the Protestant Schism, the interests of Rome and those of local activists met in the approval of miracles. This commonality of interests did not imply that every miracle was accepted as true, however. A large majority of miracles was rejected as false, and consequently, a large majority of candidates was turned down. Even so, the adjudication of miracles on the basis of local mobilization power could plant the seeds of a potential threat for Rome – the proliferation of local centers of power. An unchecked profusion of candidates could weaken the authority of the Congregatio, challenging Rome's efforts to maintain centralized control over a large territory. Yet the Church could not simply incorporate local religious elites by giving them a role in the canonization process without also sharing authority with them (Selznick 1980). The greater the number of local candidates, the more Rome would have to share its authority. The problem boiled down to who determined a candidate's sanctity: would local communities continue to establish saints, as they had for centuries, or would this become the exclusive prerogative of Rome, as the Counter-Reformed Church mandated?

The tension over who controlled the canonization process was embedded in the rules of the Congregatio. It is most notable in the title of blessed (see Chapter 1 for more details), investigations for which were carried out by local authorities. Although the status's intermediate nature does not make much sense in religious terms – what does it mean to be a blessed but not a saint? – it makes complete sense from a historical perspective that focuses on institutional processes. The title was part of a power-sharing arrangement – the price Rome had to pay in order to incorporate consensus. There was a danger that this title could come to eclipse the importance of the title of saint, which was conferred by Rome. Although external recognition remained necessary in order to institutionalize the social structure that acolytes built locally, the risk was that bishops would compete with the pope for the privilege of conferring that recognition.

The power-sharing arrangement inherent in the title of blessed does not mean that Rome did not try to control access to that title as well. The Congregatio's immediate reaction to candidates' proselytism was always the same: skepticism followed by pressure for conformity. For example, the Congregatio denied the Carmelite sisters of Maria Maddalena de' Pazzi, who died in 1607, permission to pray to her body. De' Pazzi's cult had little foothold outside Santa Maria degli Angeli, the Florentine convent where she had lived. Of the hundred witnesses who came to testify on her behalf during the ordinary trial held in 1611, the majority were sisters of her convent (ASV 767). In this and other cases, the Congregatio acted with the overall goal of slowing down access to the title of blessed.[7]

Contradictions existed, however. If a candidate's acolytes built a strong local movement quickly and received immediate support from the local authorities, the Congregatio accelerated access to beatification of the candidate so that a canonization trial, which would be under the control of Rome, could begin. This was true of two early candidates, Neri and Teresa of Jesus (Papa 2001).

In the case of Francesca Romana, an ancient case lacking official recognition (see Chapter 2), local pressure on the Congregatio was particularly evident. On March 7, 1606, Pope Paul V gave permission for a mass in her honor in *more solemni*, granted plenary pardons, and allowed the presentation of gifts in the church where she was buried, along with public prayers. Romana was treated as a de facto blessed, even though she was not officially beatified until 1608. This was not simply a by-product of the fact that Romana's cult predated the existence of the Congregatio. Although Luigi Gonzaga, a contemporary candidate, was not officially beatified until 1621, in 1605 Rome granted permission for images of him to be publicly exposed along with his *ex voto* and sanctioned an eight-day festival commemorating the anniversary of his death. The Congregatio granted permission for Gonzaga to be called blessed in 1618, three years before the status was official (Papa 2001). Or consider the striking contrast of two Congregatio decisions made on February 19, 1622. On that day, the Congregatio approved the virtues of Pasqualis Baylon, already officially blessed, and of Pietro d'Alcantara, in whose case the approval of virtues was a prerequisite to becoming blessed (ACS, *Registrum*).

All of these examples indicate the tension between Rome and local authorities and the premium that Rome placed on accommodating powerful movements in order to channel legitimacy. Essentially, Rome dealt with the pressures that religious movements placed on it by either contracting or expanding the timing of its decisions. But for how long could

[7] Eventually, the mobilization around her grew and expanded outside Florence. She became saint in 1669.

the Congregatio stave off the emergence of powerful local bishops, surrounded with their own blessed, who would question pontifical authority? Although channeling consensus was an essential condition of the Church's continued existence, it was not sufficient to preserve hegemony. Orthodox ideas and actions could produce heterodox results by fostering autonomous centers of power. The threat was acute, for instance, in the case of the Jesuits. Thus Ignatius of Loyola's miracles continued to be investigated even after he was made a saint (ACS, *Registrum*).

NEW RULES

The strategy of sharing authority with the local Church had always met with strong resistance within the Roman Curia. The history of the Congregatio's first fifty years shows the intensity of the struggle within the Curia to steer the Congregatio's policies in one direction or the other (Veraja 1992; Papa 2001). The by-product of this struggle was a constant stream of changing regulations between 1588 and 1642. After 1642, however, canonization rules stabilized, remaining essentially unaltered for the next three and a half centuries.

The Congregatio's cardinals were divided into two factions – those who favored strictly centralized control over canonization matters, and those who favored a more decentralized procedure. It was a struggle that pitted the Inquisition against recently formed secular orders, the Jesuits most notably. The latter cardinals wanted to follow the traditions of the medieval world, which would benefit their powerful order by giving more autonomy to local bishops (Bloch 1973; Gotor 2004). This position matched the spirit of the deliberations of the Council of Trent. The Inquisition meanwhile advocated strict control of new cults under the supervision of the papacy. The establishment of the title of blessed was an early victory for the Jesuits, but the victory was short-lived.

Because of pressure from local activists and the Congregatio's attempt to maintain a balanced power-sharing arrangement with local authorities, the official decisions the Congregatio made regarding the process of becoming a blessed created several inconsistencies. Rules were frequently established with the intent of regulating access to this title, but all of these rules were readily ignored locally. Thus in 1597 the Uditori stated that the title of blessed could be used only for those *probati iudicio ecclesiae*, that is, those who had passed the judgment of the Church, and that popular manifestations of veneration must be limited. Yet Ignatius of Loyola was already a de facto blessed when the Congregatio officially recognized him as such as was Teresa of Jesus. Furthermore, popular manifestations of enthusiasm were an integral part of the trials of Neri and Carlo Borromeo. Although for Rome all of these cases were "exceptional," the simple point is that the constant stream of regulations that the Congregatio issued was an attempt to resist the pressure that a locally driven process put on Rome in an effort to speed its response.

Starting in 1628, the Congregatio began to promote reforms more aggressively in order to reduce the power of local authorities and better insulate the decisions of central officials. This renewed effort coincided with the ascension of the Inquisition within Rome during the tenure of Pope Urban VIII (1623–44). Among the new rules that were introduced, of particular relevance was the decree that the Congregatio would now judge the validity only of apostolic trials, not those carried out by local authorities – implying that Rome viewed local trials as less important. The *Caelestis Hierusalem cives* of 1634 represented the most comprehensive attempt to rationalize the Congregatio's work by reducing external pressures. However, what was intended to be the last word on the matter continued to generate problems.

The confusion was not just in the local realm of the title of blessed. The Congregatio's decisions on the cases that reached Rome during the years 1630 and 1640 are notable for their absence of any consistent logic (Papa 2001; *ACS, Registrum*). Things were so complicated that from December 3, 1640, to March 12, 1642, a special commission of several high prelates met every Thursday to work on introducing new regulations and harmonizing the past procedures of the Congregatio (Papa 2001). Only six years had passed since the last attempt. The secretary of the Congregatio justified the work of the special commission by saying: "With the variety and multiplication of decrees ... regulating the causes for beatification and canonization ... ambiguities and obscurities were introduced" (ACS, *Registrum*).

The pre-1642 governing structure was not a stable equilibrium, to use a game theory concept. The 1642 reforms resolved the Curia's internal conflict regarding who had authority over the canonization process in favor of the centralizers. The rules restructured the relationship between local authorities and Rome, that is, they reorganized the governing structure of the canonization process. The new regulations also restructured the relationship between those who ruled and those who were subjected to the rules, that is, between Rome and the local acolytes (Davis and Greve 1997).

Though the changes of 1642 turned out to be the final form of the Church's canonization rules (at least until the papacy of John Paul II), their finality is clear only in hindsight. It took external events to make the changes of 1642 stick. The Peace of Westphalia, concluded in 1648, marked the beginning of a new era of religious stability for Europe. This new stability reduced Rome's need to incorporate the consensus generated by local movements and offered the centralizing forces within the Church the opportunity to make permanent the new hegemonic position they had designed for the papacy six years before.

In large part, this victory for the Curia's centralizing forces belonged to the Inquisition. From this perspective, the most significant member of the special commission that worked for two years to harmonize the Congregatio's regulations was not Giovanni B. Pamphilij – the future Pope Innocent X – but rather Cardinal Vincenzo Maculano – the future commissioner general of the Inquisition.

The main aspects of the new regulations were the following:

- Books that described the deeds, miracles, and revelations of candidates could be printed, but only with a disclosure from the author that stated that the facts narrated in the book had a human value only and did not bind the Holy See to its conclusions. Paradoxically, an author of a book about a candidate was asked to state that there was nothing divine about the events narrated. The disclosure note had to be placed at the beginning and end of the book.
- Communities were required to hold a trial to certify that no one there had worshipped the candidate since his death (*Processus Super Cultu Non Adhibito*). This type of trial had to occur before any other trials could take place. Further, fifty years had to pass between the candidate's death and the opening of this type of trial.

  The fifty-year interval was originally introduced in 1634 with the *Caelestis Hierusalem Cives*. The rule could have had devastating effects on a candidacy – who would ensure the survival of the candidate's memory in the years of imposed silence? Rome risked alienating popular support if the rule was strictly enforced. At first, the Congregatio conceded many exceptions to this rule, essentially making it optional. This was one of the inconsistencies that prompted the appointment of the special commission in 1640. The special commission devised an ingenious solution: Evidence about the sanctity of a candidate could be collected during the fifty years after his death, but it had to be sealed.
- The commission established a formula for swearing in the cardinals of the Congregatio that was similar to the formula used for the cardinals of the Inquisition. This requirement symbolized how the tasks of the two organizations had become similar in the eyes of the Curia.

Three bishops nominated by Rome became responsible for conducting the first round of trials. Their autonomy was limited, however, because they were constrained to the list of questions that the Congregatio's Promotor Fidei wrote for the trial. The list of questions was the basis for the interrogation of witnesses.

In the end, the new regulations reinforced the Holy See's complete control over the canonization process. The decree of April 1642 ruled that once a case had started, that is, once the Congregatio had granted permission for a trial, local authorities had to await instructions from Rome. The title of blessed remained part of sainthood, but instead of showing the extent of local mobilization, it now served to show that acolytes had learned the rules of how to produce true miracles. True miracles had the inclusive form described at the beginning of the chapter. The candidates before 1642 who reached the title of blessed performed (on average) more miracles than the candidates whose trials started after 1642. Fewer miracles were necessary once the rules were consolidated and access to canonization rested mainly on the form of miracles.

THE EFFECTS OF THE REFORMS ON THE CASES

The mobilizations that acolytes built after 1642 were different from earlier ones. Before 1642, acolytes used postmortem miracles to attract followers and therefore the attention and approval of Rome. That approval institutionalized the movement that the acolytes built. After 1642, once the Congregatio began to enforce the fifty-year interval between the death of the candidate and the opening of the first trial, the main task facing acolytes became preserving the memory of the deeds of their leader. Acolytes acquired the role of gatekeepers inside the monasteries or convents where the candidates had resided. They preserved their leaders' charisma among themselves, no longer using postmortem miracles to mobilize a community but instead to win Rome's approval directly. With this change in goal, the number of miracles presented in canonization trials decreased from the number needed to maximize followers to the minimum needed to satisfy Rome's requirements for canonization. Only once Rome's approval routinized the candidate's charisma did it become the basis for a larger mobilization of a community and for the flow of resources.

Besides changing the goals and roles of acolytes, the rules of 1642 affected canonization trials in several other ways: reducing the proportion of candidates who achieved sainthood, reducing the number of

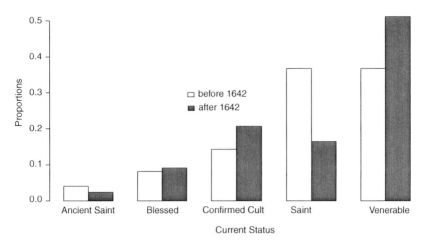

FIGURE 5.3. Career outcomes for candidates before and after 1642.

miracles in each trial, reducing the average length of a trial, increasing the share of regular clergy among the candidates, shifting the trials' focus from miracles to virtues, and allowing trials to cluster geographically, the Church spread them out before 1642.

The impact of the changes can be grasped by focusing on the institutional career of each case, or the steps a candidate had to undergo to become a saint. Of the cases that had their first trial between 1588 and 1642, 36 percent are now saints, whereas for the cases that started after 1642, only 16 percent reached canonization. Using today's status mitigates the effect of the length of time that the cases were under consideration – all of them were introduced to the Congregatio before 1751. Considering the entire population of cases, a candidate had .58 odds of becoming a saint under the old regulatory system versus .20 odds after 1642. Taking the ratio between the two odds shows that candidates were 2.9 times more likely to become saints before 1642 than after. Even assuming a background distribution of individuals with some claims to sanctity larger than the universe of cases that attracted the attention of the Congregatio, the difference in the odds is large enough to indicate a real effect caused by the new rules. The same effect remains visible, albeit in more moderate terms, when one observes the overall status of cases in 1751: 20 percent of those candidates whose trials began before 1642 were saints by 1751, versus a mere 5 percent of those who had their first trial after 1642. The Congregatio's 1642 rules had the overall effect of restricting access to sainthood. Figure 5.3 reports the proportion of cases by current status, distinguishing between individuals whose trials started before and after 1642.

The meanings of the different statuses were introduced in Chapter 1. Briefly, ancient saints were those whose cults existed for at least one hundred years before their petition for a trial reached the Congregatio. These cases could reach either of two statuses – canonization as an ancient saint or the confirmation of their cult. The former indicated acceptance by the central Church, while the latter was limited to local worship, making it analogous to the status of blessed for contemporary candidates. The proportion of ancient cases reaching the status of confirmation of their cult, as opposed to canonization as an ancient saint, rose after 1642. Besides the difference in the odds of becoming a saint before and after 1642, the other main difference was in the frequency of the outcome venerable. More than half of the cases that began after 1642 remain today at this lowest level of the celestial hierarchy. Excluding the possibility that individuals whose cases were active before 1642 had stronger supernatural capacities than those who began the path to canonization afterward, the adoption of new rules is what caused the shift in the distribution of cases across statuses. In the new institutional environment of the second half of the seventeenth century, the Church no longer needed to channel its program through local authorities to the degree it had before, and it moved decisively toward reducing the number of cases that reached sainthood.

The diminished need to attract followers and the greater knowledge of the form that true miracles had to take caused acolytes to present fewer miracles for consideration during a trial. Canonization trials averaged sixty miracles per candidate at the beginning of the seventeenth century, but they moved toward including just a few, ultimately settling around the minimum required. During the trial of Andrea Avellino in Naples at the beginning of the century, 196 *in vitam* and postmortem healing miracles were attributed to the candidate. A few decades later, during the trial of Francesco de Geronimo, also held in Naples, the number of reported healings was "just" ninety-three (Boesch-Gajano and Modica 1999).

Witnesses in post-1642 trials talked mostly about the virtues of the candidates rather than about the candidates' supernatural abilities. The 1669 trial of Caterina Vigri – a candidate who died two hundred years before and had already experienced multiple trials – provides an example. One of the nuns living in the convent where Vigri had preached in Bologna stated that she heard the candidate's "teachings" (*lettioni*) many times because the convent's nuns frequently recounted them. Vigri's teachings, not her miracles, took center stage in this trial (Spanó Martinelli

2003). Vigri's case is also instructive because, in addition to this 1669 trial, she had several trials before 1642, and miracles occupied a larger part of those earlier trials.

This marginalization of miracles was not a by-product of the fact that Vigri's case was ancient. In 1730, during the apostolic trial of Jane Frances de Fremyot in Lugdunnen, France, half the trial revolved around a single miracle, the cure of Maria Elisabetta Dronier, who suffered from a stomachache and a headache from the age of eight. When she was eleven, she joined a convent as a novice, and her pains became stronger and more frequent, until ultimately, after twenty months of diarrhea, she was forced to return home. At home, however, Dronier was very unhappy, and her pains became even worse. She started suffering from hysteria. Dronier's stubborn desire to take her vows was finally recognized, and after three years she returned to the convent, though her disease continued there as well, baffling the doctors who tried to cure her. Dronier began praying to de Fremyot, and she was suddenly healed. Thirteen witnesses testified to Dronier's healing, among them priests and doctors. Interestingly, all the witnesses had to swear that they had not heard of other miracles performed by de Fremyot (ASV 875).

Because the official number of required miracles never changed during the period from 1588 to 1751, the reduction in the number of miracles can only be imputed to the different role that social mobilization played in the new centralized governing structure. What changed was the number of miracles that acolytes had to perform before and after 1642 in order to attract the attention of Rome. The Peace of Westphalia ushered in a stability that secured the position of the papacy in southern Europe, making local mobilization before the trial irrelevant for Rome. At the same time, acolytes learned how to produce miracles of the right form by examining the decisions of the Congregatio, which were made public by papal *bolla* that described approved miracles (Veraja 1992; Delooz 1997). Separating content from form remained the cornerstone of sainthood, because it brought sainthood in line with modernity, but the need to build a large mobilization around a candidate before canonization ceased to be the concern of religious activists now that local authorities had lost their prominence.

The changes in the type of mobilization necessary to reach canonization had two direct consequences. First, canonization trials became shorter. A significant difference exists in the average length of trials before and after 1642 ($F = 13.95$, $p = .0002$). Between 1588 and 1642, trials lasted on average almost seven years, while trials between 1642 and

1751 lasted an average of four years. In the countries that had the largest number of trials – Italy, Spain and Portugal, and France – the same
dynamic operated. In Italy, trials shortened in length from 7.75 years to
4.4 ($F = 87$, $p = .0018$); in Spain and Portugal the average decreased from
6.13 years to 3.4 ($F = 5.75$, $p = .0182$); and in France there was a decrease
from 3.6 years to 3.5, though this was not statistically significant ($F = 0$,
$p = .982$).[8] Much of this reduction in trial length can be attributed to the
decline in the number of miracles in trials that started in 1642 and moved
at different paces in different macrogeographic areas.

Second, the new rules had the direct effect of moving sainthood inside
the walls of monasteries. Only there could institutional memory sustain
the candidate's reputation – allowing him to meet the seemingly paradoxical twin requirements of a large *fama* and fifty years of silence about his
deeds after his death. Although the secular clergy represented 53 percent
of all the candidates that had achieved venerable status in 1642, they represented 26 percent of the candidates of the same rank between 1643 and
1751. Similarly, 41 percent of the saints canonized before 1642 were from
the ranks of the secular clergy, in contrast to 24 percent after 1642. On
the opposite side, the percentage of candidates who were regular clergy
increased from 50 percent to 64 percent after 1642. With regard to the ideal
types of candidates defined in Chapters 3 and 4, the new rules favored the
learned monk and the folksy friar at the expense of the spiritual priest.

The New Governing Structure: Controlling Trials to Assert the Church's Authority

Perhaps the clearest indication that the rules of 1642 and their stability following the Peace of Westphalia swept away the previous power-
sharing arrangement between the Church and local bishops comes from
the differences in how the Congregatio used the Church's territorial organization into parishes before and after 1642. Groups of parishes formed
a diocese administered by a bishop. Dioceses differed in importance: if a
diocese was the metropolitan seat of a province, the bishop that administered it was called an archbishop. A province is thus composed of a

---

[8] During this period, Spain and Portugal were united under one crown. The "Iberian
Union," as the dynastic unification of the peninsula became known, began in 1581 with
the crowning of Philip II in Augsburg as king of Portugal and continued until 1640. In
December of that year, the Portuguese nobility, tired of the heavy taxation imposed on
them by the Spanish rulers, revolted and proclaimed John, Duke of Braganza, as their
king.

metropolitan seat, usually called the archdiocese, and several other dioceses, called suffragan dioceses. There are also archdioceses that are not metropolitan seats; their status reflects their past importance.

At the beginning of the seventeenth century, when grassroots movements around each candidate spread throughout southern Europe, the Congregatio had an incentive to allow trials only in provinces that were physically far from one another. By spreading out trials, the Congregatio could reduce the threat to its authority by reducing the risk that local authorities could form coalitions based on geographical proximity.

In many respects, the rules of 1642 reversed this state of affairs. The new sainthood was based more on virtues than on miracles and was composed largely of members of the regular clergy, who were removed from the public eye. This could render the clustering of territories with supernatural activity either irrelevant to or else necessary for canonization. Complete centralization might be expected to make territorial aggregation irrelevant because the establishment of sainthood no longer involved local authorities. However, now that acolytes appealed directly to Rome for recognition, territorial aggregation might be necessary for approval because it could give universal substance to local worship. In either case, Rome's central authority was no longer challenged locally, and physical separation was no longer necessary.

By dictating the time and the place where canonization trials could begin, the Church used its territorial organization to reaffirm its authority before and after 1642. But whereas during the first period the Congregatio would spread out trials to reduce threats, during the second period it would group trials more closely together in order to increase dominance.

To test this hypothesis, I looked more closely at the case of Italy. In Italy the Church was organized into 284 small dioceses and forty-one provinces. To achieve a fine territorial division that could still sustain a broad analytical perspective, I created seven extra provinces by dividing up the large province that encompassed Central Italy. I considered the activation of a territory to be the Congregatio's permission to have a first trial there (Land, Blau, and Deane 1991; Strang 1991; Morris 1993).[9] Focusing on the time (in years) that a province waited before being activated, I defined a province's yearly hazard of having a trial at time t,

---

[9] I divided Umbria into two provinces, Perugia and Spoleto; the northern part of the region outside Rome I called Lazio. I separated the provinces of Chieti and Lanciano from Abruzzi. I created two new provinces, Ferrara and Piacenza.

on the condition that it had not yet experienced a trial prior to t. For instance, the yearly hazard measure for province X at time 10 is the ratio between the probability of experiencing a trial at exactly time 10 and the probability of experiencing a trial at a time greater than 10.

If maintaining authority was the Congregatio's concern, having an active neighbor will affect a province's hazard in opposite directions before and after 1642 – negatively during the first period and positively during the second. To be of any significance, the effect of the rules in restructuring authority must hold after considering the size of the province's population. Territories with large populations had a greater demand for miracles; that is, they were home to many recipients of a candidate's miracles, who strengthened his reputation, thus creating more pressure on the Congregatio. Furthermore, territories with large populations were more likely to have many movements operating at the same time. The overall expectation is that more populated territories could exercise greater pressure on Rome for permission to open trials, and that more trials occurred in more populated territories as a result of more opportunity.

Table 5.3 reports the effect of having an active neighbor on a province's hazard, controlling for the size of the population (log), the number of neighbors, and other covariates. Two models were fit separately for the two periods. For both, the unit of observation is the province in time. For instance, if Florence had its first trial in the year 1600, it would contribute twelve observations (1588–1600) during the first period of the analysis (before 1642). I used the same strategy for the second period (1643–1751).

The presence of the Inquisition is expected to decrease the activity of acolytes and thus delay the activation of a province. The proceedings of the trials in the period under study (especially in the first part) listed in great detail how the witnesses talked, dressed, and crossed themselves (see Chapter 3). A canonization could easily become an opportunity to discover heretics. In provinces where the Inquisition was strong, there was a risk that the miracles described could be found to be the work of the devil, and the witnesses might be associated with the devil and brought to trial for heresy. The presence of Jesuits in a province is expected to have the opposite effect, strengthening acolyte activism instead. Despite being loyal soldiers of the papacy, the Jesuits were very protective of their autonomy and became the representatives of local bishops' interests vis-à-vis the Roman Curia. The Jesuits saw in the canonization trial an opportunity to protect their independence from the Curia.

A large concentration of female regular clergy is expected to have a negative impact on a province's chance of opening a trial. One of the

TABLE 5.3. *Hazard of Having a Canonization Trial*
A: Survival Probability Estimates (Cox Time Dependent
Model): Italy, 1588–1642

	Coefficient	Exp(coef.)	Se(coef.)	Z	p
Population (log)	0.27	1.31	0.04	6.91	0.00
Inquisition	0.03	1.03	0.09	0.31	0.75
Regular Clergy: Male < Female	0.15	1.16	0.13	1.11	0.27
Regular Clergy: Male = Female	0.25	1.29	0.11	2.36	0.02
Jesuits	0.63	1.87	0.08	7.48	0.00
Active Neigh.	−0.70	0.50	0.09	−7.76	0.00
Number of Neigh.	0.04	1.04	0.03	1.48	0.14
Time Interaction: Number of Neigh.	−0.00	1.00	0.00	−0.28	0.78

Note: N = 1768; Likelihood Ratio Test = 233 (8 d.f.) *p* < .00; Wald Test = 277 (8 d.f.) *p* < .00.

B: Survival Probability Estimates (Cox Time Dependent
Model): Italy, 1643–1751

	Coefficient	Exp(coef.)	se(coef.)	Z	p
Population (log)	0.01	1.01	0.04	0.17	0.87
Inquisition	0.37	1.44	0.09	4.16	0.00
Regular Clergy: Male < Female	−0.43	0.65	0.13	−3.41	0.00
Regular Clergy: Male = Female	−0.14	0.87	0.09	−1.57	0.12
Jesuits	0.50	1.65	0.08	6.39	0.00
Active Neigh.	0.04	1.05	0.16	0.28	0.78
Number of Neigh.	0.13	1.14	0.01	9.83	0.00
Time Interaction: Active Neigh.	0.00	1.00	0.00	0.59	0.56

Note: N = 2833; Likelihood Ratio Test = 364 (8 d.f.) *p* < .00; Wald Test = 376 (8 d.f.) *p* < .00.

main consequences of the establishment of the Congregatio was that a sanctity based on visions and prophecies was displaced in favor of one based on healings (see Chapter 1). Healings built local consensus but also alienated women from access to sanctity, because most of their miracles were of the type no longer tolerated (see Chapter 2).

In Table 5.3 the effect of interest is that of neighboring provinces: did the hazard of having a trial increase if a neighboring province was already active? For the period from 1588 to 1642, holding other factors constant, having an active neighboring province reduced the yearly hazard of having a trial by .5 (the exponentiated coefficient), that is, by 50 percent on average. For the period after 1642, however, having an active neighbor becomes largely irrelevant. The Congregatio was less concerned with avoiding the clustering of active provinces after 1642.

Somewhat surprisingly, the Inquisition's presence increased the hazard of having a trial in the second period, whereas it was an irrelevant factor in the first. The Inquisition's counterintuitive role can be interpreted in light of the events described in the previous section. After 1642, the Inquisition's control over the canonization process reduced the challenges that trials previously presented – local authorities were no longer relevant and trials became an opportunity to show Rome's control. In this respect, there was not much difference between the spectacle of condemned heretics burned at the stake in Piazza della Minerva in Rome and a triumphant canonization. After 1642, both displays showed the unquestioned authority of the papacy, control of the Curia, and power of Rome (Mecklin 1941; Gotor 2004).

Furthermore, the significant negative effect of having a majority of female regular clergy in a province indicates again the gender bias that historians have highlighted – modern sainthood, whether in the public eye or away from it, is a male-dominated world. Finally, as expected, the size of the population significantly increases the chances of having a trial, and the presence of Jesuits remains significantly correlated with the hazard of a trial in both periods. Although no longer a threat to the control of the Congregatio, the Jesuits continued to use their militarily disciplined order to defend their independence from Rome (Wright 2004).

The evidence implies that the new rules had effects at multiple levels. During the first part of the century, Protestants showed that breaking from Rome was not just possible but an option that could succeed. As long as this option remained open, the Church reduced threats to its authority by avoiding clusters of active provinces. Once new rules excluded the local authorities from decisions about the title of blessed and a sort of cold

Panel A

FIGURE 5.4. Geographic distribution of trials.

war descended on Europe with the Peace of Westphalia, clusters of trials ceased to be a problem. A shared governing structure produced disconnected clusters of supernatural activity during the period from 1588 to 1642, while a centralized governing structure produced trials tied to the presence of the Inquisition and the display of dominance afterward.

Figure 5.4 shows the use of geographical organization concretely by plotting the first ten trials in each of the two periods. On the maps, the number indicates the order of the trial. As expected, the first period shows a wider dispersion of trials from south to north along the

Panel B: First 10 trials between 1643 and 1751

FIGURE 5.4. (Cont.)

peninsula, whereas in the second, active provinces do not appear to have a significant countereffect on their neighbors' likelihood of having a trial.

The first trial of the period from 1588 to 1642 occurred in Palermo, the second in Rome, the third in Florence, the fourth in Milan, and so forth. The Congregatio distributed trials along the peninsula. In many respects, the map of this period (Figure 5.4, panel A) is the negative image of what was occurring on the ground. Local authorities pressured Rome to have their candidates recognized, and Rome reacted by geographically dispersing trials.

During the second period, the first trial took place in Naples, the second in Siena, the third in north Lazio, the fourth in Spoleto (Umbria), and so forth. The clustering of trials in this period evidently did not cause concern for the Congregatio. The distribution of trials on the peninsula (Figure 5.4, panel B) shows where locals considered supernatural activity to be occurring, not Rome's discouragement of this activity. Once more ascendant, Rome moved toward solidifying its hegemony. Under the new governing structure, the geographical clustering of trials reinforced the status quo rather than threatening it.

A MACROLEVEL PERSPECTIVE

The lasting reforms of 1642 worked to maintain the religious hegemony of Rome precisely because they left magic at the core of the mechanism that generated saints. Until the reforms of Pope John Paul II, saints were and remained charismatic religious leaders who answered the needs of local audiences by using miracles. The Congregatio subsumed these local needs into the logical categories of a universal code. The adjudication of miracles and saints, orchestrated by the Devil's Advocate, was based on the code, not on the content of miracles.

From this perspective, the Congregatio's rules – both the pre- and post-1642 sets – resemble technological innovation. Rules are a technology of control for gaining legitimacy and for structuring the relationship between authority and the broader environment (Selznick 1979). Thus focusing on rules is key to interpreting how a thousand-year-old organization like the Church could perpetuate itself in a period marked by uncertainty. The Church developed a new technology for stabilizing the power of magic. Rules explain how the Church not only survived but also maintained its hegemony. The longevity and geographical reach of the Counter-Reformation era rules for adjudicating miracles testify to their relevance.[10] Further, the strategy of religious incorporation that the rules employed explains Catholicism's success relative to other religions in penetrating many foreign religious environments, from South America to Asia. The Church learned in Europe how to achieve control over an unstable religious environment and applied this knowledge worldwide.

---

[10] Church historians have different explanations. Warner Stark, e.g., identifies in the tension between conservative and monastic movements one of the Church's strengths during the medieval period (1966). It was this tension that made the Church more flexible and capable of adapting to local circumstances.

Conclusion

This book reconstructs the nexus of relationships that made true miracles possible during the seventeenth century. Rather than fixed content, a true miracle had a precise form: the Church deemed true the miracles that cut through existing social divisions, regardless of their content. Such recognition was beneficial to religious activists – the candidate's acolytes – who used it to defeat the competition they faced at the hands of other local activists. At the core of modern sainthood lies a structural agreement between the central officials of the Church and local religious activists.

This book develops a twofold argument to explain how the form of a true miracle came to be. On one side there is an organizational story about the emergence of the new institutional field of modern sainthood. The key characters in this story are the Church officials, bishops, and acolytes. The second story relates how the rationalization of magic made the continuance of miracles possible, rather than eliminating them from religion. The key characters in this the story are the miracles, Devil's Advocate, and doctors. The two stories in this book's argument are strongly intertwined but can nevertheless be told separately, as they will be summarized in the following text.

All of the actors in both stories were endogenous to the religious field of the time. In order to highlight this, I left the Protestant Schism deliberately in the background. This was not because I thought the impact of the Protestant Schism irrelevant but because I think of the Protestant Schism as an organic development arising from the religious unrest of the sixteenth and seventeenth centuries, one that occurred in many places in Europe, not just north and east of the Danube. In this, I follow in the footsteps of several historians who have argued against interpreting the Counter-Reformation mainly as the name suggests: a period of reaction to Protestantism (Evennett 1968). Viewing the Counter-Reformation exclusively through the lens of reaction draws a dramatically incomplete picture that marginalizes the powerful religious reformers who operated within Catholicism before and after the Protestant Schism. Among those reformers were the candidates to sainthood whose stories are central to the arguments of this book. Taking a broader view, *Counter-Reformation* is an unfortunate term that, were it not in such common usage, might be better replaced by *Catholic Reformation*. My positioning of the Protestant Schism in the background of my arguments about the transformation of sainthood is therefore quite deliberate. The transformation I describe occurred endogenously.

THE EMERGENCE OF MODERN SAINTHOOD: A STRUCTURAL ARGUMENT

The argument that this book makes about how the field of modern sainthood came to be can be recast succinctly in structural terms. The emergence of the new institutional field involved four actors: (1) a local community of believers; (2) local Church officials; (3) central Church officials; and (4) a group of local activists, that is, the acolytes. This last actor did not play an important role before the Protestant Schism. Fervent believers always existed, but it was not until the Counter-Reformation that they acquired a relevant structural position. Before the Protestant Schism, central Church officials cared little about the relationship between acolytes and believers. At the same time, the community had little interaction with central officials; individual adherence to Catholicism was a local phenomenon, and each community practiced its own flavor of Catholicism. In the idiosyncratic medieval world, orthodoxy and heterodoxy coexisted.

The social structure of this world is depicted in Figure C.1, panel A. Church officials, whether local or central, had notions of sanctity that, while similar to each other, differed from those of local believers. Sainthood existed in a different symbolic plane for each of these actors, and every form of sainthood was tolerated. This great variation allowed the geographical and status divisions of Europe to reproduce themselves in the heavens, so that sainthood existed in both high and low forms, and the French and English each had their own lists of saints.

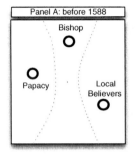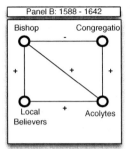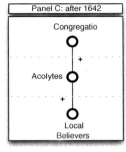

FIGURE C.1. A structural image of the transformation of sainthood.

The threat of the Protestant Schism gave the Church a need to gain and project legitimacy among its believers; miracles and the people who performed them became the primary source of that legitimacy. However, miracles had to be better regulated if the Church hoped to translate their local legitimizing force into organization-wide legitimacy in a religious environment in which Protestantism offered a viable alternative and rationalism a powerful challenge. This meant that the different versions of sainthood had to be integrated and purified. Bishops and the Congregatio's officials each carried a part of this integration effort as they both stood to lose from Protestantism and rationalism. The creation of the title of blessed at the beginning of the seventeenth century symbolizes the intention of Rome and of local authorities to reach a compromise in the interest of Catholicism. Yet the shared governing structure that regulated sainthood was politically quite complicated for Rome to navigate. Bishops and acolytes pressured the Congregatio to grant their blessed candidates access to the title of saint; the greater the local mobilization, the greater the pressure on Rome.

The structural role of acolytes grew out of tension between bishops and the Congregatio. Acolytes bridged different symbolic planes of sainthood and satisfied the Church's organizational needs. For Rome, they created and purified the connection with local communities through the institutional process of encoding. For the bishop, they organized a base of support. For local believers, they reproduced the social conditions that brought about the occurrence of miracles.

Panel B in Figure C.1 portrays the structure of sainthood during the intermediate period. Balancing theory shows readily that while the triad of bishop, acolytes, and local believers is stable, the triad of acolytes, bishop, and Congregatio is not stable. The negative tie that joins the bishop to the Congregatio will break the triad because of the tensions that the two other positive ties impose upon it. From the perspective of the Congregatio, the shared governing structure threatened to produce a scenario in which powerful religious orders, supported by bishops, could use the title of blessed to strong-arm the papacy into canonizing their leaders. The canonizations of Carlo Borromeo, Filippo Neri, and Ignatio Loyola followed paths not far from this one.

The shared governing structure not only created political tensions for Rome, it also transformed sainthood from a dichotomous to a multistage process, creating very expensive transaction costs for acolytes. The number of trials required to achieve canonization increased twofold at least, as separate investigations were required to achieve the titles of blessed and saint. The increased cost of canonization had the overall effect of reducing the number of candidates who achieved canonization. Chapter 5 shows that by the middle of the seventeenth century, the political and economic tensions embedded in the title of blessed were becoming increasingly hard to navigate.

The Church spent much of the early seventeenth century formulating new rules to address its political tension with its bishops. The solution that the rules of 1642 proposed to the political tensions around canonization proved to be a stable arrangement largely because an external event – the Peace of Westphalia – helped the Congregatio permanently reduce the bishop's role in a candidate's career toward sainthood. The key structural change was that the Congregatio took control of the title of blessed. From this time onward, sainthood finally became an indivisible good under the sole administration of Rome.

Though the new rules eliminated the autonomy of the bishop, they preserved the importance of organized local mobilization. That is to say, acolytes remained fundamental for achieving canonization under the rules of 1642. However, the de facto elimination of the title of blessed as an independent stage in the canonization process made acolytes look directly to Rome to learn how to deal with the Congregatio and thereby reduce the costs of achieving sainthood through the local support they organized. There developed something that resembled a commitment between acolytes and Rome – acolytes committed to push their candidates to the end of the process, while Rome committed to provide recognition of this effort by bestowing the title of saint. It was the birth of modern sainthood, a hierarchically organized institutional field in which powerful religious movements promote change and innovation locally, in alliance with (rather than against) the central authority of Rome. This is depicted in panel C.

Modern saints continue to perform miracles, just as their predecessors did, but modern saints perform modern miracles. In the preface, I describe a twenty-first-century miracle that the Blessed Kateri performed on a young boy near Vancouver, saving him from a skin-eating disease that seemed medically certain to kill him. Throughout the book I also provided several examples of miracles that, though certainly modern, we would have trouble recognizing as miracles today. The key to understanding how saints modernized their supernatural capacities resides not in the Weberian notion of rationalization as an immanent historical force that swept Europe but instead in viewing rationalization as an institutional tool in the hands of actors who used it to their advantage. A social world without the capacity for miracles has always been possible, during the seventeenth century as today. In such a world, individual actions sometimes succumb to chance and sheer randomness; a fundamental level of uncertainty can never be eliminated. Yet the possibility of randomness denies the divinely ordered universe of Catholic dogma, leaving space for miracles to explain the otherwise unexplainable.

During the seventeenth century, empirical science emerged as a means of explanation to rival miracles, and it is the explanatory framework with which most of us are most familiar today. However, in this book I claim that seeing miraculous events as a residual category, left over when scientific explanation fails, largely misses the point that religion and science are two interrelated yet independent fields of knowledge about the world. Leaving open a religious space for people with supernatural powers at the same time that science was becoming more empirical required that religious authorities maintain control of the process of adjudicating miracles. The empiricist turn of science, and particularly of medicine, was very troublesome to Rome not because it produced a more accurate description of how the world functions but because it produced a body of knowledge that was increasingly autonomous from religion. What religion did not control it could not effectively judge. There was a threat that papal approval would become irrelevant for sainthood.

During the intermediate period between the old version of sainthood and the new one that emerged after 1642, acolytes used the growing independence of medicine to rush Rome toward approving their candidates. Doctors-turned-acolytes mobilized their medical knowledge to pressure Rome. It is significant, as Chapter 4 reports, that the first candidate to have all of his miracles certified as true by (independent) doctors was a Jesuit. The Jesuits were a powerful new order that demanded increased autonomy from the Curia.

Rome's solution to the growing autonomy of medicine was to use its own power to create a new knowledge: the knowledge of whether a miracle was true or false. For this purpose, it created the Devil's Advocate, an institutional role devoted not to questioning that candidates could perform miracles thanks to their seats close to God in paradise, but to making sure that the Church, not doctors, had the last word in adjudicating miracles. The Devil's Advocate was at the core of the process that rationalized the magic of miracles because it excluded certain deeds like walking on water, multiplying food, and having stigmata from the realm of what was (officially) impossible. While in Protestant countries medicine (and science) took ownership of the boundary between the "possible" and the "not possible," in Catholic countries the Church maintained control of that boundary by reorganizing not just itself but also the "not possible" side of the boundary. Through this reorganization the Church was able to maintain a sprinkling of magic in its religious field.

I see magic as the connection between local needs and a sacred dimension. Emile Durkheim pointed out that a church of magic does not exist because the bonds that unite participants dissolve after the ritual. This book makes a similar argument. My claim is not that the Church became an institution that produced magic but rather that it managed to incorporate magic into a rational framework that tailored Catholicism to local needs. This process of incorporation occurred along the lines of the legal tradition of the Roman Empire. It is this process that I label the *rationalization of miracles*.

Rationalizing magic was far from an obvious outcome for Rome, and it proved to be a hard path to navigate. The fact that Rome succeeded in saving magic does not mean that things could not have gone differently. Ample scholarship has shown that several parts of Northern Italy, for example, became very open to Protestant ideas at different points during the sixteenth century. Protestant ideas existed even in the higher echelons of the Church; Cardinal Reginald Pole, who came very close to being elected pope during the middle of the century, had ideas very similar to those of John Calvin. The saving of magic was the result of a long

political struggle inside the Church and an institutional solution that created winners and losers.

The process of rationalizing magic had the side effect of giving the
Church great flexibility in colonizing foreign religious environments. The
penetration of Catholicism into vast swaths of South and Central America,
for example, cannot be imputed only to the swords of the Spanish and
Portuguese colonizers. The new religion of the dominators also had an
incredible amount of flexibility built in that allowed it to absorb local
cults and purify them along the way. This flexibility was institutionally
constructed in the process of maintaining control of the religious environment of southern Europe; like any social and political process, it not
only made Catholicism adaptable to foreign lands but also changed the
religious environments of those lands.

A SOCIAL FACT

The networks that produced true miracles were heterogeneous with
respect to kinship and status. In a social world that was highly segmented,
this social structure was a rare occurrence. As Roger Gould pointed out
in the case of the Paris Commune, a process that cuts through existing cleavages creates networks that are destined to disappear unless they
receive external institutional recognition (1991). In the context of the
development of modern sainthood, recognition from Rome provided the
necessary support to make the new structure independent of its local context. For the acolytes, the process of creating a true miracle was not one
of embedding but the opposite – a disembedding of actions from the local
fabric of relationships.

This was possible at least in part because the process of encoding gave
a meaning to the actions of the acolytes that was independent of what
local people believed. Often, established organizations fail to supplement
new actions with new meaning. For instance, during the U.S. Civil War,
locally recruited companies in the Confederate Army maintained an alliance among their members that never transcended localism. The meaning of action, in this case combat, remained embedded in existing local
networks. When war conditions deteriorated, that is, when uncertainty
arose, these companies experienced high desertion. The roots of the
Confederate Army's quick demise were in the army's failure to provide
local networks with a broader meaning disembedded from their local
alliances (Bearman 1991).

Rome's judgment of true miracles provided this meaning to the unlikely social structure that acolytes built locally; by doing so it also allowed for the routinization of the candidate's charisma into a new social structure. The new religious order that (almost always) resulted from a successful mobilization became a local manufacturing center for more miracles. Because a saint now performed these miracles, rather than a candidate, his miracles were by definition all true and required no further investigation. These miracles were true in the structural sense that I have defined: they cut across social divisions by saving people of different social statuses. Disembedded from its local context, a true miracle was an independent product, though sold only in specific locations and that consequently attracted pilgrims interested in acquiring that product. Pilgrims had the obvious by-product of generating revenues that helped the order of the new saint consolidate its control of the local religious field.

Durkheim coined the expression "social fact" to indicate every "way of acting, fixed or not, capable of exercising on the individual an influence, or an external constraint" (1982, 26). In the locations where miracles were produced, supernatural events, "sold" as true miracles, became social facts. However, though Durkheim's definition allows us to understand the persistent power of saints, it does little to illuminate the social process that created saints. The problem with using the category of social fact empirically is that we usually observe only things that succeed in becoming social facts, not all potential social facts, including those that, somehow or other, failed to become social facts. Thus we cannot know what characteristics make a fact social until we find one.

This book uses the Church's documentation of failed as well as successful candidates to sainthood – claimants to the status of social fact – to give an answer to the question of how a social fact comes to be. In sum, a social fact emerges through an alliance among several powerful actors, each pursuing its own goals, and each recognizing the higher benefits that their alliance could produce. The recognition of common interests does not necessarily have to precede the formation of the alliance. As in the case documented in this book, the key actors may recognize their common interests along the way, through conflict. For an interest-based alliance to become a social fact, the key is that the alliance, once established, must generate new interests that reinforce it. These interests single out some practices and give them new meaning. A social fact, in the interpretation given here, is a dynamic construction whose meaning is fixed.

Thus the process of updating that makes it possible for a social fact to resist the passage of time lies in detaching practices, selected according to the interests of the powerful players, from local significance, so that their meaning remains constant for everyone. A social fact is a product that although originally thought of and produced by specific people has become similar to a good, detached from the original producers.

Appendix A

Primary Sources

The following lists all the primary sources I consulted about the lives and deeds of the candidates to sainthood included in this book.

> ASV = Vatican Secret Archive
> BAV = Vatican Apostolic Library
> ACS = Archive of the Congregation for the Causes of the Saints

MANUSCRIPTS AND PRINTED

All of the ASV volumes came from the folder *Congregatio Sacrorum Rituum, Processus.*

Pasqual Baylon:	(1) BAV Barberini Latino, 2768
	(2) ASV 3393; 3399
	(3) ACS Storico, 123; 345
Alonso Orozco:	(1) ASV 3033
Antonio de Colellis:	(1) ASV 1983
Carlo Borromeo:	(1) ACS Storico, (a) Relazione Uditori di Rota, vol.1;, (b) Borromeo Summarium Miracolorum
	(2) ASV 1681
	(3) BAV Barberini Latino, 14083–84
Filippo Neri:	(1) ACS Storico, (a) Relazione Uditori di Rota, vol. 1; (b) Relationes super vitae et sanctitate Filippo Neri
	(2) Giovanni Incisa della Rocchetta, Nello Vian, eds. 1957. *Il primo processo per San Filippo Neri.* vols. 1–4. Vatican City: Biblioteca Apostolica Vaticana
Teresa of Avila:	(1) ACS Storico, (a) 63; (b) *Relazione Uditori di Rota*, vol.1

	(2) P. Silverio de Santa Teresa, ed.
	1935.Processos de Beatificacion y
	Canonizacion de Sta. Teresa de Jesus,
	vol. 1–4. Burgos: Tipografia Burgalesa
	(El Monte Carmelo)
	(3) *Libro della mia vita.* Milan:
	Mondadori, 1986
Maria Maddalena de' Pazzi:	(1) ASV 767
Rainiero of Borgo San Sepolcro:	(1) ASV 3238; 3241
	(2) ACS Storico, 223
Bernardino di Santa Lucia:	(1) ASV 2209

ACS, Registrum Decretorum in Causis Servorum Dei
ASV, Index of the Congregation of the Rites

DATA SOURCES FOR POPULATION ESTIMATES

(1) Corridore, Francesco. 1906. *La popolazione dello Stato Romano (1656–1901).* Rome: Ermanno Loescher and Co.
(2) Eubel, Conradus, ed. 1898. *Hierarchia catholica.* Munster, Germany: Librariae
   Regensbergianae.
(3) Jedin, Hubert, Kenneth S. Latourette, and Jochen Martin, eds. 1991. *Atlante universale. Storia della Chiesa.* Vatican City: Edizioni Piemme.

Appendix B

Sample-Building Procedures

The Vatican archives provide a list of people who underwent canonization trials. Because canonization required a candidate to perform miracles, the transcripts of canonization trials contain descriptions of candidates' miracles and so serve as the source of data for my analysis. Trials were recorded in Latin and in the native language of the witnesses; that is, if a trial took place in Madrid, the questions and the proceedings of the trial would be recorded in Latin and the witnesses' answers in Spanish. Trials varied in length and number of witnesses, with some documented in fewer than one hundred pages and some taking up thousands of pages. By 1642, the Congregatio had held trials on almost 180 individuals.

This relatively large number of cases requires careful interpretation. The majority of the candidates had weak local support and their acolytes used trials in an effort to generate broader consensus. Furthermore, roughly 13 percent of the cases were ancient, involving long-deceased individuals for whom the path to canonization was regulated differently from that of contemporary candidates. Thus a large number of the trials were short, involved very few witnesses, and listed few miracles. The Congregatio either ignored or rejected these weak cases without providing a systematic rationale for its decisions.

Further complicating matters, one cannot create a comprehensive list of approved and rejected miracles for all of the period's 178 cases based on the Congregatio's archives because official records exist only for cases that achieved the status of blessed or saint. Examining the Congregatio's rules relating to miracles therefore implies restricting attention to cases that already had enough support to attract the Congregatio's careful notice. This restriction had the potential to bias my findings, because the overall mobilizing capacity of a case positively correlates with the number of records that the Congregatio kept on it. In the methodological literature this problem is known as sampling on the dependent variable.

I did two things to address this problem. First, I restricted the number of cases from which to sample by defining a candidate for sainthood as an individual who died in Europe during the sixteenth century and for whom the Congregatio had approved at least one trial. By 1642 there were forty-two candidates for sainthood according to this definition. These candidates were in three states: saints, blessed, or venerable. Although I could reconstruct the Congregatio's miracle-by-miracle decisions only for saints and blessed candidates, I could assess the amount of support any candidate had by examining his trials. Despite my restriction of the number of cases, my definition of a candidate allowed enough variation for testing the research hypotheses. Second, I constructed a typology of four ideal case types by which to select candidates in order to extend the representativeness of my sample. This classification was detailed in Chapter 2. I pursue a strategy of maximizing the number of miracles included in my analysis by populating the previously constructed typology with a mix of selected and randomly chosen candidates.

Only five of the candidates who came before the Congregatio achieved canonization before 1642; of these, one (Francis Xavier) operated mostly outside of Europe and so is excluded from the analysis. The miracles recorded in the trials of three of the remaining four saints – Carlo Borromeo (1538–84) in Milan, Filippo Neri (1515–95) in Rome, and Teresa of Jesus (1515–82) in Salamanca and Avila – are included. While the first two saints hailed from urban environments in Italy and Spain, Teresa of Jesus operated in a rural environment (Avila) in addition to an urban one (Alvar 1994).[1] Both Borromeo and Neri were members of the secular clergy – the former as a priest, the latter as a bishop – while Teresa, as a nun, was a member of the regular clergy.

The remaining group of thirty-seven candidates reached canonization after 1642 or are still under evaluation. These candidates fall into two subcategories – a group of fifteen blessed and a group of twenty-two venerable. I selected one candidate who had extensive trials and came from a rural environment. Pasqual Baylon (1540–92) achieved the status

---

[1] The records of Ignatio Loyola's trials, the other saint recognized in this period, are not in the Vatican but followed Napoleon to Paris when he occupied Italy (Blouin 1988); therefore Loyola's miracles are not included in my analysis.

of blessed in 1618 and that of saint in 1690. I analyzed all of the miracles described in Baylon's trials, which were held in the village of Villa Real, Spain. I also randomly selected three candidates from the group of venerables: Alonzo Orozco (1500–91) in Madrid, Bernardino (1545–87) in Agrigento, and Rainiero of Borgo San Sepolcro (died in 1589). Orozco and Bernardino were urban candidates, while Rainiero was a rural candidate. These three venerable were members of the regular clergy: Rainiero and Bernardino were both Franciscan mendicant friars, while Orozco was an Augustinian monk.

Appendix C

Statistical Modeling

For the candidates who by 1642 were at least blessed (Teresa of Avila, Carlo Borromeo, Filippo Neri, and Pasqual Baylon), I predicted the likelihood of a miracle's approval (M = 1) with a logit model. More formally:

$$Pr(M_i = 1) = \text{logit}^{-1}(X_i\beta + \text{connected miracle}_i\theta) \qquad [1]$$

Where M_i is miracle i;
X_i is a matrix of covariates on the miracle;
connected miracle$_i$ = 1 if miracle$_i$ is connected and 0 otherwise;

and

$$\text{logit}(x) = \left(\frac{x}{1-x}\right)$$

The effect of interest is the coefficient of the dummy variable connected miracle (see Table 5.2). If significant, it suggests that Congregatio officials looked closely at the mobilizing capacity of miracles (what I refer to as their form) and less at their content.

I controlled for the fact that miracles were clustered around candidates by using clustered robust standard errors. Assuming that miracles were independent only across candidates produces the following robust variance estimates:

$$\widehat{V(\beta)} = \hat{V} \left(\frac{m}{m-1} \sum_{i=1}^{m} u_k^G u_k^G \right) \hat{V} \qquad [2]$$

where m = number of candidates
and

$$u_k^G = \sum_{j \in G_k} u_j \qquad [3]$$

That is, the pooled contributions to the robust variance estimate by candidates.

Nevertheless, even taking into account the clustering of miracles within candidates, the results of the model are limited by the nonrandom nature of the sample.

THE MODEL FOR THE TIME DISTRIBUTION OF TRIALS

The process characterized in Chapter 5, "Sainthood before the Congregatio," follows a Poisson distribution. In particular, if we let $N(s,t)$ indicate the number of trials in the time interval (s,t), then $N(s,t)$ follows a Poisson point process:

$$Pr[N(s,t) = k] = \frac{[\lambda(t-s)]^k e^{-\lambda(t-s)}}{k!} \quad \text{for} \quad k = 0, 1, \ldots \qquad [4]$$

Besides the three conditions specified in "Sainthood before the Congregatio," a Poisson point process also requires that the probability of two or more events occurring within a time interval of length h with h approaching 0 is 0. This excludes the possibility of two simultaneous trials in Rome. Furthermore, because of the change of rules of 1642, I estimated two λs: one for the period from 1588 to 1642 and one for the period from 1643 to 1751. This implies that the distribution of trials in time in Rome in the interval (s,t), that is, $N(s,t)$, is a nonhomogenous Poisson point process.

Bibliography

Abbott, Andrew. 1988. *The System of Professions: An Essay on the Division of Expert Labor*. Chicago: University of Chicago Press.

Abolafia, Mitchel Y. 2001. *Making Markets*. Cambridge, MA: Harvard University Press.

Alexander, Jeffrey C. 2006. *The Civil Sphere*. Oxford: Oxford University Press.

Alvar, Alfredo. 1994. "Vida Politica, Sociedad y Economia." Pp. 139–86 in *Historia de Madrid*, ed. Antonio Fernandez Garcia. Madrid: Editorial Complutense.

Antonelli, Francesco. 1962. *De inquisitione medico-legali super miraculis in causis beatificationis et canonizationis*. Rome: Pontificium Athenaeum Anthonianum.

Barkey, Karen. 1994. *Bandits and Bureaucrats: The Ottoman Route to State Centralization*. Ithaca, NY: Cornell University Press.

Bartley, Tim. 2007. "Institutional Emergence in an Era of Globalization." *American Journal of Sociology* 113(2): 297–351.

Bearman, Peter. 1991. "Desertion as Localism: Army Unit Solidarity and Group Normas in the U.S. Civil War." *Social Forces* 70(2): 321–42.

——. 1993. *Relations into Rhetorics*. New Brunswick, NJ: Rutgers University Press.

Bech, Ulrich. 2004. *Risk Society*. Thousand Oaks, CA: Sage Publications.

Beuchler, Steve M. 1998. "Social Movements, Sociology and the Well-Informed Citizen," *Sociological Imagination* 35: 239–64.

Blau, Peter. 2005. *Exchange and Power in Social Life*. New Brunswick, NJ, and London: Transaction Publishers.

Bloch, Mark. 1961. *Feudal Society*. New York: Routledge.

——. 1973. *I Re taumaturghi*. Torino, Italy: Einaudi.

Blok, Anton. 1974. *The Mafia of a Sicilian Village, 1860–1960*. New York: Harper and Row.

Blouin, Francis X., Jr. 1998. *Vatican Archives: An Inventory and Guide to Historical Documents of the Holy See*. New York: Oxford University Press.

Bobbio, Norberto. 1989. *Democracy and Dictatorship: The Nature and Limits of State Power*. Cambridge: Polity Press.

Boesch-Gajano, Sofia. 1999. *La santità*. Roma-Bari: Laterza and Figli.

Boesch-Gajano, Sofia, and Marilena Modica, eds. 2000. *Miracoli. Dai segni alla storia*. Roma-Bari: Laterza and Figli.

Bonfiglio, Salvatore. 1933. *La terra agrigentina e l'Italia nuova*. Milan, Italy: La Prora.

Bonnet, Henry-Marc. 1954. *Storia degli Ordini Religiosi*. Milan, Italy: Garzanti.

Bossy, John. 1976. *The English Catholic Community, 1570–1850*. Oxford: Oxford University Press.

1985. *Christianity in the West: 1400–1700*. Oxford: Oxford University Press.

Braudel, Fernand. 1992. *Civilization and Capitalism 15th–18th Century*. Berkeley: University of California Press.

Brown, Peter. 1981. *The Cult of the Saints*. Chicago and London: Chicago University Press.

Caciola, Nancy. 1996. "Through a Glass, Darkly: Recent Work on Sanctity and Society. A Review Article." *Comparative Studies in Society and History* 38: 301–9.

Carter, Thomas F. 2008. "New Rules to the Old Game: Cuban Sport and State Legitimacy in the Post-Soviet Era." *Identities* 15(2): 194–215.

Clemens, Elisabeth S. 1997. *The People's Lobby: Organizational Innovation and the Rise of Interest Group in Politics in the United States, 1890–1925*. Chicago: University of Chicago Press.

Collins, Randall. 1996. *Weberian Sociological Theory*. Cambridge: Cambridge University Press.

Cousin, Bernard. 1983. "Le miracle et le quotidien." Universite' de Provence.

Dahl, Robert Alan. 1989. *Who Governs? Democracy and Power in an American City*. New Haven, CT: Yale University Press.

D'Alfonso, Michele. 1977. *La prova in genere e la fama di santità*. Rome: Agnesotti.

Dalton, Melville. 1964. *Men Who Manage*. New York: John Wiley and Sons.

Davis, Gerald F., and Henrich R. Greve. 1997. "Corporate Elite Networks and Governance Changes in 1980s." *American Journal of Sociology* 103(1): 1–37.

Davis, Gerald F., Kristina A. Diekmann, and Catherine H. Tinsley. 1994. "The Decline and Fall of the Conglomerate Firm in the 1980s." *American Sociological Review* 59(4): 547–70.

De Angelis, Maria Antonietta. 2008. *Prospero Lambertini*. Vatican City: Archivio Segreto Vaticano.

Della Porta, Donatella, and Mario Diani. 1999. *Social Movements: An Introduction*. Oxford: Blackwell.

Delooz, Pierre. 1969. *Sociologie et canonisation*. The Hague, The Netherlands: Martinus Nijhoff.

1983. "Toward a Sociological Study of Canonized Sainthood in the Catholic Church." Pp. 189–216 in *Saints and Their Cults: Studies in Religious Sociology, Folklore and History*, ed. S. Wilson. Cambridge: Cambridge University Press.

1997. *Les miracles: un defi pour la science?* Brussels, Belgium: Duculot.

Delumeau, Jean. 1976. "De l'Aujourd'hui a l'heir de l'Occident Chretien XVI-XVIII siecles." Pp. 99–127 in *La religion populaire dans l'occident chretien: approches historiques*, ed. Bernard Plongeron. Paris: Editions Beauchesne.

De Nooy, Wouter, Anrej Mrvar, and Vladimir Batagelj. 2005. *Exploratory Social Network Analysis with Pajek*. New York: Cambridge University Press.

De Renzi, Silvia. 2002. "Witnesses of the Body: Medico-Legal Cases in Seventeenth-century Rome." *Studies in History and Philosophy of Science* 33: 219–42.

De Vries, Jan. 1974. *The Dutch Rural Economy in the Golden Age 1500–1751*. New Haven, CT: Yale University Press.

Dickens, Arthur G. 1968. *The Counter-Reformation*. London: Oxford University Press.

DiMaggio, Paul. 1991. "Constructing an Organizational Field as a Professional Project: U.S. Art Museums, 1920–1940." Pp. 267–92 in *The New Institutionalism in Organizational Analysis*, ed. Walter W. Powell and Paul DiMaggio. Chicago: University of Chicago Press.

DiMaggio, Paul, and Walter W. Powell. 1983. "The Iron Cage Revisited: Institutional Isomorphism and Collective Rationality in Organizational Fields." *American Sociological Review* 48: 147–60.

Duby, George. 1980. *The Three Orders. Feudal Society Imagined*. Chicago: University of Chicago Press.

Duffin, Jacalyin. 2009. *Medical Miracles*. Oxford: Oxford University Press.

Durkheim, Emile. 1982. *Le forme elementari della vita religiosa*. Milan, Italy: Edizioni di Comunità.

   1996. *Le regole del metodo sociologico*. Milan, Italy: Edizioni di Comunità.

   1997. *The Division of Labor in Society*. New York: The Free Press.

Eamon, William. 1998. "Cannibalism and Contagion: Framing Syphilis in Counter-Reformation Italy." *Early Science and Medicine* 3(1): 1–31.

Edelman, Lauren B. 1992. "Legal Ambiguity and Symbolic Structures: Organizational Mediation of Civil Rights Law." *American Journal of Sociology* 97(6): 1531–76.

Edelman, Lauren B., Uggen, Christopher, and Howard S. Earlanger. 1999. "The Endogeneity of Legal Regulations." *American Journal of Sociology* 105: 406–54.

Eisenstadt, Shmuel Noah. 1966. *Modernization: Protest and Change*. Englewood Cliffs, NJ: Prentice-Hall.

Eisenstein, Elizabeth. 1979. *The Printing Press as an Agent of Change*. Cambridge: Cambridge University Press.

Elias, Norbert. 1992. *An Essay on Time*. London: Blackwell.

Erikson, Emily, and Peter Bearman. 2006. "Malfeasance and the Foundation for Global Trade: The Structure of the English Trade in the East Indies, 1601–1833." *American Journal of Sociology* 112: 195–230.

Evennett, Outram H. 1968. *The Spirit of the Counter-Reformation*. Cambridge: Cambridge University Press.

Ferrero, Mario. 2002. "Competition for Sainthood and the Millennial Church." *Kyklos* 55(1): 335–60.

Firpo, Massimo, and John Tedeschi. 1996. "The Italian Reformation and Juan de Valdes." *Sixteenth Century Journal* 27(2): 353–64.

180   *Bibliography*

Fligstein, Neil. 1990. *The Trasformation of Corporate Control*. Cambridge, MA: Harvard University Press.

1996. "Markets as Politics: A Political-Cultural Approach to Market Institutions." *American Sociological Review* 61: 656–73.

Fort, Rooney, and Young Hoon Lee. 2007. "Structural Change, Competitive Balance, and the Rest of the Major Leagues." *Economic Inquiry* 45(3): 519–32.

Foucault, Michel. 2001. *Madness and Civilization: A History of Insanity in the Age of Reason*. London: Routledge.

Fox Piven, Frances, and Richard A. Cloward. 2005. "Rulemaking, Rulebraking, and Power." Pp. 33–53 in *The Handbook of Political Sociology*, ed. Thomas Janoski, Robert R. Alford, Alexander M. Hicks, and Mildred A. Schwartz. Cambridge: Cambridge University Press.

Fragnito, Gigliola. 1992. "Gli ordini religiosi tra Riforma e Controriforma." Pp. 160–205 in *Clero e società nell'Italia moderna*, ed. Mario Rosa. Roma-Bari, Italy: Editori Laterza.

Freeman, John, Glenn Carroll, and Michael Hannan. 1983. "The Liability of Newness: Age Dependence in Organizational Death Rates." *American Sociological Review* 48(5): 692–710

French, Robert. 2001. *Canonical Medicine*. Leiden, the Netherlands; Boston; and Koln, Germany: Brill.

Friedland, Roger, and Robert R. Alford. 1991. "Bringing Society Back In: Symbols, Practices, and Institutional Contraddicitions." Pp. 232–63 in *The New Institutionalism in Organizational Analysis*, ed. Walter W. Powell and Paul DiMaggio. Chicago: University of Chicago Press.

Garden, Maurice. 1986. "The Urban Trades: Social Analysis and Representation." Pp. 287–96 in *Work in France: Representations, Meaning, Organisation, and Practice*, ed. Steven L. Kaplan and Cynthia Koepp. Ithaca, NY, and London: Cornell University Press.

Gauthier, Albert. 1996. *Le droit romain et son apport a l'edification du droit canonique*. Ottawa, ON: Faculte de droit canonique Universite Saint-Paul.

Gertz, Clifford. 1966. "Religion as a Cultural System." Pp. 1–46 in *Anthropological Approaches to the Study of Religion*, ed. Micheal P. Banton. New York: Frederick A. Praeger Press.

Giddens, Anthony. 1984. *The Constitution of Society*. Berkeley: University of California Press.

Ginzburg, Carlo. 1970. *Il nicodenismo*. Torino, Italy: Einaudi.

1976. *Il formaggio ed i vermi. Il cosmo di un mugnaio del '500*. Torino, Italy: Einaudi.

Goffman, Erving. 1969. *The Presentation of Self in Everyday Life*. New York: Doubleday Anchor Books.

Gotor, Mark. 2000. "La fabbrica dei santi: la riforma urbaniana e il modello tridentino." Pp. 679–727 in *Storia d'Italia*, vol. 16, ed. L. Fiorani and A. Prosperi. Rome: Einaudi Editore.

2004. *Chiesa e santità nell'Italia moderna*. Rome: Editori Laterza.

Gould, Roger V. 1991. "Multiple Networks and Mobilization in the Parsi Commune, 1871." *American Sociological Review* 56: 716–29.

Gouldner, Alvin. 1965. *Patterns of Industrial Bureaucracy*. New York: Free Press.

Greenwood, Royston, Roy Suddaby, and C. R. Hinings. 2002. "Theorizing Change: The Role of Professional Associations in the Trasformation of Institutionalized Fields." *Academy of Management Journal* 45(1): 58–80.

Hall, A. R. 1961. "The Scientific Movement." Pp. 47–72 in *The New Cambridge Modern History*, vol. V (The Ascendancy of France), ed. F. L. Carsten. Cambridge: Cambridge University Press.

Hall, Donald John. 1965. *English Mediaeval Pilgrimage*. London: Routledge and Kegan Paul.

Hannan, Michael, and John Freeman. 1987. "The Ecology of Organizational Founding: American Labor Unions, 1863–1985." *American Journal of Sociology* 92(4): 910–43.

Hedström, Peter. 2005. *Dissecting the Social*. Cambridge: Cambridge University Press.

Hertz, Robert A. 1928. "Sociologie religieuse et folklore." Paris: Presses Universitaires de France.

Hill, Christopher. 1958. *Puritanism and Revolution*. New York: St. Martin's Press.

Hogg, Robert V., and Allen T. Craig. 1995. *Introduction to Mathematical Statistics*. Upper Saddle River, NJ: Prentice-Hall.

Hubert, Henri. 1999. *Essay on Time: A Brief Study of the Representation of Time in Religion and Magic*. Oxford: Durkheim Press.

Hubert, Jedin, Kenneth S. Latourette, and Martin Jochen, eds. 1991. *Atlante universale: Storia della Chiesa*. Vatican City: Edizioni Piemme.

Israel, Jonathan I. 1999. "Counter-Reformation, Economic Decline, and the Delayed Impact of the Medical Revolution in Catholic Europe, 1550–1750." Pp. 40–55 in *Health Care and Relief in Counter Reformation Europe*, ed. Ole Peter Grell, Andrew Cunningham, and Jon Arrizabalaga. London: Routledge.

Kaminski, Marek M. 2004. *Games Prisoners Play*. Princeton, NJ, and Oxford: Princeton University Press.

Klaniczay, Gabor. 1997. "Miraculum and Maleficium." Pp. 49–74 in *Problems in the Historical Anthropology of Early Modern Europe*, ed. P. C. R. Hsia and R. W. Scribner. Wiesbaden, Germany: Harasowitz Verlag.

Kleinberg, Aviad M. 1994. "Shared Sainthood." Pp. 167–176 in *Modelli di santità e modelli di comportamento*, ed. G. Barone, M. Caffiero, and F. Barcellona Scorza. Torino, Italy: Rosenberg and Sellier.

Knight, Frank H. 1921. *Risk, Uncertainty and Profit*. Chicago: University of Chicago Press.

Kraatz, M. S., and Edward J. Zajac. 2001. "How Organizational Resources Affect Strategic Change and Performance in Turbulent Environments: Theory and Evidence." *Organization Science* 12: 632–57.

Land, Kenneth C., Judith R. Blau, and Glenn Deane. 1991. "Religious Pluralism and Church Membership: A Spatial Diffusion Model." *American Sociological Review* 56(2): 237–49.

Le Bras, Gabriel. 1955. *Etudes de sociologie religieuse*. Paris: Universitaires de France.

Lebrun, Francois. 1995. *Se soigner autrefois: medecins, saints et sorciers aux XVIIe et XVIIIe siecles*. Paris: Seuil.

Leifer, Eric M. 1990. "Inequality among Equals: Embedding Market and Authority in League Sports." *American Journal of Sociology* 96(3): 665–81.

Lipset, Martin, Martin A. Trow, and James S. Coleman. 1956. *Union Democracy*. Glencoe, IL: The Free Press.

Locke, Richard M. 1997. *Remaking the Italian Economy*. Ithaca, NY, and London: Cor.

Lounsbury, Michael. 2007. "A Tale of Two Cities: Competing Logics and Practice Variation in the Professionalizing of Mutual Funds." *Academy of Management Journal* 50(2): 289–307..

Luhman, Niklas. 1993. *Risk: A Sociological Theory*. New York: A. de Gruyter.

McAdam, Doug. 1999. *Political Process and the Development of Black Insurgency, 1930–1970*. Chicago: University of Chicago Press.

MacMullen, Ramsay. 1984. *Christianizing the Roman Empire (A.D. 100–400)*. New Haven, CT: Yale Univerity Press.

Mecklin, John M. 1941. *The Passing of the Saint*. Chicago: University of Chicago Press.

Merelman, Richard M. 1998. "On Legitimalaise in the United States." *The Sociological Quarterly* 39(3): 351–68.

Merton, Robert K. 1996. *On Social Structure and Science*. Chicago: University of Chicago Press.

Meyer, John W., and Brian Rowan. 1977. "Institutionalized Organizations: Formal Structure as Myths and Ceremony." *The American Journal of Sociology* 83(2): 340–63.

Mols, Roger S. J. 1979. "La popolazione europea nei secoli XVI e XVII." Pp. 1–43 in *Storia economica d'Italia*, ed. C. M. Cipolla. Torino, Italy: UTET.

Mommsen, Theodor. 1861. *Storia di Roma antica*. Florence, Italy: G. C. Sansoni.

Moore, Barrington, Jr. 2000. *Moral Purity and Persecution in History*. Princeton, NJ: Princeton University Press.

Moran, James. 1973. *Printing Presses: History and Development from the Fifteenth Century to Modern Times*. Berkeley: University of California Press.

Morris, Martina. 1993. "Epidemiology and Social Networks." *Sociological Methods and Research* 22(1): 99–126.

Nicolini, Ugolino. 1993. *Scritti di storia*. edited by G. Casagrande, A. Bartoli Langeli, and N. Ottaviani. Napoli: Edizioni Scientifiche Italiane.

Olson, Mancur. 1982. *Rise and Decline of Nations*. New Haven, CT: Yale University Press.

Paciocco, Roberto. 1996. *Sublimia negotia*. Padua, Italy,: Centro Studi Antoniani.

Papa, Giovanni. 1988. "La Sacra Congregazione dei Riti nel primo periodo di attivitá." Pp. 13–52 in *Miscellanea in occasione del IV centenario della Congregazione per le cause dei santi (1588–1988)*. Vatican City: Congregazione per le cause dei santi.

2001. *Le cause di canonizzazione nel primo perido della Congregazione dei Riti (1588–1634)*. Vatican City: Urbaniana University Press.

Parigi, Paolo. 2006. "Fatti sociali e produzione di miracoli nel XVII secolo." *Polis* XX(3): 431–62.

Parsons, Talcott. 1960. *Structure and Process in Modern Socieities*. Glencoe, IL: Free Press.

Paschini, Pio. 1952. "Canonizzazione," vol. VIII. Florence, Italy: Sansoni.

Pastor, Ludwig. 1938. *The History of the Popes, from the Close of the Middle Ages*. London: K. Paul, Trench, and Trubner.

Petrocchi, Massimo. 1970. *Roma nel Seicento*. Bologna, Italy: Licinio Cappelli Editore.

Ponnelle, Louis, and Louis Bordet. 1932. *St. Philip Neri and the Roman Society of His Time (1515–1595)*. London: Sheed and Ward.

Powell, Walter W., and Paul DiMaggio. 1991. "Introduction." Pp. 1–38 in *The New Institutionalism in Organizational Analysis*, ed. Paul DiMaggio and Walter W. Powell. Chicago: University of Chicago Press.

Powell, Walter W., Kenneth W. Koput, and Laurel Smith-Doerr. 1996. "Interorganizational Collaboration and the Locus of Innovation." *Administrative Science Quarterly* 41(1): 116–45.

Prosperi, Adriano. 1986. "Dalle 'divine madri' ai padri spirituali." Pp. 71–90 in *Women and Men in Spiritual Culture: 14–17. Centuries*, ed. E. Schulte van Kessel. The Hague: Netherlands Government Publishing Office.

Putnam, Robert. 1993. *Making Democracy Work: Civic Traditions in Modern Italy*. Princeton, NJ: Princeton University Press.

Rao, Hayagreeva, Philippe Monin, and Rodolphe Durand. 2003. "Institutional Change in Toque Ville: Nouvelle Cuisine as an Identity Movement in French Gastronomy." *The American Journal of Sociology* 108(4): 795–843.

Rich, Edwin E., and Charles H. Wilson. 1977. *The Cambridge Economic History of Europe*. London: Cambridge University Press.

Richardson, Gary. 2001. "A Tale of Two Theories." *Journal of the History of Economic Thought* 23(2): 217–42.

Rosa, Mario. 2006. *Clero cattolico e società europea nell'età moderna*. Roma-Bari: Editori Laterza.

Rousselle, Aline. 1999. "Miracoli e persecuzioni: assenza e presenza." Pp. 121–50 in *Miracoli. Dai segni alla storia*, ed. S. Boesch-Gajano and M. Modica. Rome: Viella.

Rusconi, Roberto. 1992. "Gli ordini religiosi maschili dalla Controriforma alle soppressioni settecentesche. Cultura, predicazione, missioni." Pp. 207–74 in *Clero e società nell'Italia moderna*, ed. Mario Rosa. Roma-Bari: Editori Laterza.

Sallmann, Jean-Micheal. 1994. *Naples et ses saints à l'âge baroque: 1540–1750*. Paris: Presses Universitaires de France.

Sangalli, Marco. 1993. *I miracoli a Milano. I processi informativi per eventi miracolosi nel milanese in età spagnola*. Milan, Italy: NED.

Scaraffia, Lucetta, and Gabriella Zarri, eds. 1994. *Donne e fede: Santita' e vita religiosa*. Rome: Laterza.

Schneiberg, Marc, and Tim Bartley. 2001. "Regulating American Industries: Markets, Politics, and the Institutional Determinants of Fire Insurance Regulation." *American Journal of Sociology* 107(1): 101–46.

Schumpeter, Joseph A. 1947. *Capitalism, Socialism, and Democracy.* New York: Harper and Brothers.

Schwartz, Michael. 1976. *Radical Protest and Social Structure.* Chicago: University of Chicago Press.

Scott, Richard W. 1991. "Unpacking Institutional Arguments." Pp. 164–82 in *Institutionalism in Organizational Analysis,* ed. Walter W. Powell and Paul DiMaggio. Chicago: University of Chicago Press.

Selznick, Philip. 1979. *The Organizational Weapon.* New York: Arno Press.

    1980. *TVA and the Grass Roots: A Study of Politics and Organization.* Berkeley: University of California Press.

Siraisi, Nancy G. 2007. *History, Medicine, and the Traditions of Renaissance Learning.* Ann Arbor: University of Michigan Press.

Sodano, Giulio. 1999. "Miracolo e canonizzazione: processi napoletani tra XVI e XVII secolo." Pp. 171–95 in *Miracoli. Dai segni alla storia,* ed. S. Boesch-Gajano and M. Modica. Rome: Viella.

Sorokin, Pitrim. 1956. *The American Sex Revolution.* Boston: P. Sargent.

Soule, Sarah A., and Brayden G. King. 2006. "The Stages of the Policy Process and the Equal Rights Amendment, 1972–1982." *American Journal of Sociology* 111(6): 1871–1909.

Spanó Martinelli, Serena, ed. 2003. *Il processo di canonizzazione di Caterina Vigri (1586–1712).* Florence, Italy: Sismel – Edizioni del Galluzzo.

Stanko, Andric. 2000. *The Miracles of St. John Capistran.* Budapest: CEU Press.

Stark, Warner. 1966. *The Sociology of Religion: A Study of Christendom.* London: Routledge and Kegan Paul.

Stoppani, Renato. 1986. *Le grandi vie di pellegrinaggio del Medioevo. Le strade per Roma.* Florence, Italy: Centro Studi Romei.

Strang, David. 1991. "Adding Social Structure to Diffusion Model." *Sociological Methods and Research* 19(3): 324–53.

Szymanski, Stefan, and Stephen F. Ross. 2007. "Governance and Vertical Integration in Team Sports." *Contemporary Economic Policy* 25(4): 616–26.

Tanner, Murray Scot, and Eric Green. 2007. "'Principals and Secret Agents' Central versus Local Control over Policing and Obstacles to 'Rule of Law' in China." *The China Quarterly* 191: 644–70.

Tarrow, Sidney. 1996. "Social Movements in Contentious Politics: A Review Article." *American Political Science Review* 90: 874–83.

Tedeschi, John A. 1991. *The Prosecution of Heresy.* Binghamton, NY: Medieval and Renaissance Texts and Studies.

Thomas, Keith. 1997. *Religion and the Decline of Magic.* New York: Oxford University Press.

    1983. *Man and the Natural World.* London: Penguin Books.

Thompson, James D. 1967. *Organizations in Action.* New York: McGraw-Hill.

Thorndike, Lynn. 1951. *A History of Magic and Experimental Science.* New York: Columbia University Press.

Tilly, Charles. 1961. "Some Problems in the History of the Vandee." *The American Historical Review* 67(1): 19–33.

1978. *From Mobilization to Revolution*. Reading, MA: Addison-Wesley.

1985. "Models and Realities of Popular Collective Action." *Social Research Psychology* 90: 25–37.

Tolbert, P. S., and Lynne G. Zucker. 1983. "Institutional Sources of Change in the Formal Structure of Organizations: Diffusion of Civil Reform, 1880–1935." *Administrative Science Quarterly* 28: 22–39.

Turner, Victor W. 1967. *The Forest of Symbols*. Ithaca, NY: Cornell University Press.

van Dyke, Nella, SarahA. Soule, and Verta A. Taylor. 2004. "The Targets of Social Movements: Beyond a Focus on the State." *Research in Social Movements, Conflict and Change* 25: 27–52.

Vauchez, Andre. 1989. *La santità nel Medioevo*. Bologna, Italy: Il Mulino.

2000. *Santi, profeti e visionari. Il soprannaturale nel medioevo*. Bologna, Italy: Il Mulino.

Vaughan, Diane. 1999. "The Dark Side of Organizations: Mistake, Misconduct, and Disaster." *American Sociological Review* 25: 271–305.

Veraja, Fabiano. 1988. *Miscellanea in occasione del quarto centenario della Congregazione per le Cause dei Santi*. Vatican City: Libreria Editrice Vaticana.

1992. *Le cause di canonizzazione dei santi*. Vatican City: Libreria Editrice Vaticana.

Vidal, Fernando. 2007. "Miracles, Science, and Testimony in Post-Tridentine Saint-Making." *Science in Context* 20(3): 481–508.

Vigo, Giovanni. 1994. *Uno stato nell'Impero. La difficile transizione al moderno nella Milano di età spagnola*. Milan, Italy: Guerini e Associati.

von Leyden, W. 1961. "Philosophy." Pp. 73–95 in *The New Cambridge Modern History*, vol. V (The Ascendancy of France). Cambridge: Cambridge University Press.

Walder, Andrew. 2003. "Elite Opportunity in Transitional Economies." *American Sociological Review* 68(6): 899–916.

Watts, Duncan J., Peter S. Dodds, and Mark E. J. Newman. 2002. "Identity and Search in Social Networks." *Science* 296: 1302–5.

Weber, Klaus, K. Heinz, and Michele DeSoucey. 2008. "Forage for Thought: Mobilizing Codes for Grassfed Meat and Dairy Products." *Administrative Science Quarterly* 53: 529–67.

Weber, Max. 1948. *From Max Weber: Essays in Sociology*. Oxford and New York: Oxford University Press.

2000. *The Protestant Ethic and the Spirit of Capitalism*. Los Angeles: Roxbury Publishing.

Westphal, James D., and Edward J. Zajac. 2001. "Decoupling Policy from Practice: The Case of Stock Repurchase Programs." *Administrative Science Quarterly* 46: 202–28.

White, Harrison C. 1992. *Identity and Control: A Structural Theory of Social Action*. Princeton, NJ: Princeton University Press.

Woodward, Kenneth. 1990. *Making Saints: How the Catholic Church Determines Who Becomes a Saint, Who Doesn't, and Why*. New York: Simon and Schuster.

Wright, Jonathan. 2004. *God's Soldiers*. New York: Doubleday.

Zald, Mayer N., Calvin Morrill, and Hayagreeva Rao. 2005. "The Impact of Social Movements on Organizations." Pp. 253–79 in *Social Movements and Organization Theory*, ed. Gerald F. Davis, Doug McAdam, William Richard, Scott Mayer, and Nathan Zald. Cambridge: Cambridge University Press.

Zarri, Gabriella. 1991. *Finzione e santità*. Torino, Italy: Rosenberg and Sellier.

Zemon-Davis, Natalie. 1975. *Society and Culture in Early Modern France: Eight Essays*. Palo Alto, CA: Stanford University Press.

Zhou, Xueguang. 1993. "The Dynamics of Organizational Rules." *The American Journal of Sociology* 98(5): 1134–66.

Ziegler, Joseph. 1999. "Practitioners and Saints: Medical Men in Canonization Processes in the Thirteen to Fifteenth Centuries." *The Society for the Social History of Medicine* 12(2): 191–225.

Index

acolytes, 3–4, 7, 12, 21–2, 24, 40–2,
    70–3, 75–7, 80–1, 87, 89, 91–2,
    102–3, 106–7, 127, 137, 139.
    See also Congregatio Sacrorum
    Rituum, influence of acolytes on
heterogeneity of, 8, 40–1, 71–7,
    88, 102. *See also* witnesses
    to miracles, heterogeneity
    of; recipients of miracles,
    heterogeneity of; miracles, true
role in social movement, 1, 4, 8–9,
    12, 15–17, 41–2, 54, 73, 76,
    78–93, 95, 97–9, 102, 105–6,
    112, 131, 135, 146, 148, 161–4.
    See also religious activism, as a
    social movement
use of medicine by, 112–13, 121,
    164. *See also* religious activism,
    role of medicine in; canonization
    trials, role of doctors in
acts of Jesus, 21, 38, 81–2, 107, 128.
    See also miracles, changing
    content of
Agrigento, Italy, 47–8, 53
Alcantara, Pedro de, 49, 144
Alexander III, Pope, 33
Anchieta, Joseph, 60–1
*Audivimus, de Reliquiis et Veneratione
    Sanctorum*, 33
Augustine, 7

Augustine, Order of Saint, 48

barbers, 59, 108. *See also* medicine,
    development of
Barcelona, 45, 52
Barnabiti, 93, 101
Baylon, Pasqualis, 50–1, 55, 144
    death of, 15, 72
    miracles of, 51, 59–60, 68, 72, 102,
        105, 122, 128, 132–4
    network of support for, 53, 99,
        101–2, 111–12
    relics of, 15, 102
Benedict XIV, Pope, 123.
    see Lambertini, Prospero
Bernardino of Santa Lucia, 65
    head of, 13, 48
    miracles of, 48
    network of support for, 53
Besse, Saint, 28, 131
bishops, 24, 42, 133, 145, 162–3
    autonomy of, 145, 154, 163
    role in canonization, 33, 131,
        142–3, 152, 162–3
    role in early Christianity, 78–9, 86
    as saints, 31
blessed (title), 7, 26, 35–6, 99, 121,
    143–6, 148, 150, 156, 162–3
Bologna
    Univerity of, 52